SABBATH ROOTS
THE AFRICAN CONNECTION

A BIBLICAL PERSPECTIVE

CHARLES E. BRADFORD

BIBLE CREDITS

Bible texts credited to JB are from the New Jerusalem Bible, copyright 1985 by Darton, Longman and Todd, Ltd., and Doubleday company, Inc. Reprinted by permission of the publisher.

Texts credited to NEB are from The New English Bible. The Delegates of the Oxford University Press and the Syndics of the Cambridge University Press 1961, 1970. Reprinted by permission.

Texts credited to NIV are from the Holy Bible, New International Version. Copyright 1973, 1978, 1984, International Bible Society. Used by permission of Zondervan Bible Publishers.

Bible texts credited to NRSV are from the *New Revised Standard Version* of the Bible, copyright 1989 by the Division of Christian Education of the National Council of the churches of Christ in the U.S.A. Used by permission.

Bible texts credited to the RSV are from the *Revised Standard Version* of the Bible, copyright 1946, 1952, 1971, by the Division of Christian Education of the National Council of the Churches of Christ in the U.S.A. Used by permission.

PRINTED IN U.S.A.
L. Brown and Sons Printing, Inc.
14-20 Jefferson Street
Barre, Vermont 05641

The author assumes responsibility for the accuracy of all facts and quotations cited in this book.

ISBN 1-57847-056-0

TABLE OF CONTENTS

Sabbath Roots: The African Connection
A Biblical Perspective

ACKNOWLEDGMENTS

How can I say thanks to the many people, too numerous to mention, who contributed to this project? I must mention a few who deserve special commendation. William G. Johnsson, editor of the *Adventist Review*, wrote a little book called the *Wit and Wisdom of Charles Bradford* and devoted the proceeds to the Sabbath in Africa project. Harold Lee, president of the Columbia Union Conference, became a Nehemiah on the wall, rallying the troops and pressing them into action, never faltering in his interest in and support of the project. To him is due the greatest tribute of thanks.

Alvin M. Kibble, chair of the Regional Caucus and president of the Allegheny East Conference, came to the rescue at the right time. Keith Burton, associate professor of religion at Oakwood College, served for a number of years as director of the Sabbath in Africa project. I must mention Kofi Owusu-Mensa, Mary Getui, Sammy Ngetich, Josiah Okinda, and Gosnell Yorke, who labor on the African continent. And I cannot forget that James Cress, Nikolaus Satelmajer, and the General Conference Ministerial Association were willing to underwrite and publish the book, along with the presidents of the regional conferences and the African-American ministries directors of the Pacific and North Pacific unions. These good people committed themselves and their organizations to the task of bringing the project to term.

A word of appreciation should go to Ann Parrish and Joanne Stango, who toiled into the night to put the manuscript into acceptable form, and William J. Cleveland, who gave the manuscript its final going-over. Thanks to Duane McKey, Victor Wallen, and Emory Tolbert, who shared their personal library resources, and James Melancon, who served for a time as executive secretary of the Sabbath in Africa Committee.

I would remember the late Bekele Heye, beloved pastor and church leader, who gave me my first paper on Ethiopia, which he wrote. And finally, above all, thanks to my wife, Ethel, who has been this way before and, like the valiant troops of Gideon's band, is sometimes "faint, yet pursuing them" (Judges 8:4).

Charles E. Bradford
May 14, 1999

DEDICATION

This book is dedicated to Ellen Gould White, whose vision and spirit reached even unto Africa.

FOREWORD

This is an important book.

The past few years have witnessed a sharp upturn in interest in the seventh-day Sabbath. Books advocating either a return to the biblical day of worship or repudiating such a course are proliferating. The Internet has become a hornet's nest of debate on the topic.

In such a climate, *Sabbath Roots: The African Connection* makes a startlingly new and significant contribution. Amid all the current discussions I know of no other writing that touches on the area explored by this book.

Unfortunately, most of American thinking continues to be dominated by Western stereotypes and prejudices. It mines the Greco-Roman lode of history and knowledge exclusively as though there existed no other vein of precious metal into which it might tap. Thus, its mills grind the same old ideas finer and finer, blissfully ignorant of other instructive sources.

Charles E. Bradford's book has the potential of bringing about a sea change in Christian thinking and scholarly investigation. Although not written specifically for scholars, it commends itself to the probing mind that is ready to lay prejudices aside and consider new and challenging possibilities.

For the writer, the topic has been like a burr in the saddle, a load on his chest, a dream and a passion. He has had a hunch, and he has pursued it. He has followed a gleam of an idea that glows in the dark; he has tracked it down and brought it out into the light.

And I am glad very glad. I make no secret of my bias: "Brad" is an acquaintance of longstanding whom I am privileged to count as a friend. I respect, admire, and love Charles E. Bradford.

Sabbath Roots crowns a life of sterling service for the Lord, for His church, and for humanity. We are all indebted to Charles E. Bradford.

William G. Johnsson
Silver Spring
April 8, 1999

THE PROPHETIC WORD

"When Israel was a child, then I loved him, and called my son out of Egypt" (Hosea 11:1).

"Princes shall come out of Egypt; Ethiopia shall soon stretch out her hands unto God" (Ps. 68:31).

"From beyond the rivers of Ethiopia my suppliants, even the daughter of my dispersed, shall bring mine offering" (Zeph. 3:10).

"Also the sons of the stranger . . . every one that keepeth the sabbath from polluting it, and taketh hold of my covenant; Even them will I bring to my holy mountain, and make them joyful in my house of prayer" (Isa. 56:6, 7).

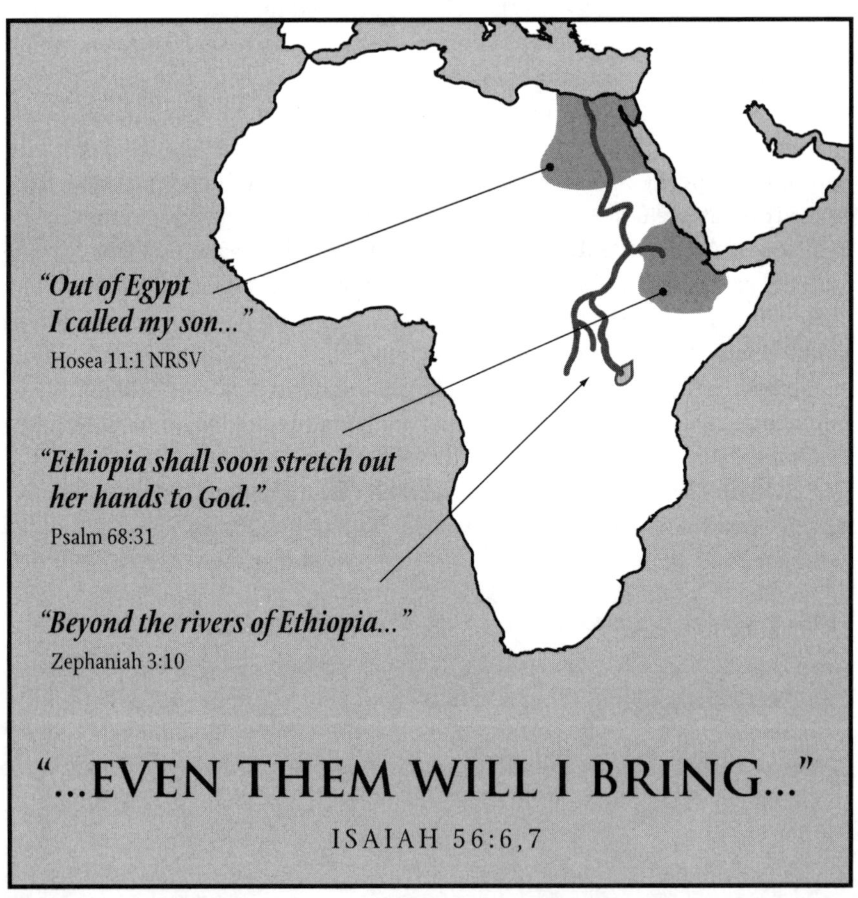

INTRODUCTION

Recently Pope John Paul II, in his pastoral letter *Dies Domini*, issued May 31, 1998, made an impassioned plea for more careful Sabbath observance (of course, he meant Sunday, the first day of the week). Protestant religious leaders joined the pope in appealing to their constituents to give more serious attention to Sabbath (Sunday) observance. Indeed, as we stand on the threshold of a new millennium, Sabbath observance, long a declining issue in Western nations, has been brought back to the table as a matter of concern.

A growing number of biblical scholars are calling for a thorough reexamination of "the Sabbath question," including the ages-old query, which day is the Sabbath: Saturday or Sunday? The Sabbath is certainly the one theological issue that will not go away.

In the light of such interest, Western scholars and theologians would be remiss if they failed to involve the insights and experience of a region that has, throughout its history, been closely identified, to an unusual extent, with the ancient biblical Sabbath the African continent and its peoples.

According to reliable estimates, the African continent is home to the largest concentration of Sabbath observers in the world. As many as 20 million people hold some measure of allegiance to the Sabbath. The Sabbath has vital roots in Africa, an African connection, if you please, carried forward by a people who bear, in some mysterious way, visceral memories of the Sabbath, however faint. This dimension should be included.

In this book I invite readers to share with me the actual account of the ancient Edenic Creation Sabbath on the African continent, among the sons and daughters of Cush, and what this can mean to us who live in what Cornel West terms the "twilight civilization."

To the question, "Why should the African experience be included in the discussion?" we must answer: because the peoples of Africa, along with the kindred of all the earth, are children of the one and same Father.

"Let no one think," observes Ellen White, "that there need not be a stroke placed upon him. There is no person, no nation, that is perfect in every habit and thought. One must learn of another."[1]

In Africa, the Creation Sabbath has been preserved for almost 2,000 years, and primarily, Ethiopia (Abyssinia) is the one nation that is defined throughout its existence by its fidelity to the Sabbath, a commitment that has brought pain and suffering to its people.

With a rich Christian history, Africa has contributed much to the church universal. John Mbiti says with understandable pride: "Christianity in Africa is so old that it can rightly be described as an indigenous, traditional, and African religion long before the start of Islam in the seventh century. Christianity was well established all over North Africa, Egypt, parts of the Sudan and Ethiopia."[2]

The North African church produced Augustine, Athanasius, Origen, and Clement of Alexandria, who "enriched Christendom with their scholarship . . . their defense of the faith. African Christianity produced martyrs, monasticism, theology, liturgy; translated the Scriptures, founded the Catechetical School of Alexandria."[3]

But the greatest gem in Africa's crown is Yahweh's Creation Sabbath, which He established as His sign of authority: "When the morning stars sang together, and all the sons of God shouted for joy" (Job 38:7).

According to the *Cambridge History of the Bible*, an ancient biblical manuscript called Africana originated in Ethiopia, the product, no doubt, of Ethiopia's highly developed monastic system, the country's intellectual and cultural center. One of the Africana manuscripts found its way to Europe and exerted quite an influence on later translations. What is interesting here is that "Africanisms" can be traced in other manuscripts, clerical blunders and all.

"One of the questions posed by the Africana [the name given to the manuscript of the old Latin version that originated from Africa] is why a manuscript like 'k' [a fifth-century African manuscript] should be found on Italian soil at all, when there were two native products, the Itala [the Italian manuscript of the old Latin version] and *die Vulgate*, apparently in general use."[4] Indeed, African scholars have had a part in preserving the Word of God that brings light and understanding to all people.

The continent that many peoples call "Mother" has evidenced an enormous ability to endure suffering. The religious power elite of the day applied great pressure in an attempt to force the Ethiopians (Abyssinians) to surrender their religious liberty, but without any lasting success. They provided a wonderful example to us in their determination to maintain their allegiance to the Sabbath and to their national integrity.

In Africa there is occurring at this moment a movement toward God that missiologists call nothing less than phenomenal. In a few years one out of every five Christians will live in Africa.[5] How exciting and fulfilling to witness Yahweh working in ways that bring glory to His name! I certainly would not give the impression that Yahweh is at work only in Africa. The word has already been spoken: "For the earth shall be full of the knowledge of the LORD, as the waters cover the sea" (Isa. 11:9).

African spirituality that almost indefinable quality that I call "openness to the unseen" is being seriously discussed in Christian circles around the world and in the academic community. Many feel that there is something here for the good of all Christians, something vital from which we all may benefit.

Are we ready to hear what the Spirit is saying to us in and through the African Sabbatarian experience? Are we willing to move beyond stereotypes and categories to a new level of understanding? Are we willing to integrate all of this into our faith and belief system in such a way as to glorify Yahweh, the God of all flesh? The issue, the main point, is not what Africans are doing in Africa, but what God is doing in Africa.

All of history and human experience is God-centered. Yahweh is in control. "God at work" is the theme, the overarching consideration that will control our study: "It is he that sitteth upon the circle of the earth, and the inhabitants thereof are as grasshoppers; that stretcheth out the heavens as a curtain, and spreadeth them out as a tent to dwell in: That bringeth the princes to nothing; he maketh the judges of the earth as vanity" (Isa. 40:22, 23).

May the hand of the Creator draw us toward eternal truths as we view the African Sabbath experience and its lessons for us today.

End Notes

[1]Ellen G. White, *Historical Sketches*, pp. 136, 137.

[2]John Mbiti, *African Religions and Philosophy* (London: Heineman, 1989), p. 223.

[3]Lukas Malisha, *Christianity in Africa* (London: Mission Book Service, 1987), p. 6.

[4]G.W.H. Lampe, ed., *Cambridge History of the Bible* (Cambridge, Mass.: Cambridge University Press, 1969), p. 347.

[5]Elizabeth A. Isichei, *A History of Christianity in Africa* (Grand Rapids, Mich.: Eerdmans, 1995), p. 1.

THE OVERVIEW: WHAT AND WHERE IS AFRICA? WHO IS AFRICAN?

Africa is both the most clearly defined of continents—in its geography—and the hardest to pin down in historical terms. Human beings originated in Africa, and as a result, there is more diversity of human types and societies there than anywhere else. It is not possible, in any nonideological way, to claim any one of these peoples or societies as more essentially 'African' than others; nor is it possible to exclude a given society as 'not really African.'"[1]

Africa is that land mass that borders on the Mediterranean on the north, the Atlantic to the west, and the Indian ocean to the south. Its eastern border is the Red Sea. Some scholars would say that Mesopotamia is "of Africa" because it is called the land of Nimrod (Micah 5:6), which includes a portion of Mesopotamia.

The people groups that occupy this vast territory are Africans. But please observe that these people are diverse, multicultural, and extremely heterogeneous. Some are indigenous to the land; others are immigrants. For the purpose of this book, we will consider Africans to be those descendants of Ham who are or were indigenous to the African continent. This is the way I am using the term.

Africa is becoming the center of the Christian world. The number of Christians in sub-Saharan Africa today is 309,639,000. And by the year 2000 the projected figure will be 338,285,000.[2] Africa also has the largest concentration of believers in the ancient Bible Sabbath, the seventh day of the week, to be found on this planet.

This is noteworthy and interesting to many, but vital and compelling to all of Yahweh's sons and daughters around the world, and, in a special way, to His children who form one community on the mother continent and throughout the globe in what African-American scholars call the "African diaspora."

The word *diaspora* is a concept basic to the discussion. Actually, it is biblical (see John 7:35;1 Peter 1:1; James 1:1). According to George Shepperson:

> "This process of Jewish migration from their homeland into all parts of the world not only created a term which could be applied to any other substantial and significant group of migrants, but also provided a concept which could be used to interpret the experience (often very bitter experiences) of other peoples who had been driven out of their native countries by forces similar to those which had dispersed the Jews; in particular, slavery and imperialism."[3]

That great prophetic word—"Princes shall come out of Egypt; Ethiopia shall soon stretch out her hands unto God" (Ps. 68:31)—brings this scattered people into the ultimate plan and purposes of Yahweh. It has been a beacon of hope for the people of the African diaspora.

The story is not finished. God has not written off the sons and daughters of Ham. They are an integral part of His earthborn family: "And it shall come to pass, that in the place where it was said unto them, Ye are not my people, there it shall be said unto them, Ye are the sons of the living God" (Hosea 1:10).

Sabbath Roots grows out of the biblical perspective, the "God's eye view"- the global, cosmic dimension. That is how we want to look at the peoples of Africa, whom Isaiah calls sons and daughters of Yahweh, who take hold of the ancient Sabbath day, the Creator's day, and thus find inclusion in the covenant. Yahweh has a contract with every branch of the human family.

This is the perspective from which Isaiah writes:

> "Thus saith the LORD, Keep ye judgment, and do justice: for my salvation is near to come, and my righteousness to be revealed. Blessed is the man that doeth this, and the son of man that layeth hold on it; that keepeth the sabbath from polluting it, and keepeth his hand from doing any evil. Neither let the son of the stranger, that hath joined himself to the LORD, speak, saying, The LORD hath utterly separated me from his people: neither let the eunuch say, Behold, I am a dry tree. For thus saith the LORD unto the eunuchs that keep my sabbaths, and choose the things that please me, and take hold of my covenant; Even unto them will I give in mine house and within my walls a place and a name better than of sons and of daughters: I will give them an everlasting name, that shall not be cut off. Also the sons of the stranger, that join themselves to the LORD, to serve him, and to love the name of the LORD, to be his servants, every one that keepeth the sabbath from polluting it, and taketh hold of my covenant; even them will I bring to my holy mountain, and make them joyful in my house of prayer: their burnt offerings and their sacrifices shall be accepted upon mine altar; for mine house shall be called an house of prayer for all people. The Lord God which gathereth the outcasts of Israel saith, Yet will I gather others to him, beside those that are gathered unto him" (Isa. 56:1-8).

Strangers, eunuchs, outcasts, are not to be denied the blessings of the contract that Yahweh offers to all people, a contract whose great seal is Yahweh's Sabbath, the seventh day of Creation's week, Creation's memorial. In an age when polarization and fragmentation of society pose a serious threat to life on the planet, we need the biblical perspective.

Sabbath, the week's end, points us forward to time's end. Sabbath speaks of fulfilment, the kind of world Yahweh had in mind when He said, "Let there be . . ." Sabbath points to the great day of Yahweh, when prophecies shall cease and time shall be no more: "For as the new heavens and the new earth, which I will make, shall remain before me, saith the LORD, so shall your seed and your name remain. And it shall come to pass, that from one new moon to another, and from one sabbath to another, shall all flesh come to worship before me, saith the LORD" (Isa. 66:22, 23).

Psalm 68:31-"Princes shall come out of Egypt; Ethiopia shall soon stretch out her hands unto God" and its reference to the exodus, was the central theme of the early African-American church. It fired the imagination of preachers and laypeople alike, lifting their spirits and giving them hope. They began to preach about the place of Ethiopia in the plans and purposes of God, looking upon the church of Abyssinia (Ethiopia) as the hidden church in the wilderness through which God had maintained for Himself a witness down through the centuries.

Theophilus Gould Steward picks up the theme in a sermon that he delivered to his congregation at the turn of the century. This hidden church, he declared, "shall come forth to lead Africa's millions, as a part of that fullness of the Gentiles which is to come to welcome the universal Christ."[4]

The African-American preaching fathers insisted that the prophecy of Psalm 68:31 had, as Albert J. Raboteau puts it, "a new global perspective." While the prophecy may seem dormant at times, even extinguished at others, it moves toward the day of complete fulfillment. Preachers and people may despair, hope may seem deferred, but this word of Scripture "cannot be broken."

"The vision is yet for an appointed time," the prophet assured, "but at the end it shall speak, and not lie: though it tarry, wait for it; because it will surely come, it will not tarry" (Hab. 2:3).

The prophecy "Ethiopia shall suddenly stretch forth her hands to God" is the operative, controlling word that addresses the gnawing, unanswered, perplexing questions of our times. It joins the purposes and plans of Yahweh with the Sabbath, the great sign and symbol of His power to create and redeem the sign of liberation.

This prophecy, inclusive, involving all people of earth, embraces the vision of the day of Yahweh, the day of consummation, when all things shall end, and justice and freedom prevail. Frank L. Peterson, eloquent spokesperson for the biblical Sabbath and an authentic visionary, writes: "Nothing can stop the glorious onward progress of the proclamation of Christ's coming everywhere throughout the earth."[5]

End Notes

[1]"Internet African History Sourcebook," Fordham University.

[2]David B. Barrett and Todd M. Johnson, *International Bulletin of Statistical Research*, Jan. 1998.

[3]Quoted in Theophilus H. Smith, "*The Spirituality of African-American Traditions*," in Louis Dupre and Don E. Saliers, eds., *Christian Spirituality* (New York: Crossroads, 1989), vol. 3, p. 403.

[4]Albert J. Raboteau, *A Fire in the Bones: Reflections on African-American Religious History* (Boston: Beacon Press, 1995), p. 54.

[5]Frank L. Peterson, *The Hope of the Race* (Nashville, Tenn.: Southern Pub. Assn., 1934), p. 141.

PART ONE
GOD OF ALL FLESH

"Behold, I am the LORD, the God of all flesh: is there any thing too hard for me?" (Jer. 32:27).

In this section we will look at the Most High God (1) from the perspective of the Hebrew prophets, (2) in African concepts of the Most High God, and (3) from the African-American (Africans in diaspora) view of God.

CHAPTER ONE
THE BIBLICAL PERSPECTIVE

The biblical perspective is God's point of view, the way things look from the lofty position that He occupies. How does God view this planet of His creation? The prophets always picture Him as occupying the best possible vantage point, dwelling in the "the high and holy place." He witnesses all from every possible dimension time, eternity, history, human relationships, the past, the present, the future as one eternal now.

Nothing can obstruct His line of vision: "The LORD looketh from heaven; he beholdeth all the sons of men. From the place of his habitation he looketh upon all the inhabitants of the earth" (Ps. 33:13, 14).

Ellen G. White adds: "Above the distractions of the earth He sits enthroned; all things are open to His divine survey; and from His great and calm eternity He orders that which His providence sees best."[1]

The biblical perspective, God's eye view, is global, inclusive, all-encompassing. Imagine a group of astronauts from several nations on a space mission. Following lift-off, as the spacecraft enters the upper atmosphere, each astronaut strains to see his or her own country, but as the craft soars higher, each can see only continents, then finally a globe with no borders no dividing lines. This is the perspective from which we must read the entire Bible; through its powerful lens we may see as God sees and interpret what is happening on this planet and how it impacts the lives of people.

The Bible Is Central

Ellen G. White makes this emphatic statement: "The Bible and the soul were made one for the other."[2]

We must agree. The Bible is absolutely indispensable to the story of humanity. This story cannot be understood, nor, indeed, written, without the wisdom and perception that fill its pages. We have to give the "Book" its due. Sons and daughters of Cush on both sides of the Atlantic owe their very existence to the light that streams from its pages. This book challenges darkness and ignorance, and the darkness flees its illumination.

Adrian Hastings, after a lifetime of study and research, makes a very perceptive comment in the *Oxford History of Christianity* about the place of the Bible in the African connection:

> "The Bible had become far more than any deed of manumission, the Charter to which one could appeal for freedom and dignity. It constituted little less than the foundation document of this new society as it shaped itself the other side of slavery. The underlying sense of African unity was wholly pervasive. The experience of the middle passage was a great unifier. Some of its leaders like Equiano and Cugoano [Africans of distinction who were educated in and lived in Europe] had been born in Africa and still knew at least something of an African language. Many others were sons of those who had been. In the late eighteenth century little distancing had been achieved from their continent of origin. The continued scale of the [slave] trade, the tens of thousands of annual new arrivals, ensured that. Yet, the diversity of their origins and their languages necessitated the adoption of English as the language of this new Africa, an Africa in diaspora, a Christian and biblical Africa, an expanded Ethiopia."[3]

The dispersed peoples of Africa came to view the Bible as the authoritative Word. They believed that the terrible dilemma in which they found themselves slavery, suffering, death—would find solution in its pages. They clung to this Book with unwavering faith, willing to suffer physical punishment in order to read its pages.

Needless to say, the Bible made a difference to them. It was their survival kit. Often today we thoughtlessly sweep away the faith of our fathers and mothers as being naive and otherworldly, as if our learning and sophistication make us wiser than they and qualify us to judge the reality of their experience. We do well to remember that a people who had no written tradition became, in every sense of the word, a people of the Book, a remarkable achievement.

African culture tends to be oral (speaking) and aural (hearing), but the sons and daughters of Africa in diaspora "adopted and adapted the sacred texts of their host cultures and learned to 'sing the Lord's song in a strange land.'" As Theophilus Smith relates:

> "The Bible has come to serve as a surrogate sacred text for an ethnic community lacking (or estranged from) indigenous literary artifacts. It is a community at the same time distinguished by a rich oral textuality and a brilliant improvisational aesthetic. This 'surrogacy' of biblical narrative for Black America (all the sons and daughters of Africa in diaspora) means that the culture inscribes its experience in the world of Scripture as an extension of that world as if the Bible were its own literary record of human participation in divine transcendence."[4]

It must be stated unequivocally: the Bible is not for theologians and scholars only. This Book belongs to all people. Unlike any other literature, the Bible speaks universally to the basic needs of human beings in any culture. Scripture comes out of the stuff that we are made of, reality. The Bible contains the deepest philosophical content, but its orientation grows out of the historical and concrete experiences of individuals and nations. It is written so that we can see the hand of God in all of history.

The message that brings salvation, wholeness, and saving knowledge is being communicated through a Book. In fact, the Bible is more like a library than a single book or collection of books. It is a one-volume library.

Scripture encompasses an essential unity. More than just a structural unity, this Book is organic, a system. The same themes, subjects, concerns, and outcomes run through its various parts. We should remember also that the Word unfolds and takes shape over a period of more than 1,500 years. The variety of circumstances and situations it records is mind-boggling. What is even more amazing is that the message, the dominant theme, filters through. It persists. It is consistent.

Yahweh speaks words of wisdom, but not of wisdom only. More to the point, He speaks words of power. His communication is vital, lifegiving.

The Bible is not a book of neat answers to life all cataloged and ready to be employed mechanically. It "is not an answer book to all of the curious questions we may ask."[5] It is made for listening, for hearing, to be absorbed, eaten, treasured in the heart, received at the very deepest level of being. The great biblical prophets regard the Word as more to be desired than physical food (Job 23:12), to be searched for like hidden treasure (Ps. 119:162), as something that brings great joy and delight (Jer. 15:16).

How that message comes to us is most fascinating. Yahweh used human instruments, people from all walks of life. While some were quite brilliant and gifted; others, by their own admission, were very ordinary. Nevertheless, the biblical writers, their themes, and their milieus represent a cross-section of humanity ethnic, cultural, sociological.

For example, speaking of the prophet Zephaniah, G. Yorke says: "We find [in his case] not only the longest genealogical list of any of the writing prophets in the Hebrew Bible, but also . . . that Zephaniah was of African descent, he being the son of Cush."[6] David J. Clark elaborates as follows:

> "The father of Zephaniah was called *Cushi* (cf. Jer. 36:14). Elsewhere in the Old Testament this name is usually found as an ethnic label, meaning a person from Cush, the Upper Nile Region which included most of modern Sudan and part of Ethiopia. Here it may mean that Zephaniah s father was an African, and that Zephaniah himself was a Black man. This possibility gains some support from the

> fact that in his short prophecy Zephaniah twice (Zeph. 2:12; 3:10) mentions the land or people of Cush (translated "Ethiopia" in RSV and "Sudan" in TEV). A Cushite dynasty had ruled Egypt 715-663 B.C., and this no doubt led to increased familiarity with Cushites in Judith and perhaps to some intermarriage with them. It was quite possible for a Cushite to settle in Jerusalem at this period. Indeed we know that a few years later, Jeremiah was rescued by Ebedmelech, the God-fearing Eunuch from Cush (Jer. 38:7-13; 39:15-18)."[7]

The Bible has a universal perspective. It is surprisingly free of any hint of classism and racism. It is totally against any ordering of humanity that would set up one part of the human family above the rest. There is no hierarchy here. All members of the family have equal worth and value.

Africa Is a Bible Land

Africa has been the host continent to believers in the One God since the time of Abraham. African Christians remind us, with pardonable pride, that the Christ child took refuge from Herod in the "land of Ham." We may find on this continent a slice of Old Testament times, "the world that then was." Before Yahweh wrote, He spoke, and we can hear the echoes of His voice in the culture, customs, stories, and speech of Africa's peoples. Our interest must be in tracing the hand of God in His world.

The amount of "hard copy" allocated to Africa in the biblical text qualifies it to be called a Bible land. The Hebrew prophets were taken with the mystique of the land "beyond the rivers of Cush" (Zeph. 3:10, NEB). In biblical terms, Africa is Ethiopia or Egypt, or as Zephaniah calls Black Africa, the land "beyond the rivers of Ethiopia" (KJV).

For a long time a school of thought insisted that Egypt was not a Black African nation and that simply by some sheer and inexplicable accident of history it just happened to be located on the African continent. But the biblical linkage between Ethiopia and Egypt is hard to overlook. More recently the accepted position seems to have shifted to the assumption that Bible writers considered Egypt and Africa synonymous.

Egypt is mentioned 611 times in Scripture. Ethiopia is mentioned 20 times. Ethiopia and Egypt are cited together eight times. Thus the Bible writers apparently considered these nations as close relations, to each other and to the land of God's people. There was no lack of contact between Israel and these giants of antiquity. Even the prophets were impressed with the accomplishments, the prowess, and the strength of their Hamitic neighbors: "Ethiopia and Egypt were her strength, and it was infinite; Put and Lubim were thy helpers" (Nahum 3:9).

In the biblical record Africa figures prominently in the plans and purposes of God: "In that day shall Israel be the third with Egypt and with Assyria, even a blessing in the midst of the land: whom the LORD of hosts shall bless, saying, Blessed be Egypt my people, and Assyria the work of my hands, and Israel mine inheritance" (Isa. 19:24, 25).

The Clutter of History

As computer hard drives seem to pick up clutter from the streams of data they are fed, so do the pages of history, often at the hands of so-called historians. From time to time we must sweep the litter away from the account of history, written, to a great extent, it would appear, with a crooked pen.

The African philosopher Okot p'Bitek used to say: "To correct error is as respectable an aim as to increase knowledge."[8] His European contemporaries observed that "P'Bitek stresses, the smelling out of error in Western scholarship and exorcising it is a primary task of the African intellectual, especially the scholar of religious studies."[9] P'Bitek even went so far as to say that "once scholarship is identified with the mission of correcting past errors, social commitment becomes perfectly compatible with high scholarship."[10]

The approach of this book is to begin with the Bible, to make Scripture the sweeping broom, the corrective. Certainly, not all historians are evil people, with a self-serving agenda, who write with malice aforethought. Nevertheless, humanity is flawed and human beings are faulty. Myths and fables have to be cleared away, and attitudes have to be corrected.

When reference is made to Africa, there is so much disinformation out there, so much fog, that even the best of scholars are sometimes taken in. As Martin Bernal says: "Research on the question usually reveals far more about the predisposition of the researcher than about the question itself."[11] These mists and myths must be dissolved if we are to see truth.

This is no attempt to refute every racist theory, nor is it an attempt to romanticize the African past or the so-called African experience. However, we have a duty to look at that part of Planet Earth which has a long, deep, rich, mostly overlooked history of God speaking to His children, even before there was a Jew or a Christian.

Growing Sabbath Consciousness

There is growing evidence from the African continent that a Sabbath consciousness exists among its peoples, and has from time immemorial. This consciousness long predates Christianity, and certainly does not derive from the European ecclesiastical establishment, which apparently strove mightily to suppress it.

Jacob Nortey, of Ghana, a veteran church leader, says: "In the Ghanaian context, and especially within the people forming the Ashanti or Akan nation, Saturday has been a traditionally accepted holy day, a day for worship of God."[12]

And according to Joel Awoniyi, a Nigerian theologian: "Among the Yoruba people, the seventh day of the week is a day when no work, no marriage, no festivities, should be performed. It is known as the forbidden day."[13]

Ethiopian Bible scholar Bekele Heye states emphatically: "The history of the seventh-day Sabbath is deep-rooted in the culture of the Ethiopian people. There is no record at any time in the history of the Ethiopian Orthodox Church that this church has officially given up Sabbath observance."[14]

Missiologists recognize a Hebraic consciousness among the African peoples, a belief that the Sabbath is their day. (Some have postulated that the African peoples are a lost tribe of Israel.) W. W. Oliphant, an African church leader in the early years of the twentieth century, says that the "Sabbath in Ethiopia [has] been kept from the days of Nimrod, about 2140 B.C. (read Gen. 10:8, 9), that is 700 years before the birth of Moses. . . . Africans or Ethiopians had been Sabbath observers from the days of Nimrod, the son of Cush."[15]

Ellen White credits Africa with being a repository of the knowledge of Yahwehism: "In lands beyond the jurisdiction of Rome there existed for many centuries bodies of Christians who . . . believed in the perpetuity of the law of God and observed the Sabbath of the fourth commandment. . . . Churches that held to this faith and practice existed in Central Africa and among the Armenians of Asia."[16]

The centuries-long presence of the Falasha, a group of Sabbathkeeping Ethiopians, is persuasive to this argument. What is striking is that these Ethiopians, Black Jews, hold to a form of Judaism that was dominant in Solomon's day. They seem to know nothing of later rabbinic Judaism. In the Falasha we have evidence that Africans have observed Sabbath at least as far back as the time of Solomon.

In a quote from Bekele Heye, the Ethiopian emperor Galawdewos (A.D. 1540-1559) spoke to the issue in his reply to European church leaders who criticized Africans for keeping the ancient Sabbath and urged them to give up their faith:

> "We do celebrate the Sabbath, because God, after He had finished the Creation of the World, rested thereon: Which day, as God would have it called the Holy of Holies, so that not celebrating thereof with great honor and devotion, seems to be plainly, contrary to God's will and precept, who will suffer heaven and earth to pass away sooner than His Word; and that especially, since Christ came not to dissolve the law but to fulfill it. It is not therefore in imitation of the Jews, but in obedience to Christ, and His holy apostles, that we observe that day."

Kofi Owusu-Mensa, an Ashante Ghanaian, notes:

"Oral traditions and modern scholars and research into Akan traditions and customs affirm Saturday as Onyamee Kwaame's special day in Akanland. Writing in the early twenties, Rattray, the British anthropologist, discovered that the Ashante name for God is Onyamee or Onyankopon Kwaame "whose day of service is a Saturday" adding that, "this Ashante God is the same as the Jehovah of the Israelites, whom they worshiped on the Sabbath or Saturday."[17]

"The Akan peoples of Ghana worshiped the Creator on Saturday long before the first Portugese ship anchored off the coast in 1471."[18]

"Ashante records have it that in the 1920s, the queen mother and women of Ashante presented a silver stool as a gift to Princess Mary of Britain, through the British governor in the Gold Coast (Ghana's colonial name), and in an accompanying message, the queen mother alluded to the Akan God of Saturday, Onyamee Kwaame:

"'We pray the great God Nyankopon, on whom men lean and do not fall, whose day of worship is a Saturday, and whom the Ashanti serve just as she [Princess Mary] serves Him, that He may give the king's child and her husband long life and happiness, and finally, when she sits upon this silver stool, which the women of Ashanti have made for their White queen mother, may she call us to mind."[19]

Speaking out of the African-American tradition, the authors and editors of the enormously popular *African Heritage Study Bible* give sympathetic attention to the ancient Sabbath in its African setting, something not done by the standard religious publications. Following are a few references:

1. *On the Ten Commandments*: "The Ashanti believe that in the beginning man acted by natural law, but sin quickly obscured the natural light of reason, and it became necessary that the same precepts and prohibitions should be given to man in clearly defined terms, that he might not plead ignorance as an excuse for transgression. That is precisely what . . . God did on Mount Sinai in giving us the Ten Commandments."[20]

2. *On Leviticus 23:32*: "The observance of the Sabbath is practiced among the Falasha of Ethiopia. In the Ethiopian language, Amharic, the Sabbath is known as Senbet. The Falasha commence preparing for Senbet on Friday afternoon."[21]

3. *On Isaiah 58:13-14*: "Sabbath rest Re Yoruba 'ako-ogo' (1st day) and similar days of rest in other West African tribes analagous to the Hebraic Sabbath with its death penalty for violations. Another African ethnic cultural tradition spoken by the prophet Isaiah."[22]

4. *On Ezekiel 20:12-13*: "Importance of the Sabbath, Leviticus 23:32."[23]

5. *On Revelation 1:10*: "'Lord's Day, Sabbath' equates the Lord's Day and the Sabbath and references Leviticus 23:32."[24]

The African Diaspora The Connection

There is a spiritual connection, a visceral unity, between and among the African peoples that is unique. Like separated twins who somehow mysteriously share the same feelings across the years, though miles apart, Africans on the continent and Africans in diaspora exhibit a symbiotic connection that W.E.B. DuBois often referred to as "the blood" or, more formally, Pan Africanism. Cheik Anta Diop, one of the greatest African scholars, was convinced that a certain global consciousness exists among the African peoples.

African-Americans cannot escape this connection; it is thrust upon them. Wrenched from their homeland and cast into new and frightening surroundings, African-Americans redefined themselves, and thus was created a new people. The middle passage was the great unifier, bringing people of different tribes and languages together, developing a commonality.

So strong is the "blood" that Africans in diaspora share Africa's pain and suffering even today. This empathy was forged in the past fires of affliction. That any survived the "middle passage," the inhuman way in which Africans were conveyed to the New World, to a life of slavery, is a miracle. That there is a remnant at all is of tremendous significance, a story worth repeating, retelling, inquiring into.

Clearly there are lessons to be learned here, even beyond the ususal historic account. Yahweh has made this suffering and coming together a part of salvation history; the Most High God has shown unequivocally that nothing is beneath His notice. His interest is worldwide, transcending national boundaries. Indeed, the poet spoke with discernment when he asked, "Is not the bond of a common fate closer than that of birth?"

For All the Saints

The Bible, like all of God's great gifts, is given to all people. No race or nation can claim it. Through the pages of the Bible, Yahweh establishes contact with His earthborn children. The Hebrew prophets may have delivered the Word, the scribes may have arranged the writings into various categories, but the Word did not originate with them. They were channels, "earthen vessels," as Paul describes them, but the treasure they bring to us is of God.

Ultimately, God intended that His Word should come into our hands, that we should have it in our possession. It is for us. The first duty of every rational human being is to know and understand this vital communication from Yahweh.

Without doubt, this Book is the most vital document ever to come into human possession. It is the supreme treasure, and Yahweh demands for it accountability and responsibility. We humans must answer, as in the Creation story, where Adam is called to account for his deeds. The Bible is a book about judgment on kings and commoners. The inner truths of the Bible, truths involving ethics and morality, cannot be grasped by those who are not willing to absorb its spirit and follow its precepts.

The Bible, with its ability to build self-esteem and self-worth, must be restored, returned, and vouchsafed, especially to Africans in diaspora. Theologians have the task of making Scripture accessible to the people.

End Notes

[1]Ellen G. White, *The Faith I Live By* (Washington, D.C.: Review and Herald Pub. Assn., 1958), p.42.

[2]———, "The Bible to Be Understood by All," *The Signs of the Times*, Aug. 20, 1894, p. 43.

[3]Adrian Hastings, "The Church in Africa: 1450-1950," *Oxford History of the Christian Church* (New York: Oxford University, 1994), pp. 176, 177.

[4]Smith, p. 404.

[5]Walter Brueggemann, *Genesis, in Interpretation: A Bible Commentary for Teaching and Preaching* (Louisville: Westminster John Knox, 1991), vol. 1, p. 43.

[6]G. Yorke, "Bible Translation in Africa: An Afrocentric Perspective," in the *Bible Translator: Technical Papers* (1999), p. 50.

[7]See David J. Clark and H. A. Hatton, *A Handbook on the Books of Nahum, Habakkuk, and Zephaniah*, United Bible Societies Handbook Series [New York: United Bible Societies, 1989], pp. 143, 144.

[8]Okot p'Bitek, *African Religions in European Scholarship* (Kampala, East Africa: East African Lit. Bureau, 1970; reprint, Chesapeake, Va.: Heritage Classical Research Studies, ECA Assn., 1997), p. 123.

[9]*Ibid.*, pp. 1, 2.

[10]*Ibid.*, p. 123.

[11]Martin Bernal, *Black Athena*, in *The Afro-Asiatic Roots of Classical Civilization: The Fabrication of Ancient Greece*, 1785-1985 (New Brunswick, N.J.: Rutgers, 1987), vol. 2, p. 241.

[12]Jacob J. Nortey, "Independent African Churches—Are They Genuinely Christian?" *Spectrum*, Dec. 1989, p. 30.

[13]Joel Awoniwi, *Sabbath in Yoruba Land Before Christianity*, 2nd ed. (Ile Ife, Nigeria, n.d.), p. 17.

[14]Bekele Heye, "The Sabbath in Ethiopia" (master's thesis, Andrews University, 1968), p. 47.

[15]Quoted in B. A. Pauw, *Christianity and the Xhosa Tradition* (Oxford: Clarendon, 1958), p. 32.

[16]Ellen G. White, *The Great Controversy* (Mountain View, Calif.: Pacific Press. Pub. Assn., 1911), p. 63.

[17]R. S. Rattray, *The Ashanti* (London: Oxford University Press, 1923), p. 80.

[18]Kofi Owusu-Mensa, "Onyamee Kwamee (The Akan Saturday God of Saturday)" (unpublished paper, n.d.), p. 17.

[19]*Ibid.*, p. 13.

[20]James Peebles, *American Heritage Study Bible* (1994), p. 119.

[21]*Ibid.*, p. 198.

[22]*Ibid.*, p. 1066.

[23]*Ibid.*, p. 1201.

[24]*Ibid.*, p. 1782.

CHAPTER TWO
GOD IS. GOD SAID. GOD DID.

The God of the Bible, the God of the African, and the God of the African in Diaspora

> "God that made the world and all things therein, seeing that he is Lord of heaven and earth, dwelleth not in temples made with hands; Neither is worshipped with men's hands, as though he needed any thing, seeing he giveth to all life, and breath, and all things; And hath made of one blood all nations of men for to dwell on all the face of the earth, and hath determined the times before appointed, and the bounds of their habitation; That they should seek the Lord, if haply they might feel after him, and find him, though he be not far from every one of us: For in him we live, and move, and have our being; as certain also of your own poets have said, For we are also his offspring" (Acts 17:24-28).
>
> "The problem of God now stands before us as the critical problem of the next decade, and it is the fundamental issue for all mankind."[1]
>
> "They [African theologians] are complaining about the failure to make God the core of church history."[2]
>
> "You need not tell a child that there is a God" (African Proverb).

God Is

The first item on the agenda is God. The existence of God is the linchpin of every religious belief system. He is the ultimate answer and the meaning of life. Without God there is no ultimacy; nothing else really matters. Without Him, man must create a belief system and invent a god. Ethics, morality, justice, and the value of human life all derive from God. In Him all things consist.

Black preachers of yesteryear, in their own unique way, would say about Yahweh's existence, "Before there was a where or a when or a there or a then, He was!"

Similarly, in speaking of Odomankoma (one of the Akan names for God), the Africans will say, "He has no beginning in time, and of course, no beginning in space, nor end. He is there always, was there, and ever will be."

As we shall see, the Hebrew prophets, Africans on the continent, and Africans in diaspora all take it for granted, and without question, that there is a great God, a Sky God, a Most High God. He exists. He is. African-Americans especially are fond of the expression "God is." By this they mean He is more than the subject of some mere philosophical discussion. God is supreme reality, the life force personified. He is existence itself, and in Him "is life, original, unborrowed, underived."[3]

God is known by His personal name, Yahweh, which means "He who was, who is, and who is to come, the I AM." African-American Christians have a favorite saying: "There is a reality in serving the true and living God."

The Hebrew Prophets

> "And God said unto Moses, I AM THAT I AM: and he said, Thus shalt thou say unto the children of Israel, I AM hath sent me unto you" (Ex. 3:14).
>
> "LORD, thou hast been our dwelling place in all generations. Before the mountains were brought forth, or ever thou hadst formed the earth and the world, even from everlasting to everlasting, thou art God" (Ps. 90:1, 2).

God is clearly the focus of the Hebrew prophets. The biblical witness, consistent from first to last, elevates God above all, as the One who demands complete homage, and calls all inhabitants of the globe to judgment.

How is this greatest of all realities, the reality of a true and living God, reflected in the ancient Hebrew prophets?

The Hebrew prophets speak about their God without restraint. They speak well of Him they laud and praise Him, memorializing His greatness in soaring language:

> "Remember the former things, those of long ago; I am God, and there is no other; I am God, and there is none like me. I make known the end from the beginning, from ancient times, what is still to come. I say: My purpose will stand, and I will do all that I please" (Isa. 46:9, 10, NIV).

"Do you not know? Have you not heard? Has it not been told you from the beginning? Have you not understood since the earth was founded? He sits enthroned above the circle of the earth, and its people are like grasshoppers. He stretches out the heavens like a canopy, and spreads them out like a tent to live in" (Isa. 40:21, 22, NIV).

African View of God

The concept of God looms large in the thinking of the African peoples, and the idea of God is the dominant reality for Africans in diaspora. The African idea of God is not identical to that of the Hebrew prophets, but neither is it antithetical. There are some striking similarities.

For instance, Africans would generally agree with the prophets' discourse about God because it is stated in terms that are familiar to them. African Christians have a strong Old Testament orientation, as do Africans in diaspora. Most African people groups believe in a High God who is perfect in knowledge and power.

Albert J. Raboteau speaks to the point and voices the sentiments of a host of scholars when he states:

> "Common to many African societies was belief in a High God, or Supreme Creator of the world and everything in it. It was also commonly believed that this High God, often associated with the sky, was somewhat removed from and uninvolved in the activities of men, especially so when compared with the lesser gods and ancestor-spirits who were actively and constantly concerned with the daily life of the individual and the affairs of society as a whole."[4]

Europeans were quick to note that Africans believed in a High God who transcended ritual relationships with humans. Describing religion on the Slave Coast, William Bosman, a Dutch factor, remarked that the Africans had an "idea of the true God, and ascribe to him the attributes of almighty, and omnipresent."[5]

West-African theologian Lamin Sanneh, speaking about transcendence and immanence, wrote: "The phrase 'God is' (Olorun mbe) affirms this dual concept of religion. God exists as an invisible force; but He also exists as efficacious power, the one who makes promises and keeps them, and may indeed be approached to fulfil human needs."[6]

The African would say He exists . . . God is!

They Worship Yahweh

There is an illuminating reference to this phenomenon, that of knowing God, in Genesis: "And to Seth, to him also there was born a son; and he called his name Enos: then began men to call upon the name of the LORD" (Gen. 4:26).

At some point in time during the antediluvian world there was a turning to God that was extensive and significant enough to be included in the record. People were moved to name themselves by the Lord God or otherwise to identify themselves as worshipers of Yahweh, belonging to Him. They gave their children names that distinguished them from those who did not believe in Yahweh. This sense of family, under God, comes to expression in Genesis 6:2, in the term "sons of God" which seems to refer to the worshipers of Yahweh.

The above-referenced revival of Yahwism compels us to be open to the possibility of other manifestations of Yahwism consciousness of the one true God in other times and places. Some Christians are perplexed and not a little distressed to think that God would work "outside" the Judeo-Christian community. A surprising number of Christians believe that all other peoples are "heathen," that they are undocumented species, disposable creatures, who have no history and no place in the plans and purposes of God. Their way of reading Scripture is to confirm their narrow view.

Yahweh, this God of care and concern, is constantly seeking to reveal Himself to the human family and to establish contact with them. We cannot negate those undocumented periods of time and places and call them "prehistory" as if their populations were not important to Yahweh, the Father of Jesus the Christ, who sees sparrows fall. Nor should we prejudge the people of these times and places as eternally lost, consigned to the outer regions.

Ellen White's view would be thought quite liberal in some theological circles: "Even among the heathen there are those who cherish the spirit of kindness, who have given all the help within their power to the missionaries that have been sent them. They worship God ignorantly, and to many of them the message of light is never brought; yet they will not perish, for they will receive the blessing, because they have wrought the works of God."[7]

He Is Also the God of Job, Melchisedek, Jethro, and Rahab

Paul insists that the knowledge of God has always been offered to the family of man, that it has always been available:

> "Then Peter opened his mouth, and said, Of a truth I perceive that God is no respecter of persons: but in every nation he that feareth him, and worketh righteousness, is accepted with him" (Acts 10:34, 35).
>
> "That they [all nations] should seek the Lord, if haply they might feel after him, and find him, though he be not far from every one of us" (Acts 17:27).

There are striking examples of non-Hebrews who were recognized by their contemporaries and by Israel's leaders as special servants of the Most High God. One of these was Job, the greatest man of antiquity.

A desert chief and not an Israelite, Job predated Moses and perhaps even Abraham (the book of Job is regarded by many as the oldest book of the Bible).

Yahweh chose Job to bear witness to His character, to reveal the kind c who is enthroned at the center of the universe. The book of Job is a pr philosophical treatise in the best sense of the word. The mysteries of [illegible] are posed and illustrated in the life experience of the "man in the land of Uz . . . and that man was perfect and upright, and one that feared God, and eschewed evil" (Job 1:1).

Then there was "Melchizedek king of Salem . . . the priest of the most high God. And he blessed him, and said, Blessed be Abram of the most high God, possessor of heaven and earth: And blessed be the most high God, which hath delivered thine enemies into thy hand. And he gave him tithes of all" (Gen. 14:18-20). Christ's priesthood is "after the order of Melchisedek" (Ps. 110:4). The book of Hebrews repeats this assertion nine times, calling him "priest of the most high God" (see Heb. 5:6, 10; 6:20; 7;1, 10, 11, 15, 17, 21). The appellation Most High God corresponds with the African idea of God.

Salem, the Canaanite city, is the site of Jerusalem, Israel's national capital. Melchizedek, himself a Canaanite, is a recognized priest of the Most High God. This passage of Scripture once again establishes Israel's Canaanite origins. It also gives credence to my assertion that Yahweh has always been in contact with non-Hebrews and chose to make "heathens" His representatives and agents, even priests according to His will.

Jethro, a priest of Midian and a Kenite, a descendant of Abraham through Keturah, his second wife, came in contact with Israel's future deliverer when Moses was a fugitive from Egypt on a murder charge. The Hebrew liberation movement was temporarily aborted (Ex. 2:11-15). Jethro gave Moses sanctuary at the lowest ebb in his career, employed the fugitive, and gave him his daughter's hand in marriage. Evidently, Jethro was a monotheist, a believer in the God of the Hebrews. He lived in the vicinity of "the mountain of God, even to Horeb" (Ex. 3:1).

(The giving of the law, the manifestation of the character of Yahweh, took place on a mountain, Sinai [see Exodus 19]. It was at this mount that God made Israel His covenant people.)

J. B. Danquah observes that Moses did not know God's personal name, Yahweh, when he went to Midian. Ellen G. White speaks of Jethro as "the priest and prince of Midian, who was also a worshiper of God."[8] White believed that "Jethro was singled out from the darkness of the Gentile world to reveal the principles of heaven. . . . Jethro helped him in many things to a correct faith, as far as he himself understood."[9] We should keep in mind that this association between Jethro and Moses spanned a period of more than 40 years.

After the Exodus Jethro came to the Hebrew encampment to bring Moses' wife and children to the now fully empowered leader of Israel. "And Jethro rejoiced for all the goodness which the LORD had done to Israel, whom he had delivered out of the hand of the Egyptians" (Ex. 18:9). It is noteworthy that Moses is still willing to be instructed by this priest of Midian in matters of organization and governance (see verses 13-27).

It is important to observe that it was during Moses's sojourn with Jethro that God's personal name, Yahweh, was revealed to him as the preferred form of address for the Deity. This name, more than any other of the many names for God, speaks to the question of His identity. "And God said unto Moses, I AM THAT I AM: and he said, Thus shalt thou say unto the children of Israel, I AM hath sent me unto you" (Ex. 3:14).

It should be further noted that this is the name that answers Pharaoh's question "Who is the LORD, that I should obey his voice to let Israel go? I know not the LORD, neither will I let Israel go" (Ex. 5:2).

This is the time when the God of Abraham, Isaac, and Jacob is about to show His power in freeing the Israelite slaves, to proclaim the law that reflects His character, to perform His most powerful action and statement about human dignity and freedom, and to establish the covenant community to whom He will give His Sabbath, the defining sign of their relationship to Him. "Moreover also I gave them my sabbaths, to be a sign between me and them, that they might know that I am the LORD that sanctify them. . . . And hallow my sabbaths; and they shall be a sign between me and you, that ye may know that I am the LORD your God" (Eze. 20:12, 20).

Yahweh uses Jethro the Kenite, who was familiar with the name Yahweh before Moses, and, in fact, helped him to understand it, to facilitate His plans and purposes for humankind. If, as a number of biblical scholars insist, the Kenites knew Yahweh by His special name, they could well have been Sabbathkeepers. Here we have a so-called heathen, Afro-Asiatic people preserving this vital intelligence before the Hebrews came on the scene!

The African mind was powerfully affected by Yahweh, the mighty name of the liberating God. He is the Sabbath God who requires special worship on His day: "And remember that thou wast a servant in the land of Egypt, and that the LORD thy God brought thee out thence through a mighty hand and by a stretched out arm: therefore the LORD thy God commanded thee to keep the sabbath day" (Deut. 5:15). By invoking that name, the believer pledges supreme allegiance to the God who has released him from bondage and becomes Yahweh's slave forever. The Sabbath serves to reinforce this relationship. By faithfully observing the Sabbath, as Yahweh has commanded, the believer is not only bound to Yahweh by a golden clasp (the Sabbath), but he or she becomes living witness to the power of the Creator God.

In terms of Old Testament societies and ancient cultures, the God fearer takes the name of his or her god as surname and becomes His possession. The believer is no longer his or her own; he or she can now say, "I am of Yahweh, 'of whom the whole family in heaven and earth is named' [Eph. 3:15]."

In His outreach to His global family, Yahweh even spoke to Gentile kings: "The LORD stirred up the spirit of Cyrus king of Persia, that he made a proclamation throughout all his kingdom, and put it also in writing, saying, Thus saith Cyrus king of Persia, All the kingdoms of the earth hath the LORD God of heaven given me; and he hath charged me to build him an house in Jerusalem, which is in Judah" (2 Chron. 36:22, 23).

It is a mistake to dismiss every religious specialist, priest, prophet, or shaman in the non-Hebrew world as a phony and a crook. There were among these nations at least a few who were honest and sincere and feared God. These are the persons Peter references when he says: "Of a truth I perceive that God is no respecter of persons: but in every nation he that feareth him, and worketh righteousness, is accepted with him" (Acts 10:34, 35).

We should also consider Rahab. Why would this Canaanite woman put herself at risk for the safety of the Hebrew scouts? How is it that her heart was softened toward the "enemy"? The answer is in her reply to the scouts: "I know that Yahweh has given you this land. . . . We have heard how Yahweh dried up the sea of Reeds before you . . . because Yahweh your God is god both in heaven above and on earth beneath" (Joshua 2:9-11, JB)."

Rahab is included in the honor roll of those who triumphed through faith: "By faith the harlot Rahab perished not with them that believed not, when she had received the spies with peace" (Heb. 11:31). A Canaanite harlot inscribed in Israel's hall of fame alongside Abraham, Isaac, and Jacob! Amazing!

This remarkable story is included in the biblical record for its teaching value, to puncture our preconceived opinions. Yahweh has always been the God of all flesh, and the biblical perspective requires us to work from this reality as our major premise. Ellen White sees in the Rahab story a revelation of the deeper purposes and plans of God: "All who, like Rahab the Canaanite, and Ruth the Moabitess, turned from idolatry to the worship of the true God, were to unite themselves with His chosen people. As the numbers of Israel increased they were to enlarge their borders, until their kingdom should embrace the world."[10]

The Hagar Narrative

Hagar, an African woman, has a most interesting association with the Hebrew people. She enters the story as Sarah's handmaid. Before the birth of Isaac, the legitimate heir, Hagar, at the request of Sarah, bares Abraham a son (see Gen. 16:1-4, 7-11).

Several observations need to be made. The "angel of the Lord" who appears to Hagar is really God. This kind of spectacular appearance is called theophany and is usually reserved for prophets and patriarchs. It is the "Angel of the Lord" who addresses Abraham (Gen. 22:11, 15) and Moses (Ex. 3:2). Jacob wrestles with this Angel, who is "even the LORD God of hosts" (Hosea 12:5). Joseph calls Him "the Angel which redeemed me from all evil" (Gen. 48:16).

Emerging Patterns

As one reviews the recent research on African traditional religions, patterns begin to emerge, some facts begin to stand out in stark contrast with myth and legend:

1. The African peoples believe in one all-powerful God. "As far as it is known, there are no images or physical representations of God by African peoples."[11] "The ever-repeated assertion that Africans are fetishists, that is worshipers of inanimate objects, is utterly false. . . . They may be superstitious but they are not fetishists. They believe in one great, invisible God who made all things and controls all things. No temples are made for Him."[12] The African elders ask the question, "What building could ever contain Him?"

2. The God of African traditional religions is transcendent and immanent. In most African societies God seems to be regarded as more transcendent than immanent. The Sky God is somewhat removed from human activities and concerns. Some African groups do believe in a God who is with us, but this is not the prevailing sentiment.

3. In Africa religion is completely integrated into all of life and suffused through the various cultures. An African teacher recently said, "To the African the whole universe breathes of God. . . . The extent of his faith . . . is locked up in spiritual capital, which the church has to learn to use." There is no dichotomy, no sharp line drawn between the secular and the sacred, no compartmentalizing of life. Africans have a wholistic view of life and the universe.

African traditional religions have no religious practice that could be called catechism or religious education. There is no formal instruction or systematic theology, per se. Thus it is difficult to understand how there can be a body of accepted truths, a belief-system substructure, but there is. However, Africans do not usually engage in theological and ideological battles.

Resonance of the African people

This pervasive religious feeling, this God-awareness, is observed throughout all of Africa, among commoners and kings. Harold Courlander gives us the story of a Xhosa who reproves a missionary for failing to deal seriously with traditional religion.

> "We had this word before the missionaries came; we had God long ago. . . . The God who is now is the one who was from everlasting, before the missionaries came. So we say there is no God who has just come to us. Let no man say, 'The God which is, is the God of the English.' There are not many gods. There is but one God. We err when we say, 'He is the God of the English.' He is not the God of certain nations; just as man is not English and Kosa; he is not Fingo and Hottentot; he is one man who came forth from one God."[14]

A Pygmy Hymn

The pygmies are looked upon as the most benighted and backward of all the African peoples. Thus it is almost incredible to find this gem of a poem floating around in Pygmy oral literature.

> "In the beginning was God,
> Today is God,
> Tomorrow will be God,
> Who can make an image of God?
> He has no body,
> He is as a word which comes out of your mouth,
> That word! It is no more,
> It is past and still it lives,
> So is God."[15]

We may conclude, with Adrian Hastings, that "there is enough evidence to suggest that belief in a single creator-god was normally foundational in their [the Africans'] worldview."[16]

African Witnesses

Two highly regarded African scholars are important to our further understanding of the African view of God, John Mbiti and J. B. Danquah. Danquah completed a major study on religious thought and practice among the Akan people, the largest, most influential people group in Ghana. A good deal of his research may be found in his book The Akan Doctrine of God.

Although his work was done more than 40 years ago, it is still highly regarded.

Mbiti was asked to write a chapter in the book Theologians in Transition, an international symposium of ranking theologians sponsored by Christian Century. His comment on the African response to the "death of God" theology that caused so much controversy in Europe and America during the 1960s helps us to get a sense of how Africans view the doctrine of God:

> "Some people tried to involve Africa in the debate. But to the disappointment of those theological exporters, this fish was not attracted by the bait. A prominent European New Testament professor visited Makerere University and interviewed me on what I thought about the 'death of God' discussion. I simply and honestly answered him that 'for us in Africa, God is not dead.' That finished the interview. On returning home, the learned professor wrote an article using my brief answer as his title.
>
> "But God's dealings with the African people are recorded, nevertheless, in living form oral communication, rituals, symbols, ceremonies, community faith. For us in Africa, God is not dead and that applies whether or not there is a written record of His relations with and concern for people.
>
> "The God described in the Bible is none other than the God who is already known in the framework of our traditional African religiosity. The missionaries who introduced the gospel to Africa in the past 200 years proclaimed the name of Jesus Christ. But they used the names of the God who was and is already known by African peoples such as Mungu, Mulungu, Katonda, Ngai, Olodumare, Asis, Ruwa, Ruhanga, Jok Modimo, Unkulunkulu and thousands more. These were not empty names. They were names of one and the same God, the Creator of the world, the Father of our Lord Jesus Christ. One African theologian, Gabriel Setiloane, has even argued that the concept of God which the missionaries presented to the Sotho-Tswana peoples was a devaluation of the traditional currency of Modimo (God) among the Sotho-Tswana."[17]

As for the Akan people, there is no doubt in Danquah's mind that they have from antiquity believed in the one true God, the God of Abraham, Isaac and Jacob, and their God. Danquah complains, along with many of his fellow African scholars, about European anthropologists who "perpetually go on creating a spate of literature about the Akan, most of it based on misunderstanding, but put forth to the world with a great show of profound learning as the result of having 'lived with the natives' for a tour or couple of tours."

Danquah's conclusion is that "Akan religious doctrine knows of only one God." Then he goes on to say, in anticipation of the questions raised about witchcraft, sorcery, and "all those gross heathen practices":

> "Everything else found in the land, in the form of religion, is nothing but superstition, and one may even make a study of the many ramifications or 'systems' of such superstitions just as many have made a study of superstitions among the European nations but, justice to the Akan, the cults of the private man desirous of short cuts to satisfy the natural craving for some religion, should not be ascribed to the Akan as their racial and national conception of God."[18]

Christaller, a European scholar, observes: "The Akan, it must be urged, should be credited as having, from the very beginning, conceived the idea that if there is to be a God, then He must have qualities and powers which are illustrious, glorious, luminous, shining and bright, and the association, but not identification, of Heaven or the Firmament with that idea is a natural and highly instructive one." He goes on to say: "The heathen Negroes are, at least to a great extent, rather monotheists, as they apply the term for God only to the Supreme Being."

Kofi Owusu-Mensa speaks authoritatively:

> "The monotheistic Akan religion recognizes only one Supreme Deity, Onyamee or Onyankopon Tweaduampon Kwaame, the . . . God of Saturday, synonymous with the Jehovah of the Jews and the Allah of Muslims. This is not denying the existence of lesser gods in the Akan traditional system. They do exist, but these sub-gods or idols (abosom) are nothing more than mere intermediaries or links between the Supreme God and man. The Akan regard them as only messengers or 'children' of God, deserving no claims to equality with Him."[19]

Owusa-Mensa believes that the practice of idol worship among the Akan was born out of sheer ignorance of the proper and ideal way of paying homage to God, the Supreme Being.

> "Because the Akan believe that the Supreme Being lives in heaven, that is, beyond the visible clouds or sky, they refer to Him as the 'Sky-God' or in the Akan rendering, 'Onyamee te soco' (literally, God lives in heaven or in the sky). In Akan antiquity, He used to live with men, His children, right here on earth, a next-door Neighbor of man, but the latter's bad neighborly stance and disrespectful attitude toward Him forced God to quit the immediate environs of man. That put a mighty gulf between them, rendering man uncomfortable and

empty of the real good things of life, and bringing him a legion of troubles, woes, and anxieties of life.

"Atheism and its allied concepts, like agnosticism and existentialism, are all alien to Akan traditional societies. The Akan hoary adage, 'Obi nkyere abofra Nysmee' (nobody teaches a child to recognize God's existence, the idea is innate with him), sums up the reality of the Supreme Being at the epicenter of life in traditional Akan societies. An atheist in a traditional Akan community would be an extremely odd person and would be readily ostracized or simply written off as thoroughly unbalanced or outright crazy. 'The belief in a Supreme Being,' says Bishop Peter Akwasi Sarpong, the famous Roman Catholic theologian of Kumase, Ghana, 'is in fact basic to the Ghanaian's traditional way of life.'

"'Onyamee nnae' (literally, God is not asleep) is the expression an Akan man uses to drive home his understanding of the immortality, immanence, omniscience, and omnipotence of God. . . . He is the quintessence of love, kindness, patience, purity, mercy, justice, and righteousness in His dealings with men, other beings, and indeed, the totality of His creation. The eternal God has perfect control over His universe, in spite of the nuisance of the devil and his associates.

"Akan traditions attribute their knowledge of God and His ways to the Supreme Being Himself. Whatever accumulated wisdom of theirs about God is a homemade heritage, given them by their great Onyamee Kwaame Himself through ancient manifestations of Himself and His ways. No foreign tutelage by man was involved. The Akan simply happened to be one of those privileged societies on earth that God, in His own wisdom, chose to bless with knowledge on some aspects of His nature and operations. The Akan God is neither inferior nor superior to any other ethnic God; rather He is perceived to be the same God everywhere, although different societies understand Him differently and from varied angles. Rattray, a British anthropologist writing about the Asante in the 1920s, affirmed that their originality on knowledge about God and His ways cannot be credited to any alien influence, Christian or Muslim."[20]

Levi Keidel became a Christian under the influence of Simon Kimbangu, one of the great African prophets and founder of the Kimbanguist Church (EKJC) in Zaire. Kimbangu and Keidel were incarcerated for many years in the same prison. Levi's comments help us to understand the thinking of the ordinary African the man in the street. He speaks of the "affairs of the Great Elder Spirit":

"Our fathers had many beautiful names with which to describe the Creator; and all of them harmonize with what the Book reveals Him to be. He is the only one who has been alive forever. He is the knower of all affairs. His pureness is brighter than the sun. The only thing that has power to clean a man from his sins before the Creator is the drained blood of a living creature offered in sacrifice. To cleanse a cursed house, our tribal diviner used two white chickens; the priest of Israel used two birds. While our diviner believed a chicken had power to carry sins away into the high grass, the priest of Israel put the same faith in a goat.

"God showed us things through dreams. He did the same to Abraham, Jacob, Joseph, Daniel and others. Israel gave the firstfruits of their harvests to God, and were careful not to neglect widows and orphans.

"The Bible now taught me more adequately great events tribal fathers had related to us: how the first man and woman sinned; how men built a tower to reach the sky; and how darkness covered the earth the day that the Son of the Great Elder Spirit was killed."[21]

African Dissent

It would be wrong to give the impression that all Africans agree with Mbiti, Owusu-Mensa, Danquah, and the host of African theologians and church leaders who believe that the God of the Bible is manifest in Africa. Many highly educated and sophisticated Africans are not in favor of any change in the position held by the traditional gods of Africa. These scholars do not want to be involved in the death of the African gods.

One of the most articulate proponents of this position is the late Okot p'Bitek, who accuses Mibiti and Danquah of putting Greek clothing on African gods. Africans who want to strengthen the role of the old traditional religions and the gods of their ancestors view Christianity as an attack on African culture. In their view, the traditional or indigeneous religions are getting a bad rap.

Some African advocates of the Most High God concept may have been a bit too quick to equate certain African names for God with the Hebrew God. I would not, however, say that they are importing Greek clothing for traditional gods. In fact, it is the other way around. Some of the early Christian fathers became so enamored with Greek philosophy that they made Christianity prisoner to Greek thought.

All of this becomes a straw man fight when we realize that there is in Africa a primeval residual revelation of Yahweh, and that tribal gods may be the imperfect memory of what was once well known. The biblical revelation is the standard, the benchmark, the rule, the canon, the precept by which we go; our guidelines are here. There need not be correspondence and borrowing, or tutelage from outside sources.

Africans may have remembrances, however faint, of the times when they knew Yahweh better. It is not the Hebrew God or the Greek gods. Yahweh is the God of all flesh and is able to reveal Himself to any and all of His children as He pleases. P'Bitek need not feel ashamed of his fellow Africans for turning to the God of the Bible.

This original knowledge of God is the premise of this book. Only the believer in the biblical account can approach the matter from this direction. Following is an encapsulation of what we are talking about:

1. There was a general knowledge of God in antiquity.
2. It was lost to a large extent.
3. A residual deposit of Yahwism a knowledge of God may be seen in other parts of the world, in many cultures.
4. It is especially strong in Africa.

Sociologists and anthropologists who do not have this biblical orientation are at a disadvantage, for they are approaching the matter from the wrong end. Knowledge of the "one God" unfortunately deteriorated with the passing of time. While much was lost in many cultures, if you go back, you find it stronger and stronger. This, possibly, is why so many ancient societies have their creation and flood stories.

The African-American Resonance

African-Americans, from the first day of the diaspora, knew that they needed a strong God, a God who could take care of business. Not the watered-down God of liberal theology, whom H. Richard Niebuhr described as "a God without wrath [who] brought men without sin into a kingdom without judgment through the ministrations of a Christ without a cross."[22] In the biblical view, the God of the Bible is adequate, quite capable of "taking care of business."

The God of the Extremity

What God concept did Africans bring to the New World the diaspora? While it is true that African traditional religion has many gods, actually lesser spirits, in the extremity of the middle passage, it was the great God to whom they appealed.

On the slave ships African people were confronted with an extreme crisis, the proportions of which called for the help of the Most High God. They did not like to bother the great Sky God with the everyday problems of life the lesser gods or spirits were considered able to care for these. But in this time of extremity only the "big God" was adequate. Hence, as H. Baumann points out, the "cry" (as distinguished from ordinary speech): "The ancient narratives, which arose in the period of oral tradition, distinguish even more clearly the two basic forms of speech, ordinary language and the cry."[23]

The cry was reserved for major crises. There is anguish, even terror, in the cry. It is a cry like the cry of the psalmist: "In my distress I called upon the LORD, and cried unto my God: he heard my voice out of his temple, and my cry came before him, into his ears" (Ps. 18:6). "Hear my cry, O God; attend unto my prayer. From the end of the earth will I cry unto thee, when my heart is overwhelmed: lead me to the rock that is higher than I" (Ps. 61:1, 2).

The Situation in the West

For a long time, Western liberal Christianity drifted away from the biblical portrait of a God who is all-powerful, absolute, who can be described only in terms of omnipotence, omniscience, and omnipresence, as classical theologians have expressed it for centuries. A few radical theologians dared to declare Him dead. A much larger crowd simply wrote Him off as irrelevant, no longer a meaningful factor in life's equations.

African-American Christians, in contrast, instinctively know, as Markus Barth states it, that "no one can cope with all the unrighteousness and injustice of the world and master it except God. Therefore it is good that God rises up for judgment."[24] The watered-down God of liberalism is not acceptable in the Black community, where people resonate to a message that is centered around the great God concept that comes out of this tradition. African-Americans view Yahweh as the Most High God and acknowledge their dependence on Him with the words of a song: "I love the Lord. He heard my cry and pitied every groan. Long as I live when troubles rise, I'll hasten to His throne."

For the African in diaspora, God is at the center. He cannot be at the periphery. He is the major player in human history, the supreme reality, the center and circumference, the one who gives consistency and substance to the story. He was and is and is to come. Without Him there is no story.

God Said, God the Speaker

> "But he answered and said, It is written, Man shall not live by bread alone, but by every word that proceedeth out of the mouth of God" (Matt. 4:4).

"That he might make thee know that man doth not live by bread only, but by every word that proceedeth out of the mouth of the LORD doth man live" (Deut. 8:3).

"In various times in the past and in various different ways, God spoke to our ancestors" (Heb. 1:1, JB).

A conference of mainly African theologians, held in Ghana in December 1977, wrote in its final communique: "The God of history speaks to all peoples in particular ways."

The Bible presents Yahweh as God the speaker. He communicates His will to humanity in a variety of ways, including dreams and visions: "And the angel of God spake unto me in a dream, saying, Jacob: And I said, Here am I" (Gen. 31:11). "And God spake unto Israel in the visions of the night, and said, Jacob, Jacob. And he said, Here am I" (Gen. 46:2). "But God came to Abimelech in a dream by night, and said to him, Behold, thou art but a dead man, for the woman which thou hast taken; for she is a man's wife" (Gen. 20:3). "For God speaketh once, yea twice, yet man perceiveth it not. In a dream, in a vision of the night, when deep sleep falleth upon men, in slumberings upon the bed; then he openeth the ears of men, and sealeth their instruction" (Job 33:14-16).

The Hebrew *dabar* is translated "word." An action word, *dabar* can mean "to speak, to subdue, to answer, appoint, bid, command, commune, declare, destroy, give, name, promise, pronounce, rehearse, say, speak, be a spokesperson, subdue, talk, teach, tell, think, use, to utter, to work."

God's Word, according to the prophet Isaiah, is alive, powerful, able to effect change: "So shall my word be that goeth forth out of my mouth: it shall not return unto me void, but it shall accomplish that which I please, and it shall prosper in the thing whereto I sent it" (Isa. 55:11).

Yahweh is the God who speaks, who communicates, who visits Adam and Eve in the garden. He keeps up His correspondence with humanity He is always communicating.

Oral Tradition, Oral Literature

One thing that Africans on the continent have bequeathed to their brethren in the diaspora is a rich oral tradition. Oral communication is part and parcel of African-American culture, the method by which history and tradition are passed forward. This is a great gift.

Jan Vansina, a Western scholar who has seen the value and usefulness of oral history, has this to say:

> "Oral tradition is so rich that one cannot study all its aspects in a single short study. I believe that the incredible wealth and versatility of this tradition are not yet fully recognized. . . . Oral traditions have a part to play in the reconstruction of the past. The importance of this part varies according to place and time. It is a part similar to that played by written sources because both are messages from the past to the present, and messages of key elements in historical reconstruction. But the relationship is not one of the diva and her understudy in the opera: when the star cannot sing, the understudy appears; when the writing fails, tradition comes on the stage. This is wrong. Wherever oral traditions are extant, they remain an indispensable source for reconstruction. They correct other perspectives just as much as other perspectives correct them."[25]

In my judgment, Western scholars have not given due attention to the fact that oral history is first. Maybe it is a display of human pride and too much faith in the idea of progress; maybe there is a playing down of oral tradition as if "those people" were lacking, "not quite as intelligent as we are." But remember, the world got along for at least a couple of millennia before a single word was written.

As the human family separated into various clans, races, and ethnic groups, and spread abroad over the face of the earth, the story became garbled and twisted and far from the original. This is why Scripture, the written Word, was needed as a corrective. It is not for us to attempt to correct the story from our own biased and inadequate view, but to stand up any story to be judged by the biblical account.

Oral transmission is a social, community event. More than a single person is involved; there are speakers and hearers. The Africans and the Hebrews were very much into oral literature (oral and aural having to do with speech and sound, saying and hearing, the mouth and the ear). Before the written Word was the spoken Word, "The spirit of the LORD spake by me, and his word was in my tongue" (2 Sam. 23:2). "O earth, earth, earth, hear the word of the LORD" (Jer. 22:29).

It has often been said that Greeks were people of the eye, but the Hebrews were people of the ear. The African and African-American ethos is closer to that of the Hebrews.

God Did

The God of the Bible is no recluse, withdrawn, apathetic, existing in splendid isolation. He is known by His works; the testimony of which is clear and abundant:

> "Many, O LORD my God, are thy wonderful works which thou hast done, and thy thoughts which are to us-ward: they cannot be reckoned up in order unto thee: if I would declare and speak of them, they are more than can be numbered" (Ps. 40:5).
>
> "They forgat God their Saviour, which had done great things in Egypt; Wondrous works in the land of Ham, and terrible things by the Red sea" (Ps. 106:21, 22).
>
> "Oh that men would praise the LORD for his goodness, and for his wonderful works to the children of men!" (Ps. 107:8).
>
> "He hath made his wonderful works to be remembered: the LORD is gracious and full of compassion" (Ps. 111:4).
>
> "All thy works shall praise thee, O LORD; and thy saints shall bless thee" (Ps. 145:10).
>
> "And they sing the song of Moses the servant of God, and the song of the Lamb, saying, Great and marvellous are thy works, Lord God Almighty; just and true are thy ways, thou King of saints" (Rev. 15:3).

The Hebrew prophets picture God as active. His name, Yahweh, suggests activity, dynamism, great energy, power to act and to perform. These prophets use the most intense verb forms to describe the Most High. He not only superintends the universe, but orders, sustains, and directs it. For the writers of the Bible, Yahweh is no recluse—He is in touch with every part of His boundless creation.

Creation, the Ultimate Deed

God has done many great and wondrous things, but Creation is His supreme act. The Hebrew prophets saw Creation as the first and primary act, the deed through which God reveals and defines Himself, His qualities of person, and all of His subsequent acts. This full-orbed vision of the great God of heaven and earth filled them with wonder, awe, and praise.

Creation takes precedence. Could we but see His handiwork, its wondrous design, in all its awesome power and operation, all else would fall into place. Even the inscrutable mysteries, questions that baffle and perplex us, would be held in abeyance to this revelation of His providence. Increasingly, modern minds have come under the tyranny of the scientific method, driven to give credibility only to what can be observed and measured. We have become, therefore, almost incapable of experiencing wonder and awe. Alas, mastery has driven out mystery!

The African and African-American Views of Creation

To a certain extent, the peoples of Africa and the diaspora share the Hebrew mind. They see God as supreme and powerful. As in the Hebrew, God is called by many names which describe His many characteristics. According to Danquah, He is "God, the Manifold" and "Nyame [popular in Akan society], or Onyame, the 'Shining One.'" Danquah continues:

> "As He grows to be worshiped and to be intimately known He is called Nyankapon, or Onyankopon, in comparison with other competitors, and distinguished as the Greater 'Shining One.' He created things, the Oboo-ade, or Boadee. The community is of Him, the entirety of it. He is 'Borebore a aboo Ade,' the great builder or excavator, who created the Thing; the Odamankoma, the Creator par excellence, beyond whom there is nothing, the Supreme of the Thing, of all that is in being."[26]

The Akan concept of God is summed up here in three appellations, Nyame, Nyankopon, and Odomankoma: "The first distinctive mark of the exalted and distinguished comprehensiveness of Odomankoma is the recognition of him as Bore Bore and Boadee."[27] Both terms mean creator, but Bore Bore means "the excavator, hewer, carver, originator, the architect. . . . Every one of the Akan conceptions of God is creative."[28]

The Akan intensifies this creative activity as much as language can, and as Danquah observes, the human mind can take: "Odomankoma is thus He who continuously and interminably or progressively excavates and creates. He invents or hews out, as it were, carving out creation into being. It is interesting to recall in this connection that the Hebrew word for 'create' also means to hew out; Bara, from BeRITH, hew out, carve, create."[29]

African-American preachers of the past were unexcelled in their preaching of the Creation story. James Weldon Johnson captures this spirit in the highly acclaimed classic God's Trombones, a poetic treatment of oft-repeated sermons he had heard since childhood. The most famous is the Creation sermon—"And God stepped out on space . . ."[30] one of those folk sermons that found their way into the psyche of the people of the African-American diaspora and into general American culture.

While the preaching curriculum of the authentic Black preaching fathers included Noah's flood, the great judgment day, and most of the familiar Bible stories, preached again and again as musicians would perform a repertoire, the Creation story took precedence, as it does in Hebrew and African primeval stories. Creation provides an anchor, a point of reference, for human beings. Creation establishes their status as God's deputies.

The Creation of Man

Scholars remark that the African people have greater interest in the creation of human beings than in the creation of the physical universe."[31] To them the creation of the physical universe and the earth were preparatory to Yahweh's crowning act, the creation of human beings. In this the Hebrew prophets concur: "For thus saith the LORD that created the heavens; God himself that formed the earth and made it; he hath established it, he created it not in vain, he formed it to be inhabited: I am the LORD; and there is none else" (Isa. 45:18). Earth is formed as a dwelling place, a habitat for humanity.

In successive stages Yahweh lifted the curtain on His handiwork. Each day new wonders and revelations unfold. At each stage He pronounces it good. On the sixth day:

> "God said, Let us make man in our image, after our likeness: and let them have dominion over the fish of the sea, and over the fowl of the air, and over the cattle, and over all the earth, and over every creeping thing that creepeth upon the earth. So God created man in his own image, in the image of God created he him; male and female created he them. And God blessed them, and God said unto them, Be fruitful, and multiply, and replenish the earth, and subdue it: and have dominion over the fish of the sea, and over the fowl of the air, and over every living thing that moveth upon the earth" (Gen. 1:26-28).

The biblical Creation narrative is seen in many nonbiblical creation stories, many of which are ancient, coming to us from the nations and cultures of Mesopotamia. Remarkably, scholars have demonstrated that many of these stories can be arranged within the framework or outline of Genesis 1-11; thus they appear to be variations on the Genesis story.

The most striking of these stories come from the most ancient African oral tradition, in which griots claimed that the first stories about the human condition ever told issued forth from the breath of the Sky God. There was even the discovery in Memphis, Egypt, of a creation story in which God creates *solo verbo*, merely by the virtue of His word.

The formation of human beings from clay is widespread in African origin stories and in all ancient cultures. The Sky God or the Most High God shapes and forms the first individuals out of clay. The Shilluks of the White Nile, who name God Tucapacha, explain the differing complexions of the various races as being determined by the color of the clay from which they were fashioned. This same theme appears in Egypt, namely, that God fashioned human beings out of clay. Mention is made of the Potter's wheel in this poem to God:

> "Thou art the master of the wheel,
> Who is pleased to model on the wheel,

> Thou art the Almighty . . .
> And thou hast made men on the wheel."[32]

This was also Job's understanding: "I too was formed from a piece of clay" (Job 33:6, RSV). Vernon Anderson wrote:

> "The Lulua (of Zaire) believe, as most Africans traditionally believe, that man was created by God. The origin of all mankind, then, is God. In genealogies the Lulua people will recite long lists of names as they go back to their earliest ancestors many generations back. Usually after some 16 or 20 names have been given, they will say that so and so was the son of Huntu, who was the son of God . . . thus, Huntu, though a simple word for man, also signifies the first man."[33]

The Creation of Sabbath

The creation of Adam and Eve on the sixth day brings the Master Craftsman's work to completion. Yahweh, having put His best into His creation, declares it very good. Then, consummate artist that He is, God takes the fabric of time and makes something special out of it the Sabbath, a cathedral in time, sculpted from hours and minutes and spun out of the stuff of eternity. A gift from His own heart.

It should be observed that God does not make the Sabbath and bring humanity to it. He creates Adam and Eve and brings the Sabbath to them. This sequence speaks volumes about how God values human beings, what each one means to Him, what God thinks of us. The gift also says something about the Giver. It pleased the Creator to make the Sabbath a vehicle for communicating His presence to His children. From the outset of human history, the Sabbath has been a gift that deepened personal relationships between God and His children (see Eze. 20:12, 20).

The first full day Adam and Eve spent was the Sabbath. It was for them a time for reflection, for enjoyment, for contemplating the wonderful works of Yahweh. Adam and Eve received God's gift with great joy, looking on it as a token of love, God's thoughtful wedding present. The Sabbath is available to every member of the human family, an unrestricted gift, a gift that cannot be stolen or intercepted, a personalized gift. The Sabbath shows that Yahweh knows us, knows our names, has not forgotten us:

> "When I consider thy heavens, the work of thy fingers, the moon and the stars, which thou hast ordained; What is man, that thou art mindful of him? and the son of man, that thou visitest him? For thou hast made him a little lower than the angels, and hast crowned him with glory and honour. Thou madest him to have dominion over the

works of thy hands; thou hast put all things under his feet: all sheep and oxen, yea, and the beasts of the field; the fowl of the air, and the fish of the sea, and whatsoever passeth through the paths of the seas. O LORD our Lord, how excellent is thy name in all the earth!" (Ps. 8:3-9).

"The seventh day marks a time of completion and Sabbath rest," observes Cain Hope Felder. He continues: "In a sense, one can find here all the elements that make for the Shalom (peace) of God: the goodness of the created order is established; the heavens and the earth are completed; the progenitors of the human family are free to develop their potentials without predetermined restraints. God is at peace with creation, and divine rest is most appropriate."[34]

End Notes

[1]Carl F. Henry, "Where Is Modern Theology Going?" *Christianity Today*, Mar. 1, 1968, p. 7.

[2]Isichei, p. 8.

[3]Ellen G. White, *The Desire of Ages* (Mountain View, Calif.: Pacific Press Pub. Assn., 1940), p. 483.

[4]Raboteau, p. 8.

[5]Quoted in Albert J. Raboteau, *Slave Religion: The Invisible Institution in the Antebellum South* (New York: Oxford University Press, 1978), p. 7.

[6]Lamin Sanneh, *West African Christianity: The Religious Impact* (Maryknoll, N.Y.: Orbis, 1983), p. 240.

[7]Ellen G. White, "Ye Did It to Me," *The Signs of the Times*, p. 614.

[8]———, in *SDA Bible Commentary*, Ellen G. White Comments, vol. 1, p. 1099.

[9]———, *This Day With God* (Washington, D.C.: Review and Herald Pub. Assn., 1979), p. 321.

[10]———, *Christ's Object Lessons* (Mountain View, Calif.: Pacific Press Pub. Assn., 1990), p. 290.

[11]*African Heritage Bible* on 2 Cor. 3:17.

[12]Heli Chatelain, "The A-M Bundu of Angola," in Harold Courlander, ed., *Treasury of African Folklore* (New York: Marlowe, 1956), p. 289.

1[3]Isichei, p. 267.

[13]Henry Calloway, "A Xhosa Reproves a Missionary," in Courlander, pp. 440, 441.

[15]Mbiti, p. 34.

[16]Hastings, p. 51.

[17]Mbiti, pp. 54, 55.

[18]*Ibid.*, p. 39.

[19]Kofi Owusu-Mensa, "Onyamee Kwamee (the Akan Saturday God of Saturday)" (unpublished paper), p. 2.

[20]*Ibid.*, pp. 17-20.

[21]Levi O. Keidel, *Black Sampson: An African's Astounding Pilgrimage to Personhood* (Carol Stream, Ill.: Creation House, 1975), chapter 1.

[22]H. Richard Niebuhr, *The Kingdom of God in America* (Hanover, N.H.: University Press of New England, 1988), p. 193.

[23]H. Baumann, *Schopfung und Urzeit des Menschen im Mythus der Afrikanischen Volker*, 2nd ed. (Berlin, 1936, 1964), p. 231.

[24]Markus Barth, *Justification* (Grand Rapids, Mich.: Eerdmans, 1971), p. 25.

[25]Jan Vansina, *Oral Tradition as History* (Madison, Wisc.: University of Wisconsin Press, 1983), pp. 199-201.

[26]Joseph B. Danquah, *The Akan Doctrine of God* (London: Lutterworth, 1944), p. 28.

[27]*Ibid.*, p. 58.

[28]*Ibid.*

[29]*Ibid.*

[30]James Weldon Johnson, *God's Trombones* (New York: Penguin Books, 1927), pp. 17-20.

[31]Claus Westermann, *Creation*, trans. John J. Scullion (Philadelphia: Fortress Press, 1974), p. 24.

[32]Ibid., p. 35.

[33]Vernon A. Anderson, "Witchcraft in Africa A Missionary Problem" (doctoral dissertation, Southern Baptist Theological Seminary, 1942).

[34]Cain Hope Felder, *Troubling Biblical Waters*, Bishop Henry McNeal Turner Studies in North American Black Religion (Maryknoll, N.Y.: Orbis, 1989), vol. 3, p. 168.

CHAPTER THREE

THE THEOLOGY AND FUNCTION OF THE SABBATH

> "Thus the heavens and the earth were finished, and all the host of them. And on the seventh day God ended his work which he had made; and he rested on the seventh day from all his work which he had made. And God blessed the seventh day, and sanctified it: because that in it he had rested from all his work which God created and made" (Gen. 2:1-3).
>
> "It is a sign forever between me and the people of Israel that in six days the LORD made heaven and earth, and on the seventh day he rested, and was refreshed" (Ex. 31:17, NRSV).

His work finished, Yahweh pronounces the planet that He has created "very good." Then, before turning it over to the first couple, the Master Designer affixes His distinctive label to the work of His hands. But first, before humankind takes possession, some things must be made clear, documented. God distinguishes this day of completion, the Sabbath, by blessing, sanctifying, and resting (literally, He "sabbaths" it). The great memorial of His prodigious work is fully established: "He hath made his wonderful works to be remembered" (Ps. 111:4).

This calls for appropriate celebration: "When I remember these things, I pour out my soul in me: for I had gone with the multitude, I went with them to the house of God, with the voice of joy and praise, with a multitude that kept holyday" (Ps. 42:4).

> "Praise ye the LORD. Praise God in his sanctuary: praise him in the firmament of his power. Praise him for his mighty acts: praise him according to his excellent greatness. Praise him with the sound of the trumpet: praise him with the psaltery and harp. Praise him with the timbrel and dance: praise him with stringed instruments and organs. Praise him upon the loud cymbals: praise him upon the high sounding cymbals" (Ps. 150:1-5).

Significant happenings and events in our lives and in history cry out to be celebrated, to be remembered, to be memorialized, "lest we forget." Birthdays, anniversaries, graduations, child dedications, baptisms, bar mitzvahs, call for remembrance. Yahweh has designated the Sabbath as a day appropriate for that purpose, of keeping His great work fresh in memory. The Sabbath is the ultimate memorial.

It Is Universal

> "Declare his glory among the heathen; his marvelous works among all nations" (1 Chron. 16:24).

Creation concerns every human being, and thus the memorial God established for it is not for the Jews alone. It is a gift for all. The event points to the God who created, as the Africans have it, "the thing." It was not done in a corner. It is on display for all to see. We are surrounded with the works of creation. We are the result of creation. How, then, could the celebration be restricted to any single tribe or nation?

The universality of the event dictates the universality of its celebration: "Let them praise the name of the LORD: for he commanded, and they were" (Ps. 148:5). "Thus saith God the LORD, he that created the heavens, and stretched them out; he that spread forth the earth, and that which cometh out of it; he that giveth breath unto the people upon it, and spirit to them that walk therein" (Isa. 42:5).

Example and Model

Sabbath is archetypical, a paradigm for all time, a model rooted in the first week of time, when Yahweh, the great exemplar, set the pattern for Planet Earth for all time to come. He rested and was refreshed. Not a provisional or temporary institution, we may speak confidently of the unchangeableness of the Sabbath. This holy day is a part of the divine constitution, along with marriage, the most ancient institution. It stems from Eden, within its sinless, pristine environment, and is tied to and rooted in Creation.

A Statement of Who He Is

Sabbath says something about the character of this God, about His person. He gives to all people liberally. Through this inestimable gift, God confers equal status on all of humanity, striking down that human pride which is based on externals physical features, bloodlines, achievements, sex, race, ethnicity. This same God who causes His sun to shine on just and unjust people alike extends the gift of the Sabbath unrestricted to every human being.

Again, there are no limitations or restrictions here. As long as the sun rises and sets, or the earth continues to revolve around the sun and spin on its axis, this day will come to us. It transcends boundaries, ignores geography, and is completely oblivious of any differences in the human family. Sabbath is the great common denominator in the human equation. No one is excluded.

About Relationships

Sabbath is a time to enhance relationships, with family and community, and especially with God. It is time for reflection on human identity, on the meaning of life and relationships, and especially our connection with God the Creator. His magnificent gift is received with great joy this token of love, this thoughtful gift.

Interestingly, a pattern for worship is established for the human pair before they are involved in the myriad of activities and responsibilities that life was soon to impose on them. At the outset a unique relationship is established between creature and Creator.

The first pair were coequals. The term "man" referred to both sexes. When this equality is accepted as fact, it becomes clear that there can be no difference of dignity, status, and worth within the human species. "This is the book of the generations of Adam. In the day that God created man, in the likeness of God made he him; male and female created he them; and blessed them, and called their name Adam, in the day when they were created" (Gen. 5:1, 2).

Our distinctive identity and status are established by creation; the Sabbath is our seal of acceptance. Racism, classism, and sexism fly in the face of the Sabbath's true meaning.

From Yahweh With Love

Sabbath was made for man. How, then, can man deny the Creator's love and concern? Sabbath speaks to the covenant relationship between God and the creature. On the sixth day He fashions two beings in His own image and makes their first day a day of delight and special communion with Himself. This speaks volumes about what human beings mean to God, how He regards them, and the relationship that He wants to establish with them. Sabbath fosters this relationship.

Self-esteem

The Sabbath develops and creates self-esteem, not on the basis of race or class or any other human criteria, but on the basis of relationship with the Creator. Every genealogy, when traced back far enough, comes to this juncture: "Which was the son of Adam which was the son of God" (Luke 3:38). This is the vital connection, the place where self-esteem begins, and its purpose is redemption:

"To restore in man the image of his Maker, to bring him back to the perfection in which he was created, to promote the development of body, mind, and soul, that the divine purpose in his creation might be realized this was to be the great work of redemption."[1]

The gift of Sabbath assures us that Yahweh will never disengage Himself from nor abandon His creation or His creatures.

Rhythm in Time and Eternity

God has built into the succession of ordinary days a movement which is a gift to the creature which has been created in His image."[2]

Sabbath is the pause that refreshes. The pattern is six days and one day. Six days of work and one day of rest. Samuele Bacchiocchi raises the question: "How did the number seven come to acquire such a meaning? Most probably as a result of its association with the seventh day of Creation."[3] Yahweh the cosmic symphony conductor orders His composition on 6/7 time. One, two, three, four, five, six, rest!

Sabbath is a promise of heavenly rest, a gift that brings with it a token or pledge of life in the eschaton, the kingdom of God. It is God's future experienced in the now. A portion of eternity set in the midst of time.

Liberation Theology The Genuine Article

It is no small wonder, then, that theologians and biblical scholars in the so-called developing countries have taken up this theme of liberation. Having looked at the account of God's great deliverance in the Exodus, they are tremendously impressed with the power that He displayed in bringing His people out of bondage. African-American theologians and theologians from developing countries consider it their duty to focus on liberation. This is understandable. They are closer to those parts of the world in which the misery index is highest.

Traditional theology, they say, is done in ivory towers by those who are identified with the "haves." "God is on the side of the poor," they say, as they send out a ringing call for justice and equity. They challenge the industrialized nations and the Western religious establishment to identify with the poor and "get on God's side."

When one hears such expressions as "Liberation whatever it takes, by whatever means," the suggestion is that even violence is in order. Conservative Bible scholars are looked upon as being accommodationists who have capitulated to the prevailing culture. Many who have espoused liberation theology now call for secular, political solutions to human problems. And a few have declared themselves radicals.

But radical liberation theology, as we understand it, is not, I would say, really radical enough. The word "radical" means to get at the root of the matter. Political solutions are not the final solution. These cannot possibly get to the root of the human dilemma, which is sin, rebellion against God. Political revolutions throw out one group of flawed creatures only to be succeeded by another.

Messiah Jesus came preaching an authentic theology of liberation: "The Spirit of the Sovereign Lord is on me, because the Lord has anointed me to preach good news to the poor. He has sent me to bind up the brokenhearted, to proclaim freedom for the captives and release for the prisoners, to proclaim the year of the Lord's favor and the day of vengeance of our God, to comfort all who mourn" (Isa 61:1, 2, NIV).

The message of Jesus, both radical and revolutionary, promises freedom to the nations total freedom. He makes the Sabbath the sign of this liberation and independence.

Sabbath Decalogue

The Ten Commandments, as found in Deuteronomy 5, are among the great proclamations about justice and human dignity, and the fourth commandment is its centerpiece. Here again we must use the word "universal". The wisdom of Yahweh comes through. In this passage, Yahweh reveals Himself as God of all flesh, the God of complete justice and equity. It is called the Sabbath decalogue, and the Sabbath and justice are forever inseparable. The essence of Sabbath is social, always relational, always covenental.

Indeed, the rendering of the Sabbath in Deuteronomy 5 speaks to the issues of fairness and justice that are relevant to any society, timeless. "Harold MacMillan, Britain's prime minister, is reputed to have called it the first great worker protection act in history."[4] Even in a patriarchal system where the lord of the estate wielded unlimited power, Yahweh established checks and balances, restraints on excessive use of power.

Sabbath comes into play here in a very practical way. What the commandment is saying is, here is how it all must work out in real life and real time. It deals in specificities. The account provides us concrete illustration of Micah's definitive statement: "He hath showed thee, O man, what is good; and what doth the LORD require of thee, but to do justly, and to love mercy, and to walk humbly with thy God" (Micah 6:8).

The commandment is not ambiguous. "Keep the sabbath day to sanctify it, as the LORD thy God hath commanded thee. Six days thou shalt labour, and do all thy work: But the seventh day is the sabbath of the LORD thy God: in it thou shalt not do any work, thou, nor thy son, nor thy daughter, nor thy manservant, nor thy maidservant, nor thine ox, nor thine ass, nor any of thy cattle, nor thy stranger that is within thy gates; that thy manservant and thy maidservant may rest as well as thou. And remember that thou wast a servant in the land of Egypt, and that the LORD thy God brought thee out thence through a mighty hand and by a stretched out arm: therefore the LORD thy God commanded thee to keep the sabbath day" (Deut. 5:12-15). This becomes a refrain in Deuteronomy 4:34; 6:21-25; 15:15; 16:12; and 26:5-10, and provides the thunder for the Hebrew prophets.

In the struggle for justice and human dignity we must not overlook the primary witness. The standard is set. It is immutable. As the lyrics to the spiritual put it, "It's so high you can't get over it, so low you can't get under it, so wide you can't get around it, you must come in at the door!" Those who claim Jesus as Lord must be confronted with Yahweh's word. The Sabbath commandment clarifies the issue. Everyone in our sphere of influence must be given the opportunity to enjoy Sabbath rest. The commandment is merciful and humane.

Christopher J. H. Wright observes that "alongside this, there is the law commanding just and prompt payment of wages to the most vulnerable workers (in Israel's case, the day 1abourers (24:14f). . . . In the Old Testament rejection of the sabbath principle was associated with exploitation and profiteering: Isaiah 1:13; Amos 8:4-6.

"The observance of the Sabbath is to be physical, concrete evidence of God's claim on us. . . . It also makes the primary relationship in our lives concrete and periodic."[5]

Sabbath is Yahweh's gift to humankind to keep them reminded of their creature status, to save them from the devastating effects of hubris on account of their achievements and accomplishments. These great prophetic words are the antidote for racism and oppression.

As Sabbath is a time to reflect on God's work in Creation, it is also a time to reflect on relationships between God and those whom He has created and between His creatures and each other:

"Thus Sabbath rest is to be available to all regardless of wealth or class, available to animals as well as humans (Ex 20:10), reminding us of our common participation and worth as a part of God's creation. Since we live in a world of inequalities, Sabbath then becomes a reminder that this is not as God intended it."[6]

When Creation was completed, the divine order was unalterably established: God, human beings, all other creatures. The biblical account allows for no other sequence. Man is subject, subordinate. We speak generically here. Human beings are an indivisible category under God. Men, women, menservants, maidservants, aliens, constitute a single class. The Sabbath commandment enjoins upon all a recognition of the divine order. Again, the focus is on Yahweh, who creates and makes covenant with His creation. He is the landlord of ultimate concern!

End Notes

[1]Ellen G. White, *Education* (Mountain View, Calif.: Pacific Press Pub. Assn., 1903), p. 15.

[2]Westermann, p. 165.

[3]Samuele Bacchiocchi, *Divine Rest for Human Restlessness* (Berrien Springs, Mich.: Bacchiocchi, 1980), p. 66.

[4]Jeffries M. Hamilton, "The Rest Is Commentary: A Reading of the Ten Commandments," *Quarterly Review 13* (fall 1993): 33.

[5]Christopher J. H. Wright, "Deuternomic Depression," *Themelios 19* (Jan. 1994): 33, 34.

[6]Bruce C. Birch, *Let Justice Roll Down: The Old Testament, Justice, and Christian Life* (Louisville: Westminister John Knox, 1991), p. 80.

PART TWO

PROBLEMS WITH THE FAMILY

"From one man he made every nation of men, that they should inhabit the whole earth; and he determined the times set for them and the exact places where they should live. God did this so that men would seek him and perhaps reach out for him and find him, though he is not far from each one of us. For in him we live and move and have our being. As some of your own poets have said, 'We are his offspring'" (Acts 17:26-28, NIV).

In this section we will develop, in the light of the biblical testimony, the story of the human family as coming out of a neighborhood, developing from a common source. We will review and point out specifically how the story became corrupted by tampering with origins and the Creation record, and the mischief that has followed.

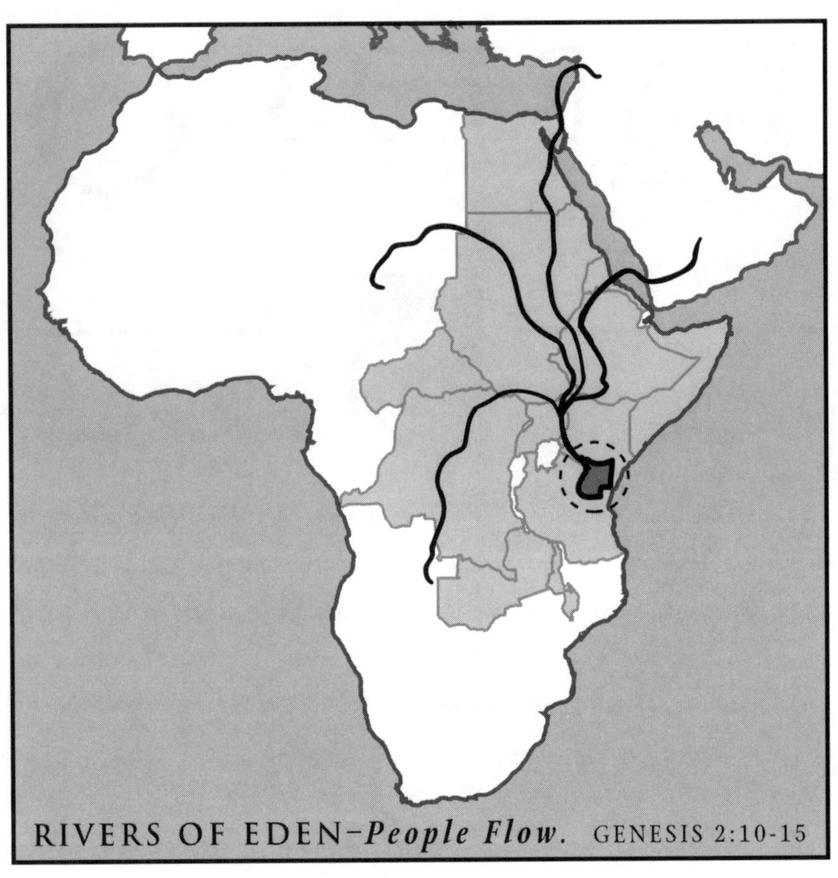

RIVERS OF EDEN–*People Flow.* GENESIS 2:10-15

CHAPTER FOUR
THE NEIGHBORHOOD OF NATIONS

From the Same Neighborhood

> "And a river went out of Eden to water the garden; and from thence it was parted, and became into four heads. The name of the first is Pison: that is it which compasseth the whole land of Havilah, where there is gold; and the gold of that land is good: there is bdellium and the onyx stone. And the name of the second river is Gihon: the same is it that compasseth the whole land of Ethiopia. And the name of the third river is Hiddekel: that is it which goeth toward the east of Assyria. And the fourth river is Euphrates" (Gen. 2:10-14).

The basic biblical declaration about the human family is that we all issue from a common stock. The river of humanity and the river of Eden are both single streams. There is only one headwater, one source. The same water flows in every branch. There are no human beings on the earth who spring from a different source. This truth, simple and at the same time profound, basic, stands behind every unfolding story and development in human history. The river, the stream of humanity, flows out of Eden. "Every nation, kindred, tongue and people (Rev.14:6)" notice how that phrase is at home in every biblical setting originates from a single source.

The first two branches of the Edenic river have a definite African orientation: "The name of the first is Pison: that is it which compasseth the whole land of Havilah, where there is gold; And the gold of that land is good: there is bdellium and the onyx stone. And the name of the second river is Gihon: the same is it that compasseth the whole land of Ethiopia."

Havilah and Ethiopia are identifiable as being of Africa. The other two are of Mesopotamia and thus Afro-Asiatic. The ancient world was an Afro-Asiatic neighborhood. This geographical area was the extent of the then-known world. Notice these considerations from Keith Burton:

> "While I do not accept the evolutionary assumptions behind the dating of fossils, I find it fascinating that archaeologists locate the oldest human fossils on the African continent. Additionally, I am intrigued by the notion that the melanin that determines the darkness of one's skin pigmentation can be lost, but never gained.

These two observations lend to the probability that the earliest humans were of a darker hue. From a biblical perspective, this is not mere assumption. In Genesis 2:10, we read of a river that flows out of Eden, which divides into four. The first, Pison, encircles the land of Havilah, the territory east of the Red Sea occupied by modern-day Saudi Arabia. The second, Gihon, encircles the land of Cush, which corresponds with modern day Ethiopia and Sudan. The third and fourth rivers, Tigris and Euphrates, run through the region of what is known today as the Middle East.

"Given the order in which the rivers are mentioned, it appears that the author lists them from south to north. If this is correct, then the garden of Eden would have been located south of Ethiopia and Saudi Arabia probably in the area of modern-day Kenya and Uganda. Some may object that the author uses post-Flood geographical markers to locate the garden. However, this does not negate the reality of its location."[1]

Monogenetic Versus Polygenetic

There seems to be genral agreement in the scientific community that all human beings come from a single source the monogenetic and that source has an African location, and though I believe the locale to be African, that is not nearly as important as the single-origin theory.

In a strange sort of way, the new scientific discipline used in archaeology, called mitochondrial DNA or molecular biology, is strongly supportive of the monogenetic, single-source idea. Scientists who do not believe in fiat creation, who may be agnostics or even atheists, are now, in effect, proclaiming that we all came from one human pair, just as the Bible says.

These researchers are suggesting the Noah's ark model rather than the candelabra model. The Noah's ark model makes its own statement all people in a single geographic location, then migration. The candelabra model speaks to the notion that human beings evolved in many places and that migration took place, followed by a coming together, and amalgamation.

Though it is not within the purview of this book to discuss the evolution theory (I, of course, accept the biblical record as authentic), I am compelled to reject Darwin on two main accounts: (1) his refutation of the Creator God as a personal being, and (2) the predictable outcome of his theory that results in the idea of superior and inferior species and races.

Social Darwinism is even worse, because this concept lays the groundwork for geneticists and biologists, under the cloak of science, to categorize human beings in a way as to support racial superiority, an idea brought to its apogee in Nazi Germany.

The biblical record puts the family together by placing them in specific areas: "From one man he made every nation of men, that they should inhabit the whole earth; and he determined the times set for them and the exact places where they should live" (Acts 17:26, NIV).

In the ancient world, where one was born and where one lived was a means of identification. If an ancient cartographer drew an accurate map of the world that then was, it would be more than a geography lesson. Such a map showing the places of residence of the people would be fascinating and revealing.

The children of Ham, and especially of Canaan and Cush, would, of course, be dominant in what is Africa and the Middle East. Palestine was occupied by the Canaanites for many centuries before the Hebrews came into the picture. Certain Hamitic tribes were longtime inhabitants of the area of the Arabian Peninsula. You can readily see why biblical scholars in the African diaspora say that most of the Middle East is northeast Africa.

The family of Ham, the largest in patriarchal times, cannot easily be discounted. Many Bible students insist that maps of the Middle Ages were drawn to minimize the African presence in the northeastern part of the continent. More recently, this has again become a point for discussion in some academic circles.

"I will record Rahab and Babylon among those who acknowledge me Philistia too, and Tyre, along with Cush" (Ps. 87:4, NIV). These names and places are all Afro-Asiatic. A brief look at any map of Bible lands reminds us that there was no Suez in those days; the land mass was unbroken.

How This Neighborhood Developed

Africa can be understood only in the light of biblical revelation. Here we have the record of Yahweh's interaction with humans and His planned future for the persons He placed upon the earth as His deputies. To get at the reality of the world that then was we shall have to think of the venue as a neighborhood. Who were the first settlers? Who were the people who lived here? Where did they come from? What was their relationship to one another? How did they get along together? How did they relate to Yahweh?

It is necessary to focus on origins: "What we think about our past will determine our futures."[2]

Genesis Is Crucial

Genesis is a name taken from the Greek that signifies "the book of generation or production"; it is properly so called, as it contains an account of the origin of all things. According to the Holmon Bible Dictionary, "There is no other history so old. There is nothing in the most ancient books which exist that contradicts it; while many things recorded by the oldest heathen writers, or to be traced in the customs of different nations, confirm what is related in the book of Genesis."[3]

The biblical view demands attention: "This is the book of the generations of Adam. In the day that God created man, in the likeness of God made he him; male and female created he them; and blessed them, and called their name Adam, in the day when they were created" (Gen. 5:1, 2). The Jerusalem Bible puts it nicely too: "This is the roll call of Adam's descendants: On the day God created Adam he made him in the likeness of God. Male and female he created them. He blessed them and gave them the name Man on the day they were created."

"And the sons of Noah, that went forth of the ark, were Shem, and Ham, and Japheth: and Ham is the father of Canaan. These are the three sons of Noah: and of them was the whole earth overspread" (Gen. 9:18-19).

You may ask, "Why is Genesis so crucial?" The answer is that Genesis sets the record straight. Earth's story has been so violently distorted that there must be a correction. And that correction must be made at the beginning, at Genesis, the book of beginnings and sources. The Genesis record is critical because:

1. It speaks clearly to the monogenetic (single-source) origin of the human family (Gen. 5:1; 9:19).

2. It establishes the patterns and norms for all the human family (Gen. 1:31).

3. It defines all relationships (Gen. 1:26, 27).

4. It strikes down the hierarchical model through its genealogies (Gen. 5:1, 2).

5. It speaks to the continuity and interrelatedness of humanity, and thus to all peoples, as the legitimate children of Noah (Gen. 10:32).

Genesis 10 begins the saga of new beginnings for Planet Earth. Yahweh has caused the Flood to cease. He resets the earth clock and renews His covenant with humanity. The command to be fruitful is repeated: "And you, be ye fruitful, and multiply; bring forth abundantly in the earth, and multiply therein" (Gen. 9:7).

God speaks to Noah's sons also this time, and, in effect, to their offspring: "And God spake unto Noah, and to his sons with him, saying, And I, behold, I establish my covenant with you, and with your seed after you; and the sons of Noah, that went forth of the ark, were Shem, and Ham, and Japheth: and Ham is the father of Canaan. These are the three sons of Noah: and of them was the whole earth overspread" (verses 8-19).

Observe that the covenant is made not only with Noah, but with his sons and "all flesh that is upon the earth" (verse 17). We need to remind ourselves often that none of the sons of Noah is excluded from the covenant.

Reflections on the Curse of Ham

It is unfortunate that it is necessary to even mention the curse on Ham/Canaan. It is only because the account of this "curse that never was"[4] has been so greatly exaggerated, and has become so much a part of the culture, that it refuses to die. In my judgment, this curse on Ham/Canaan is the most widespread, pernicious, and poisonous of all the racist myths introduced into the bloodstream of Europe and North America. Citing the Bible, its adherents treat this myth as if it were a divine edict.

There is the will on the part of many Christians to believe that some branch of the human family is cursed; sometimes it is Ham, sometimes it is Canaan. One would think that a passage of Scripture so obscure that is not connected with a command of God, that does not fit into the plans and purposes of Yahweh, would slip into the dust bin of history.

Undoubtedly, there is more here than the usual attempt to embarrass people of color, more here than meets the eye. In fact, there is something demonic about it, as Ellen White suggests: "Christ worked throughout his life to break down this prejudice. No human power alone could overcome it."[5]

Speaking in apocalyptic terms, Ellen White goes on to say: "This prejudice was created not by mere flesh and blood, but by principalities and powers; and in wrestling against it He [Christ] was wrestling against the rulers of the darkness of this world, against spiritual wickedness in high places."[6]

It could well be that the powers of evil are determined to parody the beautiful story of God's creation and to once again cast aspersions on the Creator as well.

"And Noah began to be an husbandman, and he planted a vineyard: and he drank of the wine, and was drunken; and he was uncovered within his tent. And Ham, the father of Canaan, saw the nakedness of his father, and told his two brethren without. And Shem and Japheth took a garment, and laid it upon both their shoulders, and went backward, and covered the nakedness of their father; and their faces were backward, and they saw not their father's nakedness. And Noah awoke from his wine, and knew what his younger son had done unto him. And he said, Cursed be Canaan; a servant of servants shall he be unto his brethren. And he said, Blessed be the LORD God of Shem; and Canaan shall be his servant. God shall enlarge Japheth, and he shall dwell in the tents of Shem; and Canaan shall be his servant" (Gen. 9:20-27).

Noah's outburst stems from a purely family matter. If the curse of this father were intended to figure into God's future plans for human beings, it is strange that after this simple account of a family crisis there is no further mention of it in Scripture.

Such a profusion of legends and tall tales have grown up about this incident and the development of the races of mankind that it would take a lifetime to run them all down.

First of all, Noah was drunk. Not a very good example for his sons: "Wine is a mocker, strong drink is raging: and whosoever is deceived thereby is not wise" (Prov. 20:1).

Second, Noah's outburst was against Canaan, not Ham. Most Christians insist on making Ham the recipient.

As indicated earlier, we will not attempt to refute every racist theory, because they are endless and serve evil purposes. What believers in Messiah Jesus must do is establish their dignity and self-worth in their relationship with Yahweh through His Word. So we will cite only a few of these absurd theories and fables.

For example, some of the rabbis believed that blackness of skin was an evidence of the curse of God. The Babylonian Talmud states: "Our rabbis taught: 'Three copulated in the ark, and they were all punished the dog, the raven, and Ham. The dog was doomed to be tied, the raven expectorates (his seed into his mate's mouth), and Ham was smitten in his skin.'"[7]

Another story that comes out of the rabbinic writings asserts: "Moreover because you twisted your head around to see my nakedness, your grandchildren's hair shall be twisted into kinks, and their eyes red: again because your lips jested at my misfortune, theirs shall swell; and because you neglected my nakedness, they shall go naked. . . . Men of this race are called Negroes." There is also the Midrash Rabbah on Genesis, which reads in part: "R. Huna said in R. Joseph's name (Noah declared), 'You have prevented me from begetting a fourth son, therefore I curse your fourth son.'"

Charles B. Copher, in his article on the Black presence in the Old Testament, says: "These views can be traced back among Europeans at least to the 12th century, and perhaps even to the tale of Beowulf, in which Cain's descendants are depicted as black. At any rate, Cain as black and Negroid entered European thought in theology, and became a permanent element with respect to Black peoples."[8] It seems that in some instances reason takes flight. Such outlandish ideas as these must be rejected.

But Yahweh is not involved in the marginalization or devaluation of His own creation. We must view these theories as blatant attacks on the name and character of God. It is absolutely necessary that we contend and defend earnestly the truth about God, His goodness, mercy, and steadfast love.

In his comments on the Noah incident and the Scriptural passages that follow, Gene Rice remarks:

> "Genesis has to do with all the peoples of the world known to ancient Israel and since this chapter immediately follows the episode of Noah's cursing and blessing, it would be most appropriate to express here any prejudicial feelings toward African peoples. Not only are such feelings absent, but all peoples are consciously and deliberately related to each other as brothers. No one, not even Israel, is elevated above anyone else and no disparaging remark is made about any people, not even the enemies of Israel."[9]

It should be observed that after Noah's outburst in Genesis 9:24 ("And Noah awoke from his wine, and knew what his younger son had done unto him") the Bible is silent on the matter of the "curse." This is in keeping with the character of Yahweh: "Who is a God like unto thee, that pardoneth iniquity, and passeth by the transgression of the remnant of his heritage? he retaineth not his anger for ever, because he delighteth in mercy" (Micah 7:18).

The Blessing

Genesis focuses on the idea of blessing rather than cursing. This theology of blessing is central to the story. The good news of Genesis is that the blessing of Yahweh overcomes and even reverses the effects of the curse upon Adam, his progeny, and the earth. The truth of the matter is, we are all accursed on account of sin, everyone who comes into the world. The planet is under the curse; this is the universal reality. But over and against the curse is placed the blessing of Yahweh:

"And God blessed them, saying, Be fruitful, and multiply, and fill the waters in the seas, and let fowl multiply in the earth" (Gen. 1:22).

"And God blessed them, and God said unto them, Be fruitful, and multiply, and replenish the earth, and subdue it: and have dominion over the fish of the sea, and over the fowl of the air, and over every living thing that moveth upon the earth" (verse 28).

"Male and female created he them; and blessed them, and called their name Adam, in the day when they were created" (Gen. 5:2).

"And God blessed Noah and his sons, and said unto them, Be fruitful, and multiply, and replenish the earth" (Gen. 9:1).

"And I will make of thee a great nation, and I will bless thee, and make thy name great; and thou shalt be a blessing (Gen. 12:2).

"And God Almighty bless thee, and make thee fruitful, and multiply thee, that thou mayest be a multitude of people. And give thee the blessing of

Abraham, to thee, and to thy seed with thee; that thou mayest inherit the land wherein thou art a stranger, which God gave unto Abraham" (Gen. 28:3, 4).

Yahweh is all about blessing. As African-American Christians like to say, "My God is in the blessing business."

New Phase Same Story

The story is simple. The earth has been depopulated by a flood. Now Yahweh is ready to repeople the planet, to make a new start. In this second phase everything goes back to Noah and his sons as progenitors of the race. Noah and his wife do not produce three different races of sons. The laws of nature and reproduction are not suspended. They have three normal sons, who are very much like them. It takes a great leap of the imagination to see one son as White, another son as Mongoloid, and a third son as Black, all out of the same womb, out of one man's loins.

The story is about replenishing and overspreading the earth. If we are trying to find in Genesis 10 a neatly packaged handbook as to how the human races developed, we shall be disappointed and frustrated and miss the whole point of the narrative. It is a political rather than a racial statement.

Yahweh declares that earth must again be populated. The original command and purpose of God are not abandoned or thrown aside: "And God blessed them, and God said unto them, Be fruitful, and multiply, and replenish the earth, and subdue it" (Gen. 1:28).

While it is apparent that racial groupings and categories of humanity exist, we should not be too sure or become too explicit as to how these groups developed their traits and characteristics. Racial definition is an extremely complex process. The biblical approach is safer individuals are a part of and identify with families, nations, kindreds, tongues, and peoples. Central to the biblical message is the common origin of them all (see Gen. 10:5, 20, 31).

Nimrod, First Great World Leader

> "And Cush begat Nimrod: he began to be a mighty one in the earth. He was a mighty hunter before the LORD: wherefore it is said, Even as Nimrod the mighty hunter before the LORD. And the beginning of his kingdom was Babel, and Erech, and Accad, and Calneh, in the land of Shinar" (Gen. 10:8-10).

Nimrod, the archetypical "great man," left an indelible impression on the ancient world. He is the original trailblazer, the founder of a new tradition of powerful monarchs. Nimrod sets the pace. He is unparalleled in leadership and achievement. The *Cambridge Bible Commentary* states that "Nimrod was remembered as the first man to grasp at real power, a man of might, the first totalitarian figure."

In the "table of nations," Ham's progeny is given more space than any of the other sons. And Nimrod assumes preeminence among Ham's offspring. Earlier on in the post-Flood story, it is Ham who produces Cush, whose name comes to designate the entire African continent. But it is Cush's son Nimrod who excels them all. He is described as a mighty hunter, and in the world that then was, the ability to hunt was highly prized. The people needed food, and they gravitated to the leader, the strong man, who could provide them with good hunting grounds.

Nimrod was also a great military man: "He began to be a mighty one in the earth." His bravery and strength in battle assured him of a following. The first great empire builder, he is credited with establishing a kingdom that comprised the four major cities that he founded Babylon, Erech, Accad, and Calneh. These cities were Nimrod's power base, his mainstay. He also founded Nineveh and the Assyrian kingdom.

The greatest cities of Mesopotamia, were founded by this genius. Since cities meant security and shelter, the world outside the perimeter of the original human settlements must have been forbidding. When Nimrod first made his way into Mesopotamia, there were, no doubt, wild beasts and uncivilized humans who threatened newcomers and intruders. Their territorial instinct must have been strong. This was the new territory into which Nimrod led his clan.

Westermann remarks that with the coming of Nimrod "dominion and the exercise of power coalesce completely. Nimrod's dominion is seen as something new, as an epoch making beginning."[10]

It is striking that in both Assyrian and Egyptian lore some of the most popular legends involve Nimrod as a ruler. The prophet Micah called Assyria "the land of Nimrod" (Micah 5:6).

Nimrod is the son of Cush, and the name Cush is synonymous with Ethiopia. The biblical text indicates clearly the line from Ham to Cush to Nimrod. Thus the Nimrod experience shows that the great Mesopotamian culture had its origin in the creative work of a son of Cush. It is difficult to think of a figure in all of history whose exploits equal the accomplishments of Nimrod, and that at the same time were so determinative in shaping the future of humankind.

Languages Multiplied People Scattered

Those who study the development of languages believe that language itself is a major clue in understanding the unfolding story of humanity. There is reason to believe in a common source, an early lingua franca. This theory is even more plausible when applied to the Bible lands and territories. Genesis 11:1 speaks of this "common speech."

African scholars have pointed out the occurrence of Hebrewisms in West African languages, especially in Yoruba. Some families of languages have common roots and sources. Martin Bernal, author of the audacious Black Athena, has this to say: "Recent work by a small but increasing number of scholars has convinced me that there is a genetic relationship between the Indo-European languages and those of the Afro-Asiatic language 'superfamily.'"[11]

Because our focus is the biblical perspective, the primary Scripture passage on this matter is quoted in full:

> "Now the whole world had one language and a common speech. As men moved eastward, they found a plain in Shinar and settled there. They said to each other, 'Come, let's make bricks and bake them thoroughly.' They used brick instead of stone, and tar for mortar. Then they said, 'Come, let us build ourselves a city, with a tower that reaches to the heavens, so that we may make a name for ourselves and not be scattered over the face of the whole earth.' But the LORD came down to see the city and the tower that the men were building. The LORD said, 'If as one people speaking the same language they have begun to do this, then nothing they plan to do will be impossible for them. Come, let us go down and confuse their language so they will not understand each other.' So the LORD scattered them from there over all the earth, and they stopped building the city. That is why it was called Babel because there the LORD confused the language of the whole world. From there the LORD scattered them over the face of the whole earth" (Gen. 11:1-9, NIV).

Yahweh used the multiplication of languages to accomplish His purposes in scattering the family of mankind "over the face of the whole earth." The point is clear: those who understood each other grouped together, not because of race or color but because of similar language/speech.

End Notes

[1]Keith A. Burton, "Western Imperialism and the Literary Suppression of the African Fidelity to the Biblical Sabbath" (paper presented to the Sabbath in Africa Project, 1993).

[2]Donald E. Gowan, *From Eden to Babel: A Commentary on the Book of Genesis 1 - 11* (Grand

Rapids, Mich.: Eerdmans, 1985), p. 36.

[3]"Genesis," in the *Holman Bible Dictionary*.

[4]Gene Rice, "The Curse That Never Was," *Journal of Religious Thought* 29 (1972): 13.

[5]Ellen G. White, *The Southern Work* (Washington, D.C.: Review and Herald Pub. Assn., 1956), p. 20.

[6]*Ibid.*

[7]Isadore Epstein, ed., *The Babylonian Talmud: Hebrew-English Edition*, rev. ed., Jacob Schacter and H. Freeman, trans. (London: Socino Press, 1969), p. 108B.

[8]Charles B. Copher, in Cain Hope Felder, ed., *Stony the Road We Trod* (Minneapolis: Fortress Press, 1991), p. 149.

[9]Rice, p. 13.

[10]Claus Westermann, *Creation*, John J. Scullion, trans. (Philadelphia: Fortress Press, 1974), p. 516.

[11]Martin Bernal, *Black Athena: The Afroasiatic Roots of Classical Civilization: The Fabrication of Ancient Greece, 1785-1985* (New Brunswick, N.J.: Rutgers University Press, 1987), vol. 1, p. 11.

CHAPTER FIVE
ABRAHAM AND HIS WORLD

> "Israel's relation with God is never an end in itself, nor is it ever limited to purely individualistic expressions. God acts toward Israel as a people; indeed, He Himself creates Israel as a people. But the reason for the creation is not merely in order that Israel may enjoy her relationship with God, but in order that through Israel, God may enter into loving fellowship with all men and thus restore to them the good He intended for them in the beginning. Mankind ruined God's good creation by its rebellion against His Lordship. God therefore sets out in Abraham to create a new people, which will live as a community of righteousness and obedience and trust under His Lordship, and which will then form the germ cell of that universal people in which all nations are included."[1]

If Nimrod is the archetypical secular political leader of the post-Flood world, Abraham is its spiritual leader. Abraham is God's agent for the service of the whole earth and all its clans, Yahweh's instrument for the fulfillment of His vision for humanity. The Most High God (a title similar to the African appellation for the universal ruler) demonstrates His love and care and impartiality in the call of Abraham, a call that is pro-humanity in its totality. This remarkable man becomes God's conduit of blessing and salvation to the planet and to "every nation, kindred, tongue and people" (Rev. 14:6).

> "The one who calls the worlds into being now makes a second call. This call is specific. Its object is identifiable in history. The call is addressed to aged Abraham and to barren Sarah. The purpose of the call is to fashion an alternative community in creation gone awry, to embody in human history the power of the blessing. It is the hope of God that in this new family all human history can be brought to the unity and harmony intended by the one who calls. . . .
>
> "The call to Sarah and Abraham has to do not simply with the forming of Israel but with the reforming of creation, the transforming of the nations. The stories of this family are not ends in themselves but point to God's larger purposes. . . .
>
> "Second, it is clear that Abraham and Sarah, in contrast to the resistant, mistrustful world presented in Genesis 1-11 . . . are responsive and receptive. . . . Promise is God's mode of presence in

> these narratives. The promise is God's power and will to create a new future sharply discontinuous with the past and the present. The promise is God's resolve to form a new community wrought only by miracle and reliant only on God's faithfulness. Faith as response is the capacity to embrace that announced future with such passion that the present can be relinquished for the sake of that future."[2]

With Abraham, world history takes a different tack; God establishes a new pattern. Abraham is the wave of the future for human beings and for all nations. Yahweh indicates here His indifference to bloodlines. Yahweh weans Abraham forever from his former life and surroundings, and disassociates him from the past from family and associates. It is a radical break a fresh start for everybody. It is for a reason: to redeem, to correct the devastating course of the three sons and their offspring, and to free the family of man from the inevitable repetition of their fathers' great sin before the Flood. Babel was a glaring example of this human tendency to rebellion, and the Most High intends to break the trend through the agency of Abraham, His friend.

A new line of believers in the one God is begun. Abraham, an Afro-Asiatic who lived in Nimrod's area of influence, is chosen by Yahweh to be His servant for the blessing of his brothers through his seed. Of course, God does not lose His love and concern for the family of man. It is out of this love and fatherly concern that He devises a plan, a strategy, whereby during the interim, the family of man may be preserved:

"And I will bless them that bless thee, and curse him that curseth thee: and in thee shall all families of the earth be blessed" (Gen. 12:3).

Abraham's contact with Melchisedek is interesting and instructive. The patriarch and the Canaanite priest are able to communicate well; in referring to Yahweh, both employ the appellation Most High God: "And Melchisedek king of Salem brought forth bread and wine: and he was the priest of the most high God. And he blessed him, and said, Blessed be Abram of the most high God, possessor of heaven and earth: and blessed be the most high God, which hath delivered thine enemies into thy hand. And he gave him tithes of all. . . . And Abram said to the king of Sodom, I have lift up mine hand unto the LORD, the most high God, the possessor of heaven and earth" (Gen. 14:18-22).

The God of Abraham Is Also the God of Melchizedek and the God of All Flesh

There is now a new world. The old monolingual, monocultural, parochial situation has changed drastically. The task of preserving the name of Yahweh in the earth is not limited to any particular son of Noah, not even Shem.

Abraham does come out of the line of Shem, but not because any moral superiority has been conferred on Shem. In fact, he was separated from his family and kindred in order to start a new humanity.

One man now is to act on behalf of God and humanity. The whole world must be made aware of God's plan of salvation. The kingdom of Yahweh must be proclaimed. His plan now is to include all nations. The plan and inclusion in it are based, not on ethnicity, but on covenant relationship. The plan is broad enough to include a Rahab and a Ruth. There are benefits and blessings, but they are not restricted; they are open to all humanity.

It is almost impossible to overestimate the importance and significance of this man, Abraham. He is God's confidant. He pleads with Yahweh on behalf of a city. He personally enters into the plans and purposes of Yahweh: "When the Lord chose Abraham, it was not simply to be the special friend of God, but to be a medium of the particular privileges the Lord desired to bestow upon the nations."[3]

Genesis 1-11 is prologue. Westermann observes: "The whole of the primeval story is thereby completely freed from the realm of myth."[4]

Abraham, in his life experience and in his relationship with Yahweh, sheds a great deal of light on God's intent and purpose for humankind and for history. With Abraham we begin to see more clearly the universality of Yahweh. He is concerned with history and with people. God does not deal exclusively with one nation, one ethnic group, one part of the family of man.

To quote Westermann again: "God's saving action is concerned with humanity and the world and must be bound up in some way with the sin and revolt of humankind. So sin as part of the human condition-and the primeval story is dealing with this-is linked with history; God's dealing with His people and His concern with human sin are brought into relationship."[5]

Ethiopia, Egypt, Israel

The Old Testament biblical view is that Mesopotamia is connected to Africa rather than to Europe. Isaiah's great prophecy joins "Babylonia" with lower Egypt, upper Egypt, and Cush as containing a remnant of people who receive ultimate salvation (Isa. 11:11). The so-called Middle East received nothing from Europe.

The great shakers and movers of that period of history—Nimrod, Abraham, the Hebrew patriarchs, Jacob and his progeny—were Afro-Asiatics. These were the early pacesetters. Israel's long history is defined by its African association and contact. One could say that the nations of that era were in and out of each other's habitats like neighbors' children.

Israel knew her neighbors only too well for the comfort of the prophets.

They grew up together and sat in the same classes, as it were, these Afro-Asiatic neighbors. Common ancestors taught them the stories of human origin. We cannot escape the fact that around the fireside the elders recounted the days of Creation and most certainly the day to which all others pointed, the Sabbath. The "big story" was fixed in the collective psyche of primeval peoples. Knowledge of Sabbath could be forgotten only in rebellion against the God who created all things. This is why the Sabbath command begins with "remember." Sabbath always harkens back to the Creation event (Ex. 20:8-10).

If Yahweh commands us today to remember the Sabbath, there must have been a time when He first commanded its observance. Indeed, this is the message of Israel's experience with the manna, which Yahweh sent on six days but withheld on the seventh. In this instance He does not repeat the command because, even before Mount Sinai, they knew. Every generation from Adam forward had some "griot" to keep memory alive. The fact that the word "remember" is attached to the command indicates that it has been given before and does not need to be constantly reiterated.

The point to be stressed here is that, given the interrelatedness that existed among nations and peoples in this "neighborhood" stage of development, the human family was reading essentially from the same page sharing a common experience. This interrelatedness can be seen in the world of commerce, trade, and the making of contracts. That social contacts were made with ease, including intermarriage, indicates how homogeneous the family really was. This was the world that then was a broad commonality of culture, custom, and religion that crossed cultural barriers.

As history moved toward the emergence of Israel as a separate and distinct people, with a separate and distinct mission, it became necessary for Yahweh to separate them from their neighbors in order that they might rightly represent Him before the world. Salvation history, the plan of salvation, required this new nation. It was the covenant and not some mythic ethnic or racial purity that created Israel, God's unique instrument, to be His salvific community.

Israel and the Canaanites

According to the biblical prophets, Israel's ancestry is Canaanite":

"Thus saith the Lord GOD unto Jerusalem; Thy birth and thy nativity is of the land of Canaan; thy father was an Amorite, and thy mother an Hittite" (Eze. 16:3).

"Then you shall declare before the LORD your God: "My father was a wandering Aramean, and he went down into Egypt with a few people and lived there and became a great nation, powerful and numerous" (Deut. 26:5, NIV).

The following is based on a paper written by W. T. Beckett, Jr., a young African-American with an avid interest in the interaction between Noah's progeny. Beckett points out that "Ham had four sons. Three of them, Cush (Ethiopia), Mizraim (Egypt), and Phut (Libya), migrated south into Africa. His youngest son, Canaan, settled an area known today as Palestine, west of the Jordan, originally called Canaan or Canaan Land."

The Scriptures do state that in the time of the judges "the children of Israel dwelt among the Canaanites, Hittites, and Amorites, and Perizzites, and Hivites, and Jebusites: and they took their daughters to be their wives, and gave their daughters to their sons and served their gods" (Judges 3:5, 6). Centuries later the tendency to intermarry with non-Israelite tribes still was the practice:

> "Now when these things were done, the princes came to me, saying, The people of Israel, and the priests, and the Levites, have not separated themselves from the people of the lands, doing according to their abominations, even of the Canaanites, the Hittites, the Perizzites, the Jebusites, the Ammonites, the Moabites, the Egyptians, and the Amorites. For they have taken of their daughters for themselves, and for their sons: so that the holy seed have mingled themselves with the people of those lands: yea, the hand of the princes and rulers hath been chief in this trespass" (Ezra 9:1, 2).

When Abraham first arrived at Canaan, "the Canaanite was then in the land" (Gen. 12:6). It was already occupied by the Hamitic Canaanites. Abraham, Isaac, and Jacob all dwelt in Canaan among its indigenous Hamitic inhabitants.

Ethiopia the Ancient

Ethiopia, according to Siculus, the first-century B.C. Greek historian, was thought of as the oldest of civilizations because they were the people who lived nearest "the ripening rays of the sun." Of course, to the Greeks the term Ethiopia meant Black Africa, "land of the burnt faces."

However, the dominant portrait of the Ethiopians in the Old Testament is that of a powerful and wealthy people: "Ethiopia and Egypt were her strength, and it was infinite; Put and Lubim were thy helpers" (Nahum 3:9). The patriarch Job speaks about the fabulous "topaz of Cush [Ethiopia]" (Job 28:19, NIV). Isaiah talks about "the products of Egypt and the merchandise of Cush, and those tall Sabeans" (Isa. 45:14, NIV).

The early classical writers were lavish in their praise of Ethiopia, calling it the favorite of the gods, the place where they went for rest and relaxation. Its people were praised for their good manners and bright spirits. Homer talks about the gods feasting with the blameless Ethiopians.

To sum up, Noah lived after the Flood 350 years (Gen. 9:28). The Tower of Babel episode (Gen. 11:1-9) seems to indicate that the post-Flood generation continued the rebellion against Yahweh that was begun by the antediluvians. In spite of Noah's 350 years of continued witness, the majority of his offspring chose to put God out of their thinking (see Rom. 1:19-32). But some among the human family believed Yahweh and were bold enough to call themselves by His name. They maintained their belief in the eternal Sabbath of Creation, the great reminder, the gift from Yahweh that keeps believers in the one God reminded of His sovereignty and power.

The unfolding story now has the family broken up and disbursed to all parts of the globe. Languages are multiplied. The age of beginnings is over. After the account of the dispersal, the story takes up "the generations of Shem" (Gen. 11:10).

But the knowledge of Yahweh, the true God, was carried wherever the members of the family were scattered—north, south, east, or west—by those God-fearing travelers, who were a witness that "there is a God somewhere." Again, the Most High never left Himself without a witness. Even the members of the family who chose not to worship God, who chose to rebel and put Him out of their thinking, could not completely escape Him. They had to have some knowledge of Yahweh to rebel against! How can one rebel against a God who does not exist? "Surely the wrath of man shall praise thee: the remainder of wrath shalt thou restrain" (Ps. 76:10).

Egypt, My People

We think of Egypt as Israel's nemesis and God's perennial enemy, but Yahweh speaks of Egypt also in familial terms of endearment. Isaiah sees all nations as family whom God acknowledges:

> "In that day shall five cities in the land of Egypt speak the language of Canaan, and swear to the LORD of hosts. . . . In that day shall there be an altar to the LORD in the midst of the land of Egypt, and a pillar at the border thereof to the LORD. And it shall be for a sign and for a witness unto the LORD of hosts in the land of Egypt: for they shall cry unto the LORD because of the oppressors, and he shall send them a saviour, and a great one, and he shall deliver them. And the LORD shall be known to Egypt, and the Egyptians shall know the LORD in that day, and shall do sacrifice and oblation; yea, they shall vow a vow unto the LORD, and perform it. And the LORD shall smite Egypt: he shall smite and heal it: and they shall return even to the LORD, and he shall be entreated of them, and shall heal

> them. In that day shall there be a highway out of Egypt to Assyria, and the Assyrian shall come into Egypt, and the Egyptian into Assyria, and the Egyptians shall serve with the Assyrians. In that day shall Israel be the third with Egypt and with Assyria, even a blessing in the midst of the land: whom the LORD of hosts shall bless, saying, Blessed be Egypt my people, and Assyria the work of my hands, and Israel mine inheritance" (Isa. 19:18-25).

Egypt, referred to by the psalmist as the land of Ham, adds tremendously to the universal African mystique. Israel's fascination with Egypt continued even in Jeremiah's day. Israel and Egypt knew each other well. Indeed, Israel had a love/hate relationship with Egypt of longstanding. As late as Jeremiah's day, not a few Israelites preferred to live in Egypt for one reason or another:

> "The word that came to Jeremiah concerning all the Jews which dwell in the land of Egypt, which dwell at Migdol, and at Tahpanhes, and at Noph, and in the country of Pathros. . . . Ye provoke me unto wrath with the works of your hands, burning incense unto other gods in the land of Egypt, whither ye be gone to dwell, that ye might cut yourselves off, and that ye might be a curse and a reproach among all the nations of the earth" (Jer. 44:1-8).

A realistic view of the peoples of that era is they were almost interchangeable branches on the same tree, known and accepted in all parts of the "neighborhood." Israel may have been a latecomer to that community of nations, but Yahweh demanded respect for her as a unique and equal member, with a special role to play. Politically, Israel never sustained status as a major player over long periods of time, but her role and function were above the politics of the region. Israel was not a nation in the sense of her neighbors, but a covenant people with a mission.

The ever-insightful Ellen White observes:

> "Often the Israelites seemed unable or unwilling to understand God's purpose for the heathen. Yet it was this very purpose that had made them a separate people and had established them as an independent nation among the nations of the earth. Abraham, their father, to whom the covenant promise was first given, had been called to go forth from his kindred, to the regions beyond, that he might be a light bearer to the heathen. Although the promise to him included a posterity as numerous as the sand by the sea, yet it was for no selfish purpose that he was to become the founder of a great nation in the land of Canaan. God's covenant with him embraced all the nations of earth. 'I will bless thee,' Jehovah declared, 'and make

thy name great; and thou shalt be a blessing: and I will bless them that bless thee, and curse him that curseth thee: and in thee shall all families of the earth be blessed' (Gen. 12:2, 3)."[7]

The world of the patriarchs was a distinct neighborhood inhabited mainly by a Hamitico-Semitic people and dominated by the children of Ham. With a common culture, a common history, and a common civilization, there was a good deal of travel back and forth, and there was constant borrowing from one another.

Egyptian Reference to Sabbath?

Israel, the Hebrew nation, must have made an indelible impression on Egypt during their prolonged association beginning with Abraham and continuing with Jacob's family and their subsequent sojourn, and vice versa. This is why it is not surprising to discover the following from a British explorer and scholar:

> "The pious authoress of 'Mazzaroth' wrote: 'The Babylonians, Egyptians, Chinese, and the natives of India were acquainted with the seven days' division of time, as were the Druids.' Dion Cassius derives the Egyptian days from the seven planets Sun, Moon, Mercury, Venus, Mars, Jupiter, Saturn. Montucla thought the week began on Saturday. Bailly says: 'It is to the Egyptians that is attributed the idea of dedicating each day of the week to one of the planets.' Sonnerat considered Saturday the Indian Sani or Saturn. Jahn says: 'The Egyptians consecrated to Saturn the seventh day of the week.'
>
> Pauw was of the opinion that 'the Egyptians seem to have observed it very regularly.' Bunsen, speaking of Set, adds, 'He is the [donkey] god of the Semitic tribes, who rested on the seventh day.' Hesiod, Herodotus, Philostratus, etc., mention that day. Homer, Callimachus, and other ancient writers call the seventh day the holy one, Eusebius confesses its observance by 'almost all the philosophers and poets.' Lucian notes that it was given to schoolboys for a holiday. Dr. Schmitz observes: 'The manner in which all public feriae (holidays) were kept, bears great analogy to our Sunday. The people generally visited the temples of the gods, and offered up their prayers and supplications. All kinds of business except lawsuits were suspended.' On the seventh day he appointed a holy day, and to cease from all business he commanded."[8]

If this evidence stands, there is one more indication of the knowledge of Sabbath in ancient Egypt.

End Notes

[1]Elizabeth Achtemeier, *The Old Testament and the Proclamation of the Gospel* (Philadelphia: Westminister Press, 1980), p. 43.

[2]Brueggemann, pp. 105, 106.

[3]Ellen G. White, *Thoughts From the Mount of Blessing* (Mountain View, Calif.: Pacific Press Pub. Assn., 1929), p. 67.

[4]Westermann, p. 67.

[5]*Ibid.*

[6]Timothy Beckett, "Remnant Children of Israel" (unpublished paper, 1993).

[7]Ellen G. White, *Prophets and Kings* (Mountain View, Calif.: Pacific Press Pub. Assn., 1943), pp. 367, 368.

[8]James Bonwick, *Egyptian Belief and Modern Thought* (London: African Publication Society, 1983), pp. 412, 413.

CHAPTER SIX
THE SEVENTH DAY DAWNS IN AFRICA

> "There is a need . . . to treat African Christianity as a legitimate tributary of the general stream of Christian history. The North African church of the early centuries, the Coptic Church of Egypt as well as the Ethiopian Orthodox Church should all be seen as manifestations of the ongoing history of Christianity on the continent."[1]

Ethiopia is a unique treasure trove of religious history and experience spanning the indigenous African, Jewish, and Christian religious traditions, elements that continue to exist to some degree in modern Ethiopia. All the antecedents are here. No nation on earth can go back in unbroken lines to antiquity. Ethiopia is, no doubt, among the senior citizens in the community of nations. If we want to understand Christianity in Africa and its relationship to the Creation Sabbath, we shall have to go to Ethiopia. And this is precisely where the Africa volume of the *Oxford History of the Christian Church* begins:

> "At the feast of Mary in the middle of August in the year 1449, the Emperor of Ethiopia, Zara Ya'iqob, assembled a church council in the monastery at Dabra Mitmaq in Shoa. It was called to resolve matters of great moment. Here were gathered in large numbers the Church's principal leaders, the two Egyptian metropolitans, the Abunas Mika'el and Gabri'el, the Abbots of Dabra Hayk, Dabra Libanos, Dabra Bizan, Dabra Maryam, Dabra Damo, and many other monasteries, together with the chief clerics of the royal and episcopal courts. . . . Here . . . the Emperor, surrounded by his wives, his bishops, his abbots, his generals, was resolved to settle once and for all the problem of the Sabbath."[2]

If we are going to talk about the Sabbath in Africa, Ethiopia is the place to begin. Ethiopia's history has for thousands of years been defined by her loyalty to Yahweh and to His Sabbath. The land of Cush stood up to the Western church and refused the yoke of Sunday bondage throughout the Christian era.

Consider these quotes from Frederic Perry Noble: "The Abyssinian (Ethiopian) is a truer Sabbatarian than the Seventh Day Baptist. . . . He observes the Jewish Sabbath as well as the Christian Sunday." "Protestantism shares the Abyssinian denial of papal supremacy and the right of every Christian to possess and read the Scriptures in the vernacular."[3]

Keith Burton takes the religious establishment to task:

"While pursuing my Bachelor of Arts degree, it was compulsory that I take at least one of two sections of a class entitled 'World Civilization.' The class commenced with discussions about the great Mesopotamian and Northeast African civilizations from antiquity, and then from about the fifth century B.C. the focus shifted toward Europe. We never did return to Africa. World Civilization?

"It soon became clear to me that the people who set the agenda were only concerned with that history which immediately affected them.

"One of the major episodes in the history of Christianity [is] justified by the fact that it was endorsed by the most powerful figure in the Western world at that time. The episode to which I refer is the first great Constantinian legislation in A.D. 321, which forbade townspeople from working on Sundays.

"This act legitimized the sanctity of this pagan day to honor the sun, a day that had been promoted by Christian syncretists such as Justin Martyr since the middle of the second century. The might of the state and the continued influence of Western societies throughout history have ensured that all who would read church history would be under the impression that the Lord's Day, Sunday, was the day universally accepted for worship by all who would call themselves Christian.

"This misguided notion is challenged by the history of the church in Africa, [which recognizes] that the resurrection of Christ in no way nullified the fact that "in six days the Lord made heaven and earth . . . and rested the seventh day: wherefore the LORD blessed the sabbath day, and hallowed it." This was true not only for the church in Ethiopia but also for the majority in the Egyptian church. In fact, as late as the sixth century it is recorded that the only place in Christian Africa in which Sunday was officially recognized as the Christian day of rest was the thoroughly Hellenized Alexandria.

"Even though the power of the Western papal legacy has made some indelible indentations on the churches of Africa, to this day they have refused to fully succumb. Many members of the Ethiopian Orthodox Church still observe the day which the Lord has made for all people to worship Him, and Coptic law stipulates that the seventh-day Sabbath, along with Sunday, be continuously regarded as a festal day for religious celebration (although it is not deemed a day

> of rest per se). This continued fidelity frail as it may be in some regions is a slap in the face to the racially motivated literary suppression of the Western European recorders of "church history."[4]

While the Western church was extending its hegemony over the Christian world, Ethiopia continued to refuse to accept Rome's authority as supreme. The passage cited from Hastings is worthy of our close attention. Sabbath antecedents in Ethiopia go back to Solomonic times. According to the *Kebra Negast,* the Ethiopian book of kings, when the queen of Sheba returned from her visit to hear Solomon's wisdom, she returned home to bear his child. It doesn't take a great stretch of the imagination to see this as a possibility when one thinks of Solomon's many marriages with women of gentile nations, especially of royalty.

The Ethiopians believe that after Solomon's child grew up, he was granted permission by his mother to visit his father, who urged the queen to give their son leave. But after a time in Israel he became homesick for his mother and the Ethiopian hill country. Although Solomon was enamored of the lad, he finally gave him permission to return, commissioning the brightest of Israelite young men to accompany his son.

According to the story, the party stole the ark of the covenant from Jerusalem and spirited it away to the Ethiopian capital. While this is absolutely impossible to establish as fact, it is true that most Orthodox Churches in Ethiopia have a replica of the ark housed in a kind of tabernacle. Isichei writes:

> "Each church, even the smallest, is divided into three sections. These include a Holy of Holies, where the Ark is kept, and where only priests and the king might enter. The Ethiopian liturgy, with its drumming, dancing, scriptural readings, and antiphonal singing, is a powerful amalgam of Jewish and African elements."[5]

It would be saying too much to suggest that Sheba's kingdom was converted to Judaism en masse because of her visit to Jerusalem. However, that one can find Sabbath consciousness in pre-Christian Ethiopia makes it easier to believe that this tradition does, in fact, come down from Solomon's time, from Sheba's visit.

The Falasha

The long presence of the Falasha, a group of Sabbath keeping Ethiopians, gives credence to this argument. In addition to keeping the Sabbath quite strictly, the Falasha also observe Hebrew dietary laws and keep certain feast days. What is striking is that these Ethiopians, Black Jews, hold to a form of Judaism that was dominant in Solomon's day. They seem to know nothing of later rabbinic Judaism. The Falasha are not Christians, and this has caused a great deal of friction between them and their Christian Ethiopian brethren.

Mbiti believes the Falasha to be descendants of "the Agao peoples of Ethiopia":

> "They do not know Hebrew, but their priests use the Old Testament [Jewish Bible] and the Apocrypha as their scriptures in the Geez language. Adherents of this religious system strictly observe purification laws and the keeping of the Sabbath (Saturday) as prescribed in the Bible. . . .
>
> "They are very skillful and industrious. The Falasha number about ninety thousand. It is impressive that they have kept their community and religious solidarity in spite of living in a traditionally Christian country, and can still be identified as an indigenous representative of Judaism in Africa."[6]

Mbiti's next comments give us a more complete picture of this unusual people group:

> "Missionaries who reached the Falasha in the nineteenth century treated them as Jews. In 1867 a European Jew was sent to them and confirmed for himself and others in Europe that they were genuine Jews. When the Italians conquered Ethiopia in 1936 and remained for a while as rulers, they made specific laws for these African Jews. In 1973 the chief rabbi of the state of Israel moved that they were full Jews like himself and any others, and consequently they began to receive help from fellow Jews. They also began to migrate to Israel in greater numbers than before. . . .
>
> "A strong wave of them went to Israel at the end of 1985, catapulted by a severe famine outbreak (though this is not said to have been the basic reason for their immigration to Israel). It was estimated that in 1986 there were 16,000 African Jews in Israel: the remainder of about 70,000 were still in Ethiopia. It is said by some Israelis that the African Jews have given Israel new pride and a sense of responsibility. They have reportedly been heartily received in Israel. The process of their integration had its own problems at the beginning, like that of many other Jews immigrating to Israel, but they are now numerous enough to develop their own self-consciousness and feel at home in modern Israel."[7]

More recently, during a time of severe famine in Ethiopia, the Falasha petitioned the Israeli government for permission to immigrate to Israel as citizens. This was granted by the Knesset. They still remain in Israel and have maintained citizenship. This better understanding of who the Falasha really are is furthered by an article in *Compton's Interactive Encyclopedia*:

> "On January 3, 1985, the government of Israel announced that it had been resettling Ethiopian Jews in Israel since 1977. More than 10,000 Ethiopians had been secretly airlifted to Israel in the intervening years. Israel also announced that there were 4,000 Black Jews still living in refugee camps in the Sudan and in Ethiopian villages.
>
> "The chief rabbi of Israel had ruled in 1975 that Ethiopian Jews were descendants of the tribe of Dan, one of the original 12 tribes of ancient Israel. As such they were eligible for immediate citizenship in modern Israel under terms of the Law of return. Their removal from Ethiopia in many cases meant an escape from famine."

Elizabeth Isichei is right when she says: "The Falashas are a community of Black Jews who are clearly Ethiopians, and call themselves the House of Israel . . . [who] know only the Pentateuch, not the Talmud, and do not speak Hebrew. Their liturgy is in Agaw, an ancient Cushitic tongue; their daily speech, Amharic; their history, in the centuries following their conquest by the Christian kingdom, is a tragic one of persecution."[8] But when she suggests that the Falasha were Sabbathkeepers because of "Jewish teachings via south Arabian influences,"[9] my reading of the biblical account leads me to credit Sheba's visit to Solomon as the point of reawakening Sabbath consciousness in Ethiopia. However, their prior knowledge of Sabbath stems from primeval times, even to Nimrod and Cush. That, of course, is a thesis of this book (see 2 Chron. 9:1-12).

No doubt, the exchanges between the queen and the king were intense, their discussions thorough. Sheba asked Solomon about his God—His name, who He was, and His relationship to Israel. She probably also wanted to know about this God's relationship to other nations.

Upon seeing in detail the glory of Solomon's kingdom, her response, recorded in the biblical record, suggests that she may have had a type of conversion experience: "And she said to the king, It was a true report which I heard in mine own land of thine acts, and of thy wisdom: howbeit I believed not their words, until I came, and mine eyes had seen it." Overwhelmed, she continued enthusiastically, "The one half of the greatness of thy wisdom was not told me: for thou exceedeth the fame that I heard" (2 Chron. 9:5, 6).

The Old Testament makes it clear that Yahweh made Israel responsible for interacting positively with the nations. The nation had an evangelical mission, a mission that consumed the prophets. They envisioned the day when "the earth shall be filled with the knowledge of the glory of the LORD, as the waters cover the sea" (Hab. 2:14). Israel was to be "a light of the Gentiles" (Isa. 42:6), God's way of bringing "salvation unto the end of the earth" (Isa. 49:6). God planned that through Israel "the Gentiles shall come to [His] light, and kings to the brightness of [His] rising" (Isa. 60:3).

Sheba and her people are included in God's plans, and His plans are inclusive. Yahweh declares that "the Gentiles shall see thy righteousness, and all kings thy glory: and thou shalt be called by a new name, which the mouth of the LORD shall name" (Isa. 62:2). "And they shall declare my glory among the Gentiles"(Isa.66:19).

Ethiopia and Christianity

Of all the national Christian communities, Ethiopia provides us with more of an up-close model of a nation in transition from Judaism to Christianity.

Tekele Tsadek Mekouria, an Ethiopian historical writer and specialist in the social and political history of Ethiopia, sees this solidarity with Judaism as reaching back into early Ethiopian history:

> "Even if we leave aside the fantastic story of Kebra Negast, which is the glory of the kings which the Ethiopian clerics consider as a basic work of history and literature and where all the kings of Axum are wrongly said to be linked with Solomon and Moses, certain traditions handed down through the centuries refer to the presence of believers of the Jewish faith. Indications of this are circumcision and excision at an early age, while the relative respect for the Sabbath, the sacred dance and liturgical dances, accompanied by drums, sistra and handclapping, all recall the dance of the Jews and that of King David before the Ark of the Covenant."[10]

The Eunuch, Queen Candace's Treasurer Firstfruits of a Greater Harvest

Church historians and scholars continue to ask the question, "How did Christianity come to Ethiopia?" If we take the biblical narrative as authentic and are looking for a biblical connection, the account in Acts 8:26-39 of the conversion of the Ethiopian treasurer gives us a good case for providing an answer to the question. This man apparently returned to his home with the good news about Messiah Jesus and spread it to his family, friends, and colleagues, even to the queen's palace. The New Testament evangelistic strategy was to witness in one's sphere of activity: "And ye shall be witnesses unto me both in Jerusalem, and in all Judaea, and in Samaria, and unto the uttermost part of the earth" (Acts 1:8).

Scholars identify two African kingdoms as being the Ethiopia of Bible reference. The kingdom of Meroe, to the south of the present Ethiopia, was once a very strong African nation. However, Meroe was displaced by Aksum, which is present-day Ethiopia. The Kebra Negast, the book of the kings of Ethiopia, indicates that the biblical story is concerned with Queen Makeda of Ethiopia. Of course, we could expect that the Ethiopians would be eager to connect Sheba to present-day Ethiopia. Indeed, the Kebra Negast account is the fullest account of the queen's visit, and, in my view, the most plausible.

If Western scholars have been hesitant to accept the above as historical fact, there certainly is no hesitancy on the part of the Ethiopians. The Kebra Negast credits the conversion of Queen Candace's eunuch treasurer as the event that brought Christianity to Ethiopia. The story of Philip and the eunuch is more than legend to the Ethiopians. It helps to explain how the Christian gospel was fused with their Hebrew background to produce their unique brand of Christianity.

In the scriptural account, Phillip the evangelist is directed by the angel to "arise, and go toward the south unto the way that goeth down from Jerusalem unto Gaza, which is desert" (Acts 8:26). There is a divine element, a greater-than-human dimension, to the story. An angel directs the evangelist.

This contact has teaching value for the church. All should take notice as, through this spectacular conversion, Yahweh moves events toward the fulfillment of His purpose for humankind: "This is the purpose that is purposed upon the whole earth: and this is the hand that is stretched out upon all the nations. For the LORD of hosts hath purposed, and who shall disannul it? and his hand is stretched out, and who shall turn it back?" (Isa. 14:26, 27).

What the Christian evangelist saw as he obeyed the angel's command was "a man of Ethiopia, an eunuch of great authority under Candace queen of the Ethiopians, who had the charge of all her treasure, and had come to Jerusalem for to worship" (Acts 8:27). The important point is, the treasurer had made the trek to Jerusalem "to worship." Thus the Ethiopian must have been a proselyte or a hearer, or even a full-fledged convert to Judaism.

Here is evidence of the powerful and numerous Jewish antecedents in Africa. There was still sufficient witness to the God of the universe in Ethiopia to command the treasurer's interest; the impact of Sheba's visit to Solomon continued to be felt after all these years.

An unusual amount of space is given in the book of Acts to the narrative of the treasurer's conversion. Only the account of Cornelius's conversion in some ways a parallel event gets more extensive treatment. But, perhaps significantly, the Ethiopian's story comes first.

Cornelius's conversion points toward the incursion of Christ's gospel into Europe. It follows that the eunuch's conversion foreshadows the penetration of the message into the African continent. We do not know his degree of interest and involvement in Judaism as he came up to worship. But on his return to home and responsibilities, the record confirms that he was now a baptized believer in Messiah Jesus. The fact that the evangelist baptized him immediately indicates he was not "far from the kingdom." The soil of his heart had been prepared.

This account of great significance was chosen for inclusion in the canon of Scripture to illustrate Yahweh's incorporation of the African peoples into His plan of salvation. The eunuch, an official of sufficient importance to be representative of his nation, became, in a sense, the first fruits of all the future Christian converts of Africa.

The inclusion of the story is also evidence in itself of the high esteem in which Ethiopia was held at that time in history. In the conversion of the Ethiopian, Yahweh signals a grand strategy for the inclusion of all nations.

Significantly, the eunuch was reading from one of the most gospel-oriented passages in the Old Testament, Isaiah 53. This passage became his catechism (remember, all of this took place before Saul's conversion). Many Christians in Ethiopia and elsewhere believe that Queen Candace's treasurer was the first to preach Christ in Ethiopia, the first missionary with a national constituency, the first with the possibility of reaching an entire nation, in the Christian era. At any rate, his love for Christ is unquestioned.

In the Ethiopian's experience we see an unfolding of the prophetic word for future Africans in the diaspora: "Ethiopia shall soon stretch her hands out unto God." This prophecy does not exhaust itself in a single incident or happening; it is an unfolding word that continues in force until the consummation, "until the day dawns," when Yahweh declares that all prophecy is ceased, because "it is done."

All of the African peoples, on the continent and in diaspora, may see in the conversion of the eunuch, the essential elements of which are skillfully crafted, the hand of Yahweh transcending every barrier, reaching out to His people in mercy and power: "Yet the number of the children of Israel shall be as the sand of the sea, which cannot be measured nor numbered; and it shall come to pass, that in the place where it was said unto them, Ye are not my people, there it shall be said unto them, Ye are the sons of the living God" (Hosea 1:10).

Zephaniah the Cushite makes this bold prediction about the African land mass and its peoples: "For then will I turn to the people a pure language, that they may all call upon the name of the LORD, to serve him with one consent.

From beyond the rivers of Ethiopia my suppliants, even the daughter of my dispersed, shall bring mine offering" (Zeph. 3:9, 10).

Ethiopia, Among the First Christian Nations

Ethiopians are proud of what they believe to be their unexcelled past as champions and defenders of the Christian faith, and that the worship of Christ dates from the earliest times:

> "Tsegaye Medhin Gabre [an Ethiopian playwright] tells how General Napier had been ordered by the British to overthrow the Emperor Tewodros and conquer Ethiopia. It was also a time when Queen Victoria had penned an insolent letter to Tewodros suggesting that he should invite British missionaries to spread the Christian gospel in his kingdom. Tewodros, along with his icily polite reply, had sent Victoria the copy of a Bible that had been published in Ethiopia two centuries before the English had embraced Christianity, and, as a footnote, he had pointed out that if missionaries were to be dispatched, perhaps they should be sent from Ethiopia to Britain and not the other way round."[11]

How this came to be is well known and well documented. Two young Christian brothers from Tyre, Frumentius and Edesius, were shipwrecked along with several fellow travelers on the coast of what is now known as Eritrea and taken to Axum (the ancient capital of Ethiopia; the empire took its name from the capital). The two brothers were befriended by the emperor, Ella Amida, and welcomed at the royal court:

> "[Axum] emerged sometime during the pre-Christian millennium and became the dominant kingdom in northeastern Africa during the fourth century A.D., developed a viable political state which practiced an advanced agriculture, and engaged in a vigorous trade with other Africans and inhabitants of the Middle East, produced highly skilled architects, and builders in stone, and maintained a victorious army equipped with iron weapons, a phenomenon for many ancient peoples."[12]

The shipwrecked brothers were not prohibited from speaking about their faith. Rather they made themselves useful in the palace and became friends and tutors of the king's sons. Frumentius, because of his knowledge of Greek, was made one of the king's private secretaries.

The brothers were surprised to see so many evidences of a Christian presence in Ethiopia (reference has already been made to Ethiopia's Hebraic past), which, according to ancient records, stem from an earlier intrusion of

Christianity into the country, possibly as a result, as Ethiopians believe, of the apostle Mark's ministry.

In Ethiopia at that time asylum was regularly given to dissidents and heretics from other countries. As the Ethiopian emperor, pagan in his personal beliefs, proved benign in his treatment of the Christian minority, Hansberry believes that the country became host to Christian refugees from many parts of the Roman Empire, fleeing from religious or political persecution. As hosts to foreign peoples, the Ethiopians were quite tolerant in matters of religion, as, indeed, Africans tend to be.

One can envision, during the time when Axum was a bustling center of trade and commerce, little Christian settlements here and there, especially around the population centers, made up of these refugees and traders. Many of these Christians were, like their fellow believers in Egypt, Syria, and Armenia, observers of the Creation Sabbath.

After the death of Emperor Ella Amida, the queen mother became regent and asked Frumentius and Edesius to tutor her sons, who were soon to become coregents in harmony with their father's wishes. Historians comment on this unusual arrangement: two rulers occupying the same throne. Apparently it worked well, so well that an Ethiopian poet could write:

"Peace be to Abreha and Asbeha,
They in one kingdom did the scepter sway,
And yet in love and yet in accord still
They lived as princes with one heart and will."[13]

Eventually Frumentius decided to report on the Ethiopian situation to Athanasius, patriarch of Alexandria, whose jurisdiction covered Ethiopia and North Africa. After his visit to the patriarch, Athanasius ordained Frumentius bishop of Ethiopia. Upon Frumentius's return, the Christian religion spread like a prairie fire, counting converts first by the thousands and then by the tens of thousands. Ethiopian Christians became known for their church buildings, whose architecture was quite different from the Roman or the Alexandrian style. Bekele Heye, who grew up a member of the Coptic Church, makes this comment:

"Most churches in the countryside are circular with galvanized metal roofs, and some with thatched roofs. Others are octagonal and made of stone. The internal structure of the circular or octagonal churches consists of three concentric rings. The innermost ring is the sanctuary (Makdas) and contains the Holy of Holies, a representation of the Ark of the Covenant. The area is screened off from the second circle, of which it actually forms a part. Only the priests and deacons may enter the sanctuary."[14]

At the outset Ethiopia seemed intent on maintaining a certain degree of independence from the major Christian centers, Alexandria and Rome. Eventually, though the emperor's sons reigned jointly for a time, one of them, Ezana (Abreha's throne name), emerged as the acknowledged leader of the nation. It was Ezana who, after his conversion to Christianity, proclaimed his empire a Christian nation.

King Ezana

Ezana's conversion experience must have been spectacular, as, indeed, inscriptions in stone seem to bear out. Early in his reign these inscriptions attributed his victories and achievements to pagan gods. But at some point the stone inscriptions cease to extol the pagan gods, but extol the God of heaven as supreme. One of these later inscriptions reads:

> "Through the might of the Lord of heaven, who is victorious in heaven and on earth over all! Aezenes, the son of Ella Amida, of the tribe of Halen, the king of Axum and Himyar and of Raiden and of Saba and of Salhen and of Siyamo and of Bega and of Kasu, the king of kings, the son of Ella Amida, who will not be defeated by the enemy. Through the might of the Lord of heaven, who has created me, by the Lord of All, by whom the king is beloved."[15]

After his conversion even the king's coins reflected his newly professed faith. Whereas in the past they had borne pagan inscriptions, they now displayed Christian symbolism:

> "The Orthodox Church of Ethiopia was organized into the National Church in the year A.D. 331. Frumentius, who was consecrated by Athanasius of Alexandria, was its first bishop. Emperor Ezana, who reigned in the fourth century, was made titular leader of the National Church."[16]

The late Bekele Heye was proud of his national heritage, and rightly so, and felt it necessary to keep this matter of the ancient beginnings of Christianity in Ethiopia before the world. Speaking of fourth-century Ezana, a contemporary with Constantine, he notes:

> "Emperor Ezana is one of the most important figures in the history of Ethiopia. He was the only emperor from this period who has made known his exploits to posterity in a series of inscriptions. One of these inscriptions was in Sabean alone. The rest were in Geez,

> or Ethiopic, as it is sometimes called. The last inscription has a great interest for us. It is the first Christian document of Ethiopia."[17]

The Ethiopians were committed Sabbathkeepers, many of them before Christianity ever came to their country. But when the nation became Christian, the Sabbath was observed as the national day of rest. As we shall see, this practice brought the nation into conflict with Rome, which was at this time vigorously promoting Sunday as the preferred day of rest.

One of the most beloved stories of Ethiopia's Christian past is that of the revered Philip, who stood up for the ancient Sabbath at peril of his life in opposition to the king, Prester John:

> "There is a tomb in this monastery which they say is of an abba or provincial of this monastery who is named Philip, and they give him the merits of a saint, saying that there was a King Prester John who commanded that Saturday should not be observed in his kingdoms and lordships, and this Abba Philip went to that King Prester with his friars, and undertook to show how God had commanded that Saturday should be kept, and that whoever did not keep it should die by stoning, and that he would maintain this before all the fathers of Ethiopia; and he made it good before the King. Therefore they say that he was a saint for making Saturday to be kept, and they treat him as a saint, and they hold a feast for him every year, in the month of July, which they call Castor Philip, which means funeral or memorial of Philip."[18]

When interrogated by missionaries who would destroy their ancient faith, Ethiopian Christians declared that their practice of keeping Sabbath was, in the words of King Galawdewos, "as our fathers the apostles have instructed us in the Didascalia."

The amazing aspect of this story is that Ethiopia, isolated, cut off from the Latin church and its theologians' guild, and looked on as theologically unsophisticated, managed to develop its own theological framework an indigenous theology. Christian by all means, but at the same time not dominated by Alexandria or Rome.

The Ethiopian Bible

The Ethiopian Bible is one of those mysteries that have continued to confound Western scholars. Hastings calls it "a remarkable achievement": "We do not know just how or when or by whom the Scriptures were translated into Ethiopic. . . . We can be certain the New Testament was translated from Greek at quite an early stage in the history of the Church of Aksum, certainly before the end of the fifth century. The Old Testament was at least no later and may well have initially been translated, at least in parts, direct from Hebrew."[19]

Reference has already been made to the remarkable Africanus manuscript, which found its way to Rome and was copied into a later manuscript, scribal errors and all! A number of other significant sources have contributed to Ethiopia's development and religious history. Heye points out:

> "The ancient Ethiopian canon of Scripture contains books not included in that of the other churches. Among these books are the books of the Shepherd of Hermas, the Ascension of Isaiah, the book of Enoch and the book of Jubilees. The book of Enoch proved to be important to the Western Christians, as there was not a complete version available in any other language. This was made available to Westerners after the manuscript brought back from Ethiopia by the traveler James Bruce was translated by R. Laurence in 1821. . . .
>
> "The most interesting book occurring at the beginning of the literary work by the Ethiopian Orthodox Church is the book called Kebra Negast, which means "Glory of Kings." The book is a combination of mythical history, allegory, and apocalypse. The central theme of the book is the visit of the Queen of Sheba to King Solomon and the birth of a son, Menelik, who became the founder of the Ethiopian Solomonic dynasty.
>
> "Of the same period are two other ecclesiastical books highly valued in Ethiopia. They are known as the Sinodos and Didascalia. They are collections of canons, constitutions, and statues. Sinodos is reckoned as a canonical book of the New Testament, some of its ordinances being attributed to Christ Himself. . . . Emperor Galawdewos, who ruled from 1540 to 1559, refers to [the Didascalia] in his defense of Sabbath observance."[20]

National Conversion The Aftermath

News of the explosion of Christianity in Ethiopia reached the entire Christian world, including the Alexandrian see and the Church of Rome. A time of great theological discussion, lines were being drawn and sides were being taken on many issues. Church councils were called to settle disputes. Each school of theology had its champions and its enemies. It was the Council of Chalcedon that affected Ethiopia and the Eastern churches most directly.

The churches of Egypt, Syria, Nubia, and Ethiopia refused to accept the decision of the council that proclaimed as dogma that Jesus had two distinct natures. The Eastern churches thought this blasphemous and declared Messiah Jesus to be both human and divine, but the two aspects of His person, for all practical purposes, were one. With the proclamation of this doctrine as the Church's official position, Christendom was in serious schism.

Modern scholars have come to see the controversy as more political than theological. It was, no doubt, a power play on the part of the European ecclesiastical establishment to strengthen its position, but Ethiopia was caught in the crossfire. (Their view much later came to be called Monophysitism.) When Rome heard that Frumentius had accepted the doctrine of the single nature of Jesus, he was summoned to the Holy See. The Ethiopian people did not appreciate what they looked upon as high-handedness on the part of Rome and an infringement upon their national integrity. They rallied to protect their bishop. Frumentius stayed with his flock; the Roman Church was too busy and too far away to carry out its summons.

The church continued to flourish in the land of table mountains. Monastic orders were established, which became the teaching centers of the nation. So many churches were built during this period that astonished travelers could take back to their homelands the tale of the Ethiopians, whose devotion and sheer religiosity put Europeans to shame.

Even the Jesuits, who tried desperately to change Ethiopia's faith and practice, were forced to admit:

> "No country in the world is so full of churches, monasteries, and ecclesiastics as Abyssinia; it is not possible to sing in one church or monastery without being heard by another, and perhaps by several. . . . The instruments of musick made use of in their rites of worship are little drums, which they hang about their necks and beat with both their hands. . . . They have sticks likewise with which they strike the ground . . . when they have heated themselves by degrees, they leave off drumming and fall to leaping, dancing and clapping their hands. . . . They are possess'd with a strange notion that they are the only true Christians in the world."[21]

The Ethiopians were separated by many miles from the great centers of Christianity, Alexandria and Rome. This proved to be a blessing. After Frumentius, Ethiopia dropped off the map and out of history. Left providentially to plot her own course, for 1,000 years the people who looked on themselves as the Israel of God kept the faith. Their devotion to the Ark of the Covenant (an account has the ark transported to Aksum and installed securely in the cathedral) was surely a sign of their chosenness? The Ethiopians' European neighbors might regard them as pagans and heathen, objects for missionary incursions and spiritual crusades, but their self-understanding was unshakeable. They were the Zion of God.

The continuing story of Ethiopia is of a country always under attack by hostile powers, ecclesiastical and political. When in conflict with Rome, it was usually over the Ethiopians' ecclesiastical practices and theological views, especially the Sabbath. Ethiopia's Muslim neighbors waged wars of conquest against them. The great crises of the sixteenth and seventeenth centuries, which were ecclesiastical in nature, and the nineteenth and twentieth centuries, which were political struggles, show that Ethiopia's history has been one ongoing struggle for independence, both religious and political.

Nevertheless, Ethiopia's enormous influence on the rest of the African continent remained larger than her actual political or military strength. People of other African nations knew of this nation whose soldiers were almost always victorious in battle. Traders, religious specialists and griots, no doubt, told the story.

"When the king [of Ethiopia] marched forth at the head of his armies," writes Adrian Hastings, "the tabot carried by monks in their midst, their confidence rested in the certainty of divine protection, in the frequently quoted line of Psalm 68: 'Ethiopia shall soon stretch out her hands unto God.'"[22] Surely, they also sang the rest of the lyrics of the psalm:

> "Sing unto God, ye kingdoms of the earth; O sing praises unto the Lord; Selah: to him that rideth upon the heavens of heavens, which were of old; lo, he doth send out his voice, and that a mighty voice. Ascribe ye strength unto God: his excellency is over Israel, and his strength is in the clouds. O God, thou art terrible out of thy holy places: the God of Israel is he that giveth strength and power unto his people. Blessed be God" (Ps. 68:32-35). "Thou hast given a banner to them that fear thee, that it may be displayed because of the truth" (Ps. 60:4).

The Ethiopians and the peoples of Africa and the diaspora can identify with Psalm 87:

"Yahweh loves His city
Founded on the holy mountain;
He prefers the gates of Zion
To any town in Jacob
He has glorious predictions to make of you,
city of God!

I will add Egypt and Babylon
to the nations that acknowledge me.
Of Philistia, Tyre, Ethiopia,
Here so and so was born men say.

> But all call Zion 'Mother,'
> since all were born in her.
>
> It is he who makes her what she is,
> he, the Most High, Yahweh;
> and as he registers the peoples,
> 'It was here' he writes 'that so and so was born.'
> And there will be princes dancing there.
> All find their home in you" (JB).

Their confidence in Yahweh as their leader and their Sabbatarian faith, a sign of allegiance to Yahweh, were the bedrock which gave stability to the children of Cush. As Yahweh's new Zion, all the promises given to Israel of old were now transferred to them.

The North African Christian Experience

> "That we should continue to use Western charts to navigate this new confluence of the gospel and Africa is one of the paradoxical legacies of an ethnocentric Western worldview. . . . We need a shift in our categories of data compilation and analysis to take adequate account of the new African Christian material."[23]
>
> "Christianity in Africa is so old that it can rightly be described as an indigenous, traditional and African religion. Long before the start of Islam in the seventh century, Christianity was well established all over North Arica, Egypt, parts of the Sudan and Ethiopia. It was a dynamic form of Christianity, producing great scholars and theologians like Tertullian, Origen, Clement of Alexandria and Augustine."[24]

North Africa produced a firmament of Christian witnesses. Many of the early Church Fathers had their roots on the African continent. Augustine was born in North Africa. Athanasius, bishop of Alexandria, was an Egyptian. Perry Noble notes:

> "Christianity civilized Abyssinia and made Nubia an African power. If early missions had done nothing else than produce an Athanasius and an Augustine, the one a full-blooded Egyptian, the other a native Numidian, the former the founder of theology proper through his vindication of the divinity of Jesus, the latter the father of Western theology through his justification of the ways of God with man these giants repaid the church and the world a thousand times.

. . . Of the 20 most prominent leaders of the Christian church during the third, fourth and fifth centuries, its formative period intellectually, nine were African. . . . The African followers include Clement, Origen, Tertulian, Cyprian, Dionysius, Athanasius, Didymus, Augustine and Cyril."[25]

North Africa not only produced great theologians and scholars but also stalwart laypeople. We find stirring stories of these heroic Christians who gave the supreme witness:

"The passion of Saints Perpetua and Felicity is a moving account of two young African woman martyrs. Perpetua is of noble birth. Felicity is a slave. Both are in their twenties and mothers of infants. They are both sentenced to death for their faith. Perpetua's diary tells of her father's pleading with the magistrate for her life, but she is adamant in her decision to accept martyrdom.

"Perpetua, Felicity, and their companions were martyred in the arena at Carthage in March 203. Perpetua guided the executioner's sword to her own throat. 'Perhaps so great a woman . . . could not otherwise be slain except she willed it.'"[26]

The Situation in Egypt

Most North African Christians were for centuries Sabbatarian. We can say this because the Coptic, Ethiopian, and Syrian Churches resisted Rome's attempts to establish Sunday as the required day of rest. To be Christian was to follow Jesus in all things, including His reverence for the Edenic Sabbath: "The Son of man is Lord even of the Sabbath day" (Matt. 12:8). This text the Ethiopians quoted in answer to their European brethren who were critical of their Sabbath observance.

A rift seems to have developed between the Alexandrian church and the rest of the Egyptian Christian community. Perhaps the Copts resented or felt uneasy with the intellectualism of the catechetical school at Alexandria, which was so influential throughout early Christendom. To simple believers, Alexandria must have appeared a hotbed of endless disputes and doctrinal controversies, all very irrelevant to them. The Sabbath question may have come into play, because Alexandria soon sided with Rome in promoting Sunday worship. As a result, a mass flight of Coptic Christians into the desert ensued.

Coptic Christianity was forged in persecution, and its most distinctive expression was in the lives of these "desert people." In Egypt, as in North Africa, a mass turning away from the old religion toward Christianity seems to have begun in the middle of the third century A.D. and to have been virtually complete by 400, with the exception of a few neo-pagan aristocrats. The Egyptian people accepted Christianity with tremendous enthusiasm. Historians marvel at the speed with which the faith spread through the country.

The churches of Egypt, Nubia, and Ethiopia had close links with the rest of Eastern Christendom. A great unity of spirit existed between Egyptian and Syriac Christians. The Syrian Christians rejoiced in the fact that their language was closest to the Aramaic spoken by Jesus. After Chalcedon, the spiritual unity of Ethiopian, Nubian, Egyptian, and Jacobite Syrian Christians was cemented by their adoption of a Monophysite Christology.

The Coptic Contribution

Did the Egyptian Copts totally reject out of hand their longstanding regard for the seventh-day Sabbath? As in certain periods in Ethiopian history, the elite may have become infatuated with the new idea of Sunday sanctity. The Egyptian Copts' allies in Syria, Ethiopia, and Armenia did not abandon Yahweh's rest. In all other matters, such as the monophysite teaching, they stood together. We do know that the Egyptian Copts suffered terrible periods of persecution for their faith.

The Copts were a breed apart. They were not numbered among the Alexandrian elite. They took their Christianity literally and seriously. Having accepted banishment to the desert, they made the best of it, refusing to give up their simple faith. The word Coptic can refer to a people, a language, or a church. Both Copt and Egypt come from a Greek word, Aigyptos, which, in turn, comes from the ancient Egyptian name for Memphis, "the house of Ptah."

The Christian community in Egypt has a record of notable accomplishments, foremost of which was the development of the monastic life. The Egyptian brand was not reclusive, withdrawing from the people, although some groups and individuals did go to excess. Their missionary monks went as far as to Britain, teaching the tenets of their faith. Whether there is a direct connection here, the practice of observing the ancient Sabbath continued in Scotland and Ireland for centuries. Rome complained about those churches who persisted in "Judaizing," that is, observing Sabbath rest. Could it be that the strongly Sabbath-oriented Coptic Christians kept this flame alive in Europe?

Nubia the Suffering Church

Africa has no Sunday tradition. All of the African churches accepted the ancient Sabbath of the Bible as ordered by the commandment. Nubia (an ancient kingdom that occupied what is presently Sudan and southern Egypt), Egypt's southern neighbor, was not the richest country in the region, but its people were rugged and had character.

Nubia was originally the kingdom of Meroe. It later was extended into three separate states: Nobatia, Makouria, and Allwa. Many church historians believe that the Ethiopian eunuch came from this area rather than the territory of present-day Ethiopia. Of course, Ethiopian tradition continues to vigorously refute this assertion. Ethiopia did conquer Meroe about A.D. 300. (As already pointed out, the Bible uses the name Ethiopia to mean all of sub-Sahara Africa.) Syrians evangelized Ethiopia and Egypt, and it seems also that Egypt sent proselytizers to Nubia. (Syrian Christians stood firm for Sabbath observance through the centuries.)

The Nubian church held to the faith and practice of the Eastern churches. Observance of the first day of the week was not enforceable by commandment. All of the African churches accepted the ancient Sabbath of the Bible as ordered by the commandment, including Nubia.

It was Chalcedon's definition of the nature of Christ with which the Ethiopians, Egyptians, and Syrians disagreed. In substance, the churches of the East and West were not far apart. The Ethiopians argued "that perfect unity resulted from the union of the two natures forming one united nature. Their opponents called them Monophysites, and the two sides engaged in a protracted struggle which disturbed the peace hoped for after the council."[27]

After the council, lines were drawn and positions hardened, but most theologians would agree that it was more a matter of semantics than substance.

Lamin Sanneh, an African scholar who converted from Islam to Christianity, finds that Ethiopian Christians, until this day, think it unfair for their church to be called *monophysite,* because the expression used by them and the churches of Egypt, Nubia, and Syria "was always *mia-physis* not *mono-physis*: *mia* meaning complete unity, unlike *mono,* which stands for an elemental unity."[28] As proves to be the case so often, the Latin Church defined a doctrine, made a label, and plastered it on all who disagreed with it, going so far as to excommunicate any who dissented.

During the spread of Islam, the Arabs were not able to conquer Nubia completely. They were repelled by Nubia's archers in two battles at Dongola, a setback they doubtless accepted the more readily because of the poverty of the country. They recognized the independence of Nubia in a baqt, the only non-Muslim state so recognized. Aswan was their only officially accepted frontier.

"Nubia was one of the few countries in the ancient world that was converted to Christianity without a prior experience of Roman rule; Ethiopia was another."[29]

In 543 Theodora sent the Monophysite monk Julian to Nubia, instructing the governor of the Thebaid to stop any other mission. Julian converted Nobatia to Christianity, beginning with the court. So rapid and complete was the process that it suggests either that the king wielded great power or that a considerable degree of prior Christian influence existed. The fact that Monophysites converted Nubia to the faith is reason to believe that Nubian Christians were Sabbath observers:

> "The whole country of Nubia had been converted by the last quarter of the sixth century and archaeologists have found a brilliant Christian civilization flourished there, in Alodia at least, until the beginning of the sixteenth century. Nubian liturgy was highly developed notwithstanding the lack of a common liturgical language. There was no uniformity: Greek, old Nubian and Coptic all being used. Nor was it certain to which of the patriarchs allegiance was owed. Who assigned the metropolitan? Alexandria, Constantinople or the emperors?
>
> "This and other questions lost their significance when Islam swept from East to West with the all but invincible Arab armies, to conquer Egypt in 640 onwards and to attack Nubia in 651. This last was inconclusive and ended in a Nubian agreement to pay annual tribute to Egypt and to boost trade between the two countries.
>
> "Faced with this adversary in the north, the Nubians united their three kingdoms and grew strong enough to pose as protector of Christians harassed in Egypt. Their newfound strength enabled the Nubians to remain independent for eight hundred years. Even that did not outlast Islam."[30]

The extinction of Christianity in the Maghreb (north Africa) is one of the great mysteries of African history. The spread of Islam in Arabia, Egypt, Nubia, and throughout the Middle East meant that Christian Ethiopia became increasingly isolated. The remnant Christian communities were driven farther and farther into the desert. In spite of the severity of their persecution, they were not completely annihilated; they did not go silently into the darkness. Travelers to Nubia during the centuries after Constantine, and as late as the tenth century, report finding enclaves of Christians and Christian churches here and there, living out their faith in spite of isolation. It must have been a severe blow to the Nubians when Egypt became an Islamic nation.

The Demise of Christianity in North Africa

Muslim powers are charged with destruction of Christianity in the

Maghreb, Roman-controlled North Africa. This is true to a certain extent, but careful study indicates that the constant bickering among Christians over theological issues and church polity sapped the strength of a once strong church that flourished along Africa's northern frontier. Christians did themselves in. It did not take the kind of aggressive action that most of us associate with the rise of Islam in north Africa. Eventually, only Ethiopia was left, the last bastion of Christianity on the continent.

However, Ellen White insisted: "In lands beyond the jurisdiction of Rome there existed for many centuries bodies of Christians who remained almost wholly free from papal corruption. They were surrounded by heathenism and in the lapse of ages were affected by its errors; but they continued to regard the Bible as the only rule of faith and adhered to many of its truths. These Christians believed in the perpetuity of the law of God and observed the Sabbath of the fourth commandment. Churches that held to this faith and practice existed in Central Africa and among the Armenians of Asia."[31]

The Adaption Process Toward a New Brand of Christianity

Any review of Christianity in its European setting reveals trends and changes and departures from the primitive Christianity of the apostles' day. Theologians and historians have taken note of this phenomenon and seek to analyze it. Even Gibbon, the secular historian, reports this in his *Decline and Fall of the Roman Empire.*

Slippery Slope

Douglas Hall calls our attention to what he calls the adaptation process: "Still readily traceable [is] the manner in which many of the feast days and holy seasons of the pagan, Gentile world were 'baptized' with Christian names and meanings, though they frequently continued to carry the deep undertones of the original pre-Christian festivals and events."[32]

J. N. Andrews, in his monumental study on the Sabbath in history, traces the attempts of the Latin Church to transfer the holiness of the ancient Sabbath to Sunday. It seems that the African churches resisted this move. But Rome went to great lengths to achieve its ends, so far as to make the seventh-day Sabbath a gloomy day of fasting and penance. Toward the end of the fourth century, the change was in place throughout most of the empire except the Ethiopian, Eastern, north African, and Syrian churches.

Writes Andrews:

> "The holy doctors of the church had by this time very effectually

despoiled the Sabbath of its glory, transferring it to the Lord's day of Pope Sylvester; as Augustine testifies; yet was not Sabbatical observance wholly extinguished even in the Catholic Church?"

The historian Socrates [Scholasticus], who wrote about the middle of the fifth century, thus testifies:

> "For although almost all churches throughout the world celebrate the sacred mysteries on the Sabbath of every week, yet the Christians of Alexandria and at Rome, on account of some ancient tradition, refuse to do this. The Egyptians in the neighborhood of Alexandria, and the inhabitants of Thebais, hold their religious meetings on the Sabbath, but do not participate of the mysteries in the manner usual among Christians in general for after having eaten and satisfied themselves with food of all kinds, in the evening making their oblations they partake of the mysteries."[34]

As the church of Rome had turned the Sabbath into a fast some 200 years before this in order to oppose its observance, it is probable that this was the ancient tradition referred to by Socrates. And Sozomen, the contemporary of Socrates, speaks on the same point as follows:

> "The people of Constantinople, and of several other cities, assemble together on the Sabbath, as well as on the next day; which custom is never observed at Rome or at Alexandria. There are several cities and villages in Egypt where, contrary to the usages established elsewhere, the people meet together on Sabbath evenings; and, although they have dined previously, partake of the mysteries."[35]

Not on Ethiopian Soil

Bekele Heye reported on a visit that he and a group of clergy paid to the bishop of west Ethiopia in his office at Lekempti, the provincial capital of Wollenga. They had a long interview with the bishop regarding the position of the Ethiopian Orthodox Church on the seventh-day Sabbath. The bishop told them plainly that the Coptic Church has never given up Sabbath observance. He referred to Matthew 5:17, 18 and said that the Decalogue is still binding."[35] Heye also points to Edward Ullendorff, who makes this comment:

> "The history of Sabbath observance in Abyssinia is fairly checkered, and the sources are often ambiguous or even contradictory, but the retention of the Sabbath drew support from a number of unimpeachable authorities. The Ethiopic *Didascalia* as

well as Gregory of Nussa whose prestige among Ethiopians stands high enjoin the keeping of the Sabbath and Sunday. And most significant is the continued validity of the Decalogue and the law expressly prescribed in Matthew 5:18 that 'one jot or one tittle shall in no wise pass from the law.'"[36]

Further, says Heye:

"It is interesting to note that the word 'Ehud' for Sunday is derived from the Ethiopian word 'Ahadu' meaning 'one,' and the Arabic word 'Wahid' also meaning 'one.' So the word 'Ehud' for Sunday really means the first day of the week. The name used for Wednesday means the fourth day, and also the name used for Thursday means the fifth day. The Galla tribe, which is the largest ethnic group in Ethiopia, has a very interesting name for the Saturday Sabbath 'the original Sabbath.' The name this tribe has given to Sunday is 'the little Sabbath,' or 'the second Sabbath.'

"These and many other factors indicate that the history of the seventh-day Sabbath is deep-rooted in the culture of the Ethiopian people. There is no record at any time in the history of the Ethiopian Orthodox Church that this church has officially given up Sabbath observance."[37]

Was Anti-Semitism a Factor in the Acceptance of Sunday as the Preferred Day of Worship?

Europeans have never been comfortable with things Jewish. The presence of Jews among them has been an irritant and almost always erupts in some kind of violence or persecution. The question must be asked, Does this have anything to do with Europe's attitude and action toward the "Jewish" Sabbath? In the context and purpose of this book, the question must enlarge to include African-American concerns. Do African-Americans have a vital interest in the attempted change of the day of rest from Saturday to Sunday?

We need to take a fresh look at the evidence from the biblical and historical perspective. What is at stake here? Did the Latin Church do us a good service in this instance, or otherwise? What do Greek philosophy and old Nordic superstitions have to do with it? Whatever could lead the church to cast aside this gift (Sabbath)? Did Messiah Jesus give any warning? Was this change envisioned in Paul's writing? Does it make any real difference, or is it merely a war of words?

First of all, the Jews were not regarded as the best of neighbors in the Greco-Roman world. They were suspected of being seditious and a threat to the empire. Stereotypical profiles painted Jews as grasping, pushy, and conniving. Christians were deathly afraid of being identified with the Jews, as seems to have been the case in the burning of Rome, for which Nero blamed the followers of "one Chrestus, a Jew." The church also feared becoming known as a Jewish sect.

It probably seemed fortuitous to the early Church Fathers, who had to deal with the Jewish question, that the wild solar holiday of the pagans (Sunday) coincided with the day of the Resurrection.

The church erred in granting the Jews exclusive rights to the Sabbath, God's universal gift; in inventing a counter day of worship the leaders effectively disfranchised their people: "The Sabbath was made for man" (Mark 2:28). Yahweh had said through Isaiah that Sabbath was for Gentiles, for all peoples (Isa. 56:4-6).

Remember, the Sabbath existed before there was ever a Jew. Even though the Jews would seemingly try to confiscate the Sabbath, it was given also to the sons and daughters of Cush the Ethiopians and Africans. Christians should not have capitulated and abdicated their responsibility for holding aloft the banner of truth the day which God chose, to call to mind His creative acts.

What was and is at stake here is loyalty to Jesus Christ. In matters of this magnitude, Christ's church should not give in to the prevailing culture or follow the course of expediency. But alas, in this case the fear of stigma proved too strong. The hierarchy caved in and, having done so, used every method, argument, and ruse, including the strong arm, to make it stick.

Arguments for Sunday keeping were and still are very weak. The Church Fathers were, of course, unable to come up with a single scripture in support of this major departure from the ancient faith. It was in honor of the Resurrection, they said, in spite of Paul's insistence that baptism is the true memorial of the Resurrection (Rom. 6:3-5). One of the "salient" reasons was that the sanctity of the first day of the week was taught by the apostles, all in spite of a plethora of scriptural references in which the apostles observed the Sabbath and preached to Jews and Gentiles on that day (Acts 13:14, 27, 42, 44; 16:13; 17:2; 18:4).

Ecclesiastics even resorted to the use of allegory and pure pagan sentiment, citing the Greek myth about the Phoenix to enhance the position of Sunday. It was all a concession, a pitch to the prevailing culture, accelerated by Constantine's conversion.

From the Author of the Baptist Manual

We have in more recent times the well-known statement of Edward

Hiscox, author of the *Manual of Baptist Churches*, who summarizes the question brilliantly in an address given to a group of Baptist clergy in New York City:

"There was and is a commandment to keep holy the Sabbath day, but that Sabbath day was not Sunday. It will be said, however, and with some show of triumph, that the Sabbath was transferred from the seventh to the first day of the week, with all its duties, privileges, and sanctions. Earnestly desiring information on this subject, which I have studied for many years, I ask, where is the record of such a transaction to be found? Not in the New Testament, absolutely not. There is no scriptural evidence of the change of the Sabbath institution from the seventh to the first day of the week.

> "I wish to say that this Sabbath question, in this aspect of it, is the gravest and most perplexing question connected with Christian institutions which at this time claims attention from Christian people; and the only reason it is not a more disturbing element in Christian thought and religious discussions is because the Christian world has settled down content on the conviction that somehow a transference has taken place at the beginning of Christian history.
>
> "To me it seems unaccountable that Jesus, during three years intercourse with His disciples, often conversing with them upon the Sabbath question, discussing it in some of its various aspects, freeing it from its false glosses, never alluded to any transference of the day; also, that during forty days of His resurrection life, no such thing was intimated. Nor, so far as we know, did the Spirit which was given to bring to their remembrance all things whatsoever that He had said unto them deal with this question. Nor did the inspired apostles, in preaching the gospel, founding churches, counseling, and instructing those founded, discuss or approach this subject.
>
> "Of course, I quite well know that Sunday did come into use in early Christian history as a religious day, as we learn from the Christian fathers and other sources. But what a pity that it comes branded with the mark of paganism, and christened with the name of the sun god, when adopted and sanctioned by the papal apostasy, and bequeathed as a sacred legacy to Protestantism!"[38]

John Nevins Andrews comments:

> "This extraordinary edict of Constantine [A.D. 321] caused Sunday to be observed with greater solemnity than it had formerly been. Yet we have the most indubitable proof that this law was a heathen enactment; that it was put forth in favor of Sunday as a heathen institution and not as a Christian festival; and that

Constantine himself not only did not possess the character of a Christian, but was at that time in truth a heathen. It is to be observed that Constantine did not designate the day which he commanded men to keep, as Lord's day, Christian Sabbath, or the day of Christ's resurrection; nor does he assign any reason for its observance which would indicate it as a Christian festival. On the contrary, he designates the ancient heathen festival of the sun in language that cannot be mistaken."[39]

Andrews then quotes a Dr. Hessey, who sustains his statement:

"Others have looked at the transaction in a totally different light, and refused to discover in the document, or to suppose in the mind of the enactor, any recognition of the Lord's Day as a matter of divine obligation. They remark, and very truly, that Constantine designates it by its astrological or heathen title, Dies Solis, and insist that the epithet venerabilis with which it is introduced has reference to the rites performed on that day in honor of Hercules, Apollo, and Mithras."[40]

Capitulation to a Pagan Ruler

The Latin Church accuses the African of gross superstition, even to the point of caricature, but it is Western historians who have documented the fact that Sunday comes to us through an edict of a pagan ruler whose conversion to Christianity, according to the historian Mosheim, came two years after he issued the edict establishing the new universal day of rest.[41] It needs to be said with great emphasis that the institution of the day was not an initiative of Church leaders, but of a pagan ruler whose perception of Christ's gospel was abysmally dim. Mosheim further says:

"He [Constantine] had previously considered the religion of one God as more excellent than the other religions, and believed that Christ ought especially to be worshiped: yet he supposed there were also inferior deities, and that to these some worship might be paid, in the manner of the fathers, without fault or sin. And who does not know, that in those times, many others also combined the worship of Christ with that of the ancient gods, whom they regarded as the ministers of the supreme God in the government of human and earthly affairs."[42]

Constantine worshiped Apollo or the sun, and therefore, enjoins the people of the empire to observe the venerable day of the sun. Where were the

Church Fathers when all of this was taking place? Were they already in alliance with the political power? Had they completely abdicated their role as protectors of the faith? Gibbon says:

> "The devotion of Constantine was more peculiarly directed to the genius of the Sun, the Apollo of Greek and Roman mythology; and he was pleased to be represented with the symbols of the god of light and poetry. . . . The altars of Apollo were crowned with the votive offerings of Constantine; and the credulous multitude were taught to believe that the emperor was permitted to behold with mortal eyes the visible majesty of their tutelar deity. . . . The Sun was universally celebrated as the invincible guide and protector of Constantine."[43]

The Hebrew-African Connection

The African peoples did not have this anxiety about Jewish practices and Hebraisms that plagued their European brethren. The early civilizations of man were, as we have seen, Afro-Asiatic. The descendants of Cush were thoroughly exposed to the Semitic peoples of the region. They all shared a common geography. Europe came later into the family of nations.

This brings us to conclude that the African connection is key, that African Christians were prepared by their unique position within the community of nations from antiquity, unspoiled by Hellenism and the biases of the Latin Church, able to hear all sides of the question. African Christians were prepared to serve as a nexus between European Gentile Christianity and Judaism. Elizabeth Isichei makes this very insightful observation:

> "The Ethiopian church's strong Hebraic elements give it a unique role in Christian/Jewish dialogue. It has grown directly from Christianity's Jewish roots, without the admixture of Hellenism. The world of the Hebrew Bible clearly has much in common with African cultures, in the importance placed on dreams and visions, and the felt need to establish boundaries with ritual prohibitions. Many modern African prophetic churches keep the Sabbath holy, and adopt dietary and other prohibitions similar to those laid down in Leviticus, as the Ethiopians do."[44]

One can only ask what the experience of Christendom might have been if the Western church had been willing to learn from the Ethiopian church. Would there have been such a radical discontinuity from Christianity's Jewish roots as to lead the Roman Church to reject all things Jewish? Would there have been the fertile field so conducive to the growth of anti-Semitism?

Would European Christianity have felt compelled to adopt and baptize Sunday, the "wild solar holiday of the heathen" as a substitute for the Bible Sabbath? Had the Sabbath been retained, there would not have been the necessity to enforce the new day of rest with such a heavy hand.

No doubt, the development of the church's theological system would have been radically different. We would have probably seen a kinder, gentler face on the emerging church. The whole experience of Christianity would have been radically different.

The Great Schism and the Year A.D. 1054

Mervyn Maxwell calls the year A.D. 1054 "a watershed, not only in Christian history as a whole, but also in the history of Sabbath observance." R. L. Odom, writing on the "Sabbath in the Great Schism of 1054," states: "One of the main issues involved in that controversy was the matter of fasting on the Sabbath, the seventh day of the week."[45] Disagreement on the issue had became "verbally violent" the year before, Odom continues. By 1054 Orthodox Christians and Catholic Christians were excommunicating each other. The Great Schism which resulted lasted until 1967."[46]

Says Maxwell:

> "One of the principal issues which led to this tragic separation in 1054 was Rome s opposition to the Sabbath. Patriarch Michael Cerularius and his associates in Constantinople insisted in 1053 and 1054 that the Roman Catholics ought to abandon their gloomy Saturday fasts. They said that the way the Catholics treated the Sabbath had no foundation in Scripture and seriously altered the intended character of the Sabbath as a day of joy.
>
> "Pope Leo IX refused to make the requested change. He insisted instead that because he was the successor of Peter, his word was law for all faithful Christians to obey.
>
> "Tempers flared, and Pope Leo ordered his representative, the papal legate Cardinal Humbert, to present the patriarch of Constantinople with an official document denouncing his Orthodox Christians as being on a level with 'the devil and his angels.'
>
> "[There were] six major branches of Christianity [that] existed in 1054: Catholic, Orthodox, Armenian, Nestorian, Egyptian (or Coptic), and Ethiopic. In the . . . Orthodox, Armenian, and Ethiopic [areas] the Sabbath was honored, along with Sunday, by regular worship services. In addition to holding meetings, Armenian and Ethiopic Christians also honored the Sabbath by resting on that day as well as on Sunday.

"From the seventh century onward the Nestorian, Armenian, and Egyptian (Coptic) churches were out-rivaled in influence by Islam as a result of the Muslim conquests. (Contrary to popular belief the early Muslims, unlike some later ones, did not compel Christians and Jews to accept Islam or die; they stipulated instead that Christians and Jews had to pay extra taxes; then they resisted the conversion of Christians to Islam as causing an erosion of the tax base. Nonetheless, Islam greatly diluted the influence of Christianity in the lands it conquered.)

"Thus the Catholics emerged as *the primary Christian opponents of the seventh-day sabbath*. This helps explain why Daniel 7 portrays the Catholic Church as 'thinking to change the times and the law.'

"The fact that Sunday is observed by Christians in most parts of the world today, to the exclusion of the Sabbath, is explained by the vigorous missionary work conducted by Catholics and Protestants after the Reformation. Both Catholic and Protestant missionaries carried with them around the world the Catholic opposition to the Sabbath."[47]

Europe's Attitude Toward Africa and Africans

The presence of Egypt on the African continent has caused great consternation to the European intellectual community. It stood as an embarrassment to those scholars who were determined to paint Africa as the black hole of the planet, the dregs of humanity. This antipathy toward Africa and things African fevered the thinking of the nations of northern Europe and produced a mind-set that colored the development of every discipline in the university from archaeology to theology and zoology.

Historians now had to become revisionists, because all of the ancient writers and historians readily acknowledged Egypt as the first great flowering of human thought and achievement.

Perhaps this is the point at which to look at the development of racist attitudes among northern European peoples. "The curse causeless shall not come." "All cultures have some degree of prejudice for, or more often against, people whose appearance is unusual," says Martin Bernal. "However, the intensity and pervasiveness of Northern European, American and other colonial racism since the 17th century have been so much greater than the norm that they need some special explanation."[48]

Black scholars have contended all along, unheard and unheeded by the power centers of academia for many years, that the truth about Africa should be acknowledged. Cheikh Anta Diop said forthrightly that this acknowledgment must begin with Egypt:

"If Egypt is a dilemma in Western historiography: it is a created dilemma. The Western historians, in most cases, have rested the foundation of what is called 'Western Civilization' on the false assumption, or claim, that the ancient Egyptians were White people. To do this they had to ignore great masterpieces on Egyptian history written by other White historians who did not support this point of view such as Gerald Massey's great classic, *Ancient Egypt, the Light of the World* (1907) and his other works, *A Book of the Beginnings and the Natural Genesis*. Other neglected works by White writers are *Politics, Intercourse, and Trade of the Carthaginians, Ethiopians, and Egyptians*, by A.H.L. Heeren (1833), and *Ruins of Empires*, by Count Volney."[49]

Interest in Egypt and its civilization was awakened and developed concurrently with the slave trade and the colonial system. At the same time the academicians severed Egypt from Africa and made it Europe south. This is why Diop insists that Egypt is key. Indeed, "African history is out of kilter until ancient Egypt is looked upon as a distinct African nation."[50]

The French writer Count C. E. Volney, in his important work *The Ruins of Empires*, said that the Egyptians were the first people to "attain the physical and moral sciences necessary to civilized life." Volney further states that "it was on the borders of the Upper Nile, among an African race of men, that was organized the complicated system of worship of the stars, considered in relation to the productions of the earth and the labors of agriculture; and this first worship, characterized by their adoration under their own forms and national attributes, was a simple proceeding of the human mind."[51]

A galaxy of African-American scholars, including Carter G. Woodson, W.E.B. DuBois, Willis N. Huggins, J. A. Rogers, and Charles C. Seifort, were familiar with the works of these radical historians and began to build on their findings. Today their numbers include such names as John G. Jackson (*Introduction to African Civilizations,* 1970), Yosef ben-Jochannan (*Black Man of the Nile,* 1972), and Chancellor Williams (*The Destruction of Black Civilization: Great Issues of a Race From 4500 B.C. to 2000 A.D.,* 1971). Until the publication of James G. Spady's article "*Negritude, PanBanegritude and the Diapian Philosophy of African History*" (in *A Current Bibliography on African Affairs,* vol. 5, no. 1, Jan., 1972) and the interview by Harun Kofi Wangara (published in *Black World* Magazine, Feb. 1974), Cheikh Anta Diop was known to only a small group of Black writers and teachers in the United States. For more than seven years his books were offered to American publishers, with no show of interest.

Then two of his books were published in the United States within one year: The Third World Press in Chicago brought out his book *The Cultural*

Unity of Negro Africa. All of his books were originally published by Presence Africaine, the Paris-based publication arm of the International Society of African Culture.

The extent to which the historians' guild went to write Africa out of history is almost unbelievable. Martin Bernal has written two large volumes tracing the rise of European antipathy toward Africa and the extent to which it has penetrated and controlled the thought processes of Europe and America. His thesis is that two paradigms or models are used to look at Egypt.

One, which Bernal calls the ancient model, follows the lead of the ancient classical scholars, who unanimously agreed that Egypt was a Black nation ruled through most of her history by Black pharaohs except for brief periods of time: "Egyptian civilization is clearly based on the rich Predynastic cultures of Upper Egypt and Nubia, whose African origin is uncontested."

The other, which came out of the European academic community, is the Aryan model. This model found it difficult to accept the ancient model, especially after Egypt was rediscovered in the eighteenth century. To accept Egypt as the founder of civilization as we know it, and to admit that the Egyptians tutored Greeks in mathematics and philosophy, was a bit too much for the Teutonic mind. Thus the rise of the Aryan, or new model, which glorified Greece as the mother of modern civilization.

In fact, Greece, under this model, became the mythical ideal community whose people were beautiful and gracious. Its women were pure and lovely, and its scholars extremely brilliant. Odes to the glories of ancient Greece rolled from the pens and flowed from the lips of writers and orators. A whole school of historians earned the name romantic in their adoration of a society that never existed in real time.

This approach to the past can be traced and charted: "The centrality of racism to European society after 1700 is shown by the fact that this 'polygenetic' view of human origins continued to grow in the early 19th century, even after the revival of Christianity."[53]

This polygenetic view is the same as the *candelabra* theory of human origins. I accept the more biblically friendly Noah's ark model. The *polygenetic* would allow numerous beginnings of human species in many places: Asia, Europe, Africa, etc. The *monogenetic* restricts human origins to one common source. We cannot long escape the scriptural dictum: "And he made from one every nation of men to live on all the face of the earth, having determined allotted periods and the boundaries of their habitation that they should seek God, in the hope that they might feel after him and find him. Yet he is not far from each one of us" (Acts 17:26, 27, RSV).

It has been established that Ham is the father of Black people, but the *Interpreter's Bible* does not count Black people as Hamitic. How, then, can the

Negro people be non-Hamitic? All people trace back their origin to Noah, and to one of his sons. This leads one to believe that the European ecclesiastical establishment, the theologians' guild, the academic elites, are cohorts in denying legitimacy to Black Africa by refusing to grant them lineage with any of Noah's sons.

Notice that Hamites included Egyptians, Lybians, and Cushites. According to some historians, Negroes infiltrated from some mysterious land to the south after the third millennium B.C., some pre-Adamic creation.? Other unfortunate theories concerning the origin of Black people were taught with vehemence in Reconstruction America. The important thing to remember is, the human family began as a single family, and all were earth colored. From that original group all nations and races sprang, before the Flood and after.

End Notes

[1]Sanneh, p. xviii.

[2]Hastings, pp. 3, 4.

[3]Frederic Perry Noble, *The Redemption of Africa: A Story of Civilization* (Chicago: Revell, 1899), pp. 192, 193.

[4]Burton.

[5]Isichei, p. 50.

[6]Mbiti, p. 248.

[7]*Ibid.*, pp. 248, 249.

[8]Isichei, p. 50.

[9]*Ibid.*

[10]Tekele Tsadek Mekouria, *Ancient Africa*, in G. Moktar, ed., *General History of Africa* (Berkeley, Calif.: University of California, 1980), pp. 492, 493.

[11]Ivan Van Sertima and Larry Williams, eds., *Great African Thinkers* (New Brunswick, N.J.: Transaction, 1986), vol. 1, p. 24.

[12]Harris.

[13]*Ibid.*

[14]Heye, p. 8.

[15]Harris.

[16]Heye.

[17]*Ibid.*, p. 6.

[18]Rubem A. Alves, *Tomorrow's Child: Imagination, Creativity, and the Rebirth of Culture* (New York: Harper, 1972), pp. 23, 24.

[19]Hastings, p. 19.

[20]Heye, p. 11.

[21]Isichei, p. 52.

[22]Hastings, p. 21.

[23]Sanneh.

[24]Mbiti, p. 223.

[25]Noble, p. 33.

[26]Isichei, p 35.

[27]Malisha, p. 56.

[28]Sanneh, p. 56.

[29]Isichei, pp. 30, 31.

[30]Sanneh, p. 63.

[31]White, *The Great Controversy*, p. 63.

[32]Douglas J. Hall, *The Stewardship of Life in the Kingdom of Death* (Grand Rapids, Mich.: Eerdmans, 1992), p. 54.

[33]John Nevins Andrews, *History of the Sabbath and the First Day of the Week*, 2nd ed. (Battle Creek, Mich.: Adventist Pub. Co., 1873), pp. 366, 367.

[34]*Ecclesiastical History*, quoted in ibid., p. 367.

[35]Heye, p. 45.

[36]Edward Ullendorff, *The Ethiopians: An Introduction to the Country and People* (London: Oxford University Press, 1960), p. 105.

[37]Heye, p. 45.

[38]*New York Examiner*, Nov. 16, 1893.

[39]Andrews, p. 342.

[40]Quoted in *Ibid.*

[41]*Ibid.*, p. 347.

[42]*Ibid.*

[43]Edward Gibbon, *The Decline and Fall of the Roman Empire* (London: Dent Everyman, 1910), chap. 20.

[44]Isichei, p. 49.

[45]R. L. Odom, "The Sabbath in the Great Schism of A.D. 1054, *Andrews University Seminary Studies* 1 (1963): 74.

[46]*Ibid.*, pp. 74-80.

[47]C. Mervyn Maxwell, *The Message of Daniel* (Boise, Idaho: Pacific Press Pub. Assn., 1981), pp. 141, 142.

[48]Bernal, p. 20.

[49]Cheikh Anta Diop, *The Cultural Unity of Black Africa*, 2nd ed. (Chicago: Third World Press, 1989), p. 114.

[50]*Ibid.*, p. 115.

[51]Quoted in *Ibid.*, pp. 115, 116.

[52]Bernal, p. 15.

[53]*Ibid.*, p. 204.

CHAPTER SEVEN

A FLICKERING FLAME

Augustine warned his fellow Christians against the fallacy of thinking the second advent of Christ was at hand on the basis that the gospel had been preached throughout the world. "Even in the heart of our own Africa," said he, "how many tribes there are of which we have no knowledge and no access."[1] His brethren failed to heed his passionate plea for "his Africa" and became bogged down in minutia, in endless theological wrangling and disputes, and the door of opportunity was shut, the moment passed. After a time of faithfulness to the gospel, the north African and Egyptian churches became hidebound, moribund, and, like the dinosaur, doomed to extinction and oblivion. What persecution and sword could not accomplish, internecine struggles and obsession with theological trivia could. These brought down the once-flourishing churches and, sadly, caused the demise and almost total eclipse of the church of Perpetua and Felicity!

The Rise of Islam

Did Islam, in its origin more than 600 years after the birth of Christ, seek to fill the gap created by a failed Christianity?" The Prophet Muhammad and his reformer cohorts, after all, declared that their work was to reclaim the faith of Abraham, to preserve this high view of God in a world that had lapsed into superstition and gross darkness.

Islam is a monotheistic religion, and early on, Muslims made accords with Christians and did not seem bent on the annihilation of the faith of Messiah Jesus.

Nevertheless, the rise of Islam in Egypt and north Africa effectively silenced the voice of Christianity on the African continent, except for Ethiopia, which was able to escape the dominance of the Roman Church and somehow survive the spread of Islam. Thus the saga of perennial struggle and resistance, so familiar to Africans on the continent and in diaspora, continues.

The impression must not be given, however, that Yahweh's purposes were thwarted in the rest of Africa; they were not. The Egyptian Coptic Church, once a proud stronghold of the faith, did survive, but only as a minority. The Coptic Christians have not completely lost their Sabbath consciousness. God maintains His remnant; He will not leave Himself without witness.

Children of Ishmael: The Muslim Connection

> "And the angel of the LORD said unto her, Behold, thou art with child, and shalt bear a son, and shalt call his name Ishmael; because the LORD hath heard thy affliction. And Hagar bare Abram a son: and Abram called his son's name, which Hagar bare, Ishmael. And Abram was fourscore and six years old, when Hagar bare Ishmael to Abram" (Gen. 16:11).

Ishmael, Abraham's son by his Egyptian wife, Hagar, is also a product of the "neighborhood," the area peopled by Afro-Asiatics. The neighborhood is northeast Africa Ethiopia, Egypt, and Nimrod's territories in Mesopotamia where existed a commonality of language, culture, and religion.

Islam, like Judaism, is a religion of the book, the Koran. The Prophet Muhammad is a product of this admixture of peoples. Islam, having taken root in this soil, draws its nourishment from its Judeo-Christian antecedents. Yahweh made covenant also to the children of Ishmael. They, like Isaac's descendants, also practiced circumcision, as did many of the sons of Ham. Circumcision has been known and practiced among African peoples from earliest times.

For centuries Islam and Christianity have been in head-to-head competition for Africa. Edward Blyden points out that Islam is, in some ways, more appealing to the African because it seems to bring with it less racial and cultural baggage than Western Christianity,[2] and is more easily adapted to local cultures. Blyden observes that in Islam there are no pictures of deities, angels, or saints that suggest that salvation is only for Whites. In fact, Muslims believe that they have kept the commandments better than Christians with respect to not worshiping graven images.

Of course, Christians can counter with observations on Islam's faults and failures, including the fact that Muslims were at the forefront of the African slave trade, that they stole land and goods from Africans, and that they were particularly ruthless and brutal in their slave raids. This may all be true, but all the same, the Muslim appeal was greater in the African setting.

"Islam claims to be the religion of Abraham," says Jerald Whitehouse, a specialist in Islamic studies:

> "The early reformers in Arabia during the time of Muhammad (there were several) were called Hanif. They were calling their people back to the faith of Abraham to a worship of the one true God, calling their people away from idolatry, worship of ancestors, and human sacrifices. In the Koran, Abraham is referred to in several places as a Hanif. Further, Muhammad, the messenger of Arabia, traces his lineage directly back to Nabaioth, the first son of Ishmael, son of Abraham."[3]

When Muhammad and his followers were being persecuted in Mecca, he urged them to flee to Ethiopia for refuge. Indeed, it is a matter of record that one of the kings of Aksum (early Ethiopia) gave sanctuary to the first Muslims. Since that time an Islamic presence has existed in Ethiopia. Relations between the religions were rather amicable at first, but when the Portugese seemed poised to occupy Ethiopia, the Muslims attacked, more in defense of their own position than out of antipathy toward the Ethiopians. Nevertheless, in his lifetime Muhammad was sympathetic to the Ethiopians.[4]

The Sabbath and the Koran

In keeping with the thrust of this book, I asked Jerald W. Whitehouse if there are references to Sabbath in the Koran. He assured me that there are several, and that the Koran teaches that Allah is Creator. In fact, there is in the Koran an easily recognized resonance to the Hebrew Scriptures, but not a precise articulation of Hebrew-Christian teachings. The Koran is charitable in its assessment of Judaism and Christianity, as the following quote indicates:

> "We believe in Allah and in that which has been sent down to us and that which was sent down to Abraham and Ishmael, and Isaac and Jacob and his children, and that which was given to Moses and Jesus, and that which was given to all other Prophets from their Lord, we make no distinction between any of them."[5]

In the Koran the children of Ishmael have knowledge of Israel's history. Abraham, Isaac, Jacob, Moses, Aaron, Noah, David, Solomon, etc., are claimed as a part of their heritage. Jesus is acknowledged as a great prophet; Islam affirms the truth and righteousness of all the prophets, insisting that Allah, through them, has sent guidance to all people:

> "We have sent thee with enduring truth, as a bearer of glad tidings and as a warner. There is no people to whom a warning has not been sent."[6]
>
> "Be ye Jews; or be ye Christians; that you may be rightly guided. Tell them: Nay not so; let us agree to follow the religion of Abraham, who was ever inclined towards Allah and was not one of those who set up partners with Him. Affirm: We believe in Allah and in that which has been sent down to us and that which was sent down to Abraham and Ishmael, and Isaac and Jacob and his children, and that which was given to Moses and Jesus, and that which was given to all other Prophets from their Lord, we make no distinction between any of them. To Him do we wholly submit ourselves."[7]

Reference is also made to Israel's apostasy at Mount Sinai:

> "Because of their presumption they were afflicted with a destructive chastisement. Then, after clear Signs had come to them, they took to worshiping the calf, but We pardoned even that and We bestowed manifest authority upon Moses. We raised high above them the Mount whilst making a covenant with them, and We commanded them: Enter the gate submissively; and We also commanded them: Transgress not in the matter of the Sabbath. We took from them a firm covenant."[8]

The Koran reminds its readers of the seriousness of God's Sabbath: "You have surely known the end of those from amongst you who transgressed in the matter of the Sabbath. We condemned them: . . . . Thus We made this event a lesson for their contemporaries and for those who came after and an admonition for the God-fearing."[9]

According to the Koran, the creation of the universe and of humankind has been done with a purpose: "Allah is the Creator of all things and He is Guardian over all, to Him belong the keys of the heavens and the earth."[10] "He has created everything and has determined its measure."[11] "He says concerning it: Be and it is."[12]

The concepts of a last judgment and of the life to come are addressed by the Koran, but on the matter of the sonship of Messiah Jesus there is sharp variance with the Christian doctrine and a leaning toward Jewish understanding of the matter. The Koran says:

> "To insist upon Allah having a son in any but a purely spiritual or metaphorical sense is to insist upon an utter incongruity and impossibility. They have appointed partners of Allah, out of the jinn, whereas He has created them; and they falsely attribute to Him sons and daughters without any knowledge. Holy is He and exalted far above that which they attribute to Him. Originator of the heavens and the earth! How can He have a son when He has no consort, and He has created everything and has full knowledge of all things."[13]
>
> "Proclaim-'He is Allah, the Single; Allah, the Self-Existing and besought of all. He begets not, nor is He begotten; nor is there anyone like unto Him or His equal.'"[14]

Muslim dietary laws are very similar to the Hebrew Levitical prohibitions against certain articles of food: "He has made unlawful for you only that which has died and blood and the flesh of swine."[15] Not only did the Koran forbid the use of swine's flesh; it also spoke out against liquor and gambling.

Forgotten Continent

> "The Christians of Central Africa were lost sight of and forgotten by the world, and for many centuries they enjoyed freedom in the exercise of their faith."[16]

The Middle Ages saw a decline of the Western church during which sub-Saharan Africa found itself beyond the influence of the European ecclesiastical establishment. What of the Sabbath? How did it fare? Is there evidence of Sabbath awareness in Black Africa before the arrival of Christian missionaries? Is there any hint or intimation that the African peoples had any sense of Yahweh's day of rest and worship? Without a written record, how can we know?

First, Yahweh has never relinquished the right to speak to the sons and daughters of Adam in any part of His domain. One of the prophets refers to a system of communication that defies explanation: "No utterance at all, no speech, no sound that anyone can hear; yet their voice goes out through all the earth, and their message to the ends of the world" (Ps. 19:3, JB). Just as scientists can detect invisible bodies in space, there are ways we can know that knowledge of the Creation Sabbath is present in Africa.

First are the widespread evidences of Hebrew influence and antecedents on the continent. The idea of the one God and revealed religion is held to a certain extent by all people groups and in all areas of sub-Saharan Africa. This huge deposit of Yahwism is proof positive that the knowledge of Sabbath is pervasive on the continent. And we must not credit this to Hebraic influences alone. This knowledge of Yahweh is from Creation itself, and though it may be faint in racial memory, it is never completely destroyed.

Certainly, the very essence of Sabbath is memory: "*Remember* the sabbath day, to keep it holy" (Ex. 20:8). "He hath made his wonderful works to be *remembered*: the LORD is gracious and full of compassion" (Ps. 111:4).

Scholars are both fascinated and perplexed by these strong Hebrew influences in all parts of the African continent, especially West Africa. All people knew Yahweh at one time, and this knowledge, though dimmed by the ages, still persists. Joseph Williams insists: "An influence of Hebraic culture found its way along the same lines from Egypt to the heart of [sub-Saharan Africa]." So Williams, challenged by this phenomenon, dedicated his life to the study of possible contacts between the Hebrews and the tribes of West Africa.

Jewish Diaspora

THE Jewish people in diaspora may be found everywhere. From earliest times the children of Israel were dispersed by war and persecution. Historians of antiquity report the presence of Jews in such faraway places as India and

China. From some descriptions, many of these Israelites were of dark complexion. At one time they poured into Egypt in great numbers, establishing businesses and learning centers in Alexandria and elsewhere.

During New Testament times, Jewish immigrants were scattered throughout the Roman Empire. Their existence in foreign lands generally took on a pattern: for a time they would prosper they are usually astute and industrious—but they would seldom be fully accepted. Sabbath observance, dietary laws, and culture set them apart. Their apparent prosperity made them targets of demagogues ready scapegoats.

Characteristically, they would cling to the Sabbath of Yahweh, and are known for their devotion to this day. Inevitably, the Jewish people are associated with Sabbath. The Sabbath is, therefore, a universal mark of Jewish identification, a badge.

When hostile neighbors would invade their host states, the Jews were forced to flee and begin all over again in more favorable locations. This can account for the widespread presence of Jews in Africa. Driven from Egypt by Roman conquerors, they escaped to the south, to Nubia and the Sudan. And when the Muslims extended hegemony over all of the northern part of Africa except Ethiopia, they migrated further south into sub-Saharan Africa. Those Jewish people who have sought sanctuary in Africa have generally been tolerated and often been made welcome.

As a result of this immigration, many African people groups display in their culture Hebrew customs reminiscent of Hebrew society. And wherever there is acknowledgment of the one God, there is also Sabbath awareness. Wherever we see these strong Hebrew manifestations, we have indications of the Sabbath. The people who hold this great truth proclaim their belief in Creation and the Creator God.

With the exception of the influence Philip the evangelist had through his encounter with the Ethiopian eunuch (Acts 8), the consciousness of God and the reverence to the Sabbath that we are speaking of cannot be properly attributed to the entrance of Christianity into Africa, which occurred in the fifteenth century A.D. at the earliest. Unfortunately, when they came, they brought a zealous devotion to the so-called Lord's Day, Sunday, in direct opposition to the biblical Sabbath. (In fact, in Ghana the missionaries were called *broni*, "Sunday people.")[17]

This opposition to the Bible Sabbath on the part of the European ecclesiastical establishment and its academic auxiliaries poses a conundrum avowed followers of Messiah Jesus have embraced a day of rest that is without His sanction. People of the Book supposedly brought the knowledge of Jesus to Africa. The whole missionary effort seems suspect when these people of the Book insist on the sanctity of a day not sanctioned by the Book. But the people of Africa, who did not have the Book, have caused consternation for missionaries when, upon being taught to read the Book, they soon began inquiring, "Why do you differ from this Book?"

Further, the pious missionaries—highly motivated, altruistic, fully persuaded that they bring God's special revelation to this continent are taken aback when they discover traces of Yahweh's footprints in unexpected and out-of-the-way places. Missionaries find it difficult to account for the presence of Hebrewisms throughout Africa, memories of a great Sky God, the *Bore Bore* who created the "thing" (Akan for the earth) and man upon it.

Clearly, Yahweh has not ceased to visit the African peoples in ways that we cannot anticipate or journalize. Nor should we be surprised to discover wherever we go that He has already been there: "In the past God spoke to our forefathers through the prophets at many times and in various ways" (Heb. 1:1, NIV).

Joseph Williams is one of those scholars who believes strongly that Africans and Jews have had continuing contacts since pre-Christian times. He cites the Ashanti of West Africa as an example of an African people whose culture is permeated with reminders of Old Testament culture.

Williams quotes, with approval, Philo Mills when he speaks in opposition to the popular belief that humankind originally was either "atheistic, or, if in possession of any religion at all, that the idea of God was developed out of the ghost or the magical nature cult."[18]

He sees in his own research what Mills found in his:

> "[There are] an enormous array of religious facts which have only recently been unearthed but which in their united force point to conclusions of precisely the opposite character. . . . It is the all-Father belief which precedes the totemic or animistic cult by indefinite ages. Primitive man believed in God, and only in later times was the belief corrupted."[19]

Williams's greatest interest is in the Ashanti people, among whom he finds many Hebrewisms. Along with J. B. Danquah, Williams looks at several Ashanti words that bear "striking resemblance to those of equivalent Hebrew meaning. Finally, the Supreme Being of the Ashanti gave strong indication of being the Yahweh of the Old Testament"[20]:

> "The question naturally rose, how to explain these parallels of cultural beliefs? Should they be ascribed to mere coincidence to independent development? Or, have we here a remarkable instance of diffusion across the entire breadth of Africa? Is it possible to establish even a partial historical contact between the Ashanti of today and the Hebrews of fully two thousand years ago or more?
>
> "The problem might be approached, either by trying to trace the

story of the Dispersion of the Jews, usually called the Diaspora, or by the study of tribal beliefs and practices and the records of early African travellers, particularly of those who had written of the manners and customs of [Black people] before the inroads of Islamism had tended to utterly destroy all traditions of the past.

"It was finally decided to attack the question from both angles. The worldwide diffusion of the Jews was followed in its manifold ramifications with a view of establishing every possible influx of Hebraic culture that might possibly at any time have reached the shores of Africa. After a general consideration of the Diaspora itself, the first line of investigation led from the Abyssinian centre of Hebraic influence, that dates back to a more or less legendary origin, and which eventually built up the distinctively Jewish Falashas.

"Then again, long before the destruction of Jerusalem by Titus, the Mediterranean shore of Africa had become lined with influential Jewish colonies which undoubtedly were in constant mercantile relations with the interior of [Africa]. But Egypt especially had been the haven of the refugees from Jerusalem at the time of the Babylonian Captivity, and for many subsequent centuries the Jewish element in the land of the Pharaohs continued to increase and prosper.

"From all three of these sources, an Hebraic influence might well have penetrated to the very heart of Western Africa, especially along the general lines of commerce.

"It was here that the study of the West African tribes themselves was undertaken, and every vestige of evidence recorded. It was indeed supprising how many Hebrewisms, either real or at least apparent, were to be found among the unislamised tribes."[21]

Then there is the presence of the Falasha in Ethiopia, still one of the strongest evidences of Hebrew influence in Africa. These uncompromisingly singular, Old Testament kind of people trace their ancestry back to Solomonic times and claim to be possessors of the religion of the one true God. The Falashas, ethnically Ethiopian, accuse their Ethiopian brethren of departing from the faith when they accepted Christianity. They still speak of King Ezana's conversion as the great apostasy. Williams concludes:

"The Supreme Being not only of the Ashanti and allied tribes, but most probably of the whole of [Africa] as well is not the God of the Christians which, at a comparatively recent date, was superimposed on the various tribal beliefs by ministers of the gospel: but, the Yahweh of the Hebrews, and that too of the Hebrews of preexilic times, that either supplanted the previous concept of divinity in the

African mind, or else clarified and defined the original monotheistic idea which may have lain dormant for many centuries, or even perhaps been buried for a time in an inexplicable confusion of polytheism and superstition."[22]

The Lemba of Southern Africa

In several places on the continent there are people groups who almost seem counterculture, they are so different from the surrounding society. Such a group are the Lemba people. H. A. Stayt, in his book The BaVenda, comments that the "life and customs of this peculiar people [The Lemba] are strangely reminiscent of the wandering Jews of medieval times."[23]

The Lemba follow Jewish practices, including kosher preparation of meat and circumcision, and close their prayers with amen. They claim to have built the great Zimbabwe, and once had a book, perhaps the book of the Jews, Stayt said, but it was lost a long time ago with the great Lemba drum.

The Lemba people, the so-called Black Jews of southern Africa, are found in the Transvaal and Zimbabwe. They live among the VhaVenda people. Paul Kruger, pioneer Africaner leader, recognized the Lemba's Jewishness. This is probably why they are called "Kruger's Jews." Although the Lemba are Black, they have endeavored to maintain their identity and apartness from their Venda neighbors.

Estimates of the number of Lemba range from 150,000 to 500,000. Lemba villages are called clean places, and they are proud of their apparently Semitic origins. Western observers report that they have Semitic features, "thin noses," and could "pass easily for dark Yemite Jews."[24]

Photographs of Lembas, according to some anthropologists, suggest that what these people have claimed all along is true that they are Jews, with a history as long and as proud as Jews anywhere else in the world. In fact, there are Israeli scholars who maintain that the Lemba are indeed Jews who should be acknowledged as such and admitted to the ranks of world Jewry.[25]

The Lemba believe they are kin to the Falasha of Ethiopia. Margaret Nabbarro, an ethnomusicologist who for many years has supported the Lemba's claims, reports:

> "They have a musical instrument called the Bush piano, which, unlike those used by the VhaVenda, is played inside of a gourd decorated with shells. The only other people who have an instrument like that are the Falashas. I believe that the Lemba and the Falashas are related and perhaps formed part of the same original migration. Some stayed on in Ethiopia as Falashas; the rest made their way down through Africa until eventually they came to Zimbabwe. If you want

more evidence their tribal symbol is the star of David with an elephant inside of it."[26]

Both the Falashas and the Lembas believe they came from "Senna," which could be the city Sennar on the Nile river. R. Wessmann concludes:

"One cannot avoid the often striking similarity between the African and the Jewish types. Again and again we find laws and customs among the African which force the impression that there has been at some former time some kind of connection between Blacks and the ancient Hebrews. . . . In the [Lemba] tribe, one may find, especially, distinct traces of such contact or connection."[27]

The Lemba were featured in an article in the New York Times:

"Genetic tests on the Lemba people of southern Africa show convincing evidence the Bantu-speaking tribe may be of Jewish ancestry. . . . A team of geneticists have discovered that Lemba men carry a DNA sequence that is distinctive to the cohanim, a hereditary set of Jewish priests. . . . The Lemba, who practice circumcision, keep one day a week holy and avoid eating pork or pig-like animals, have long asserted they are of Jewish heritage.

"The discovery of the common DNA sequences stemmed from research being done into the Jewish tradition that priests are the descendants of Aaron, the elder brother of Moses. An analysis of the male Y chromosome found in 1997 that a particular pattern of DNA changes was much more common among cohanim priests than among lay Jews. David B. Goldstein, a population geneticist at Oxford University in England, took that discovery one step further. 'In studying the priesthood, we happened into this tool for distinguishing Jewish from non-Jewish populations,' Goldstein said. . . .

"Unlike in other chromosomes, the genetic material of the Y chromosome remains more or less unchanged from generation to generation, making it a useful tool in discovering heritage.

. . . "Goldstein found a particular set of genetic mutations that was strongly associated with the priestly caste, not so common among lay Jews and very rare in non-Jewish populations. He then tested DNA samples collected from the Lemba. Goldstein's research showed that the proportion of Lemba men carrying the genetic signature of the priests [was] similar to those found among the major Jewish populations, strongly supporting the Lemba tradition of Jewish ancestry. . . .

"The DNA sequences were particularly common among Lemba men who belong to the Buba clan, the senior of their 12 groups. The

Lemba, from South Africa and Zimbabwe, believe they were led out of Judea by a man named Buba."

Many African people groups have memories of migrating from the north and have brought with them customs and words that can be attributed to Egyptian or Ethiopian places. The Venda say that they "have a Jewish language which only our priests and traditional witch doctors know. A professor from Bar Ilan University in Israel has proved that there are many Hebrew words in this old Shona Language of ours."[28]

Mary Getui, from the Abagusii people of Kenya, speaks about the significance of Misiri. The Abagusii tell stories about the place of their origin, which they call Misiri. Getui believes that Misiri is Egypt, and would thus place the origins of the Abagusii people in Egypt.

The Incubation Period

Among the effects the Dark Ages had on Christian faith in Africa and Europe was a diminishing of interaction between Christians on the two continents. What contacts remained were not sufficient to foster that mutual support that is the hallmark of Christianity. Nevertheless, Ethiopia's seclusion may have contributed to the survival of Christianity there.

By the time of the Middle Ages, Africa, in general, had dropped off the Christian map. Egypt/Alexandria, North Africa, Carthage, and the Nubian Christian strongholds were virtually wiped out. There was no Christian presence on the continent except for Ethiopia and for small remnant communities in the areas aforementioned. Islam completely controlled North Africa and the south and east coasts of the Mediterranean.

Lamin Sanneh calls this the "period of incubation," by which he means that Christianity in Africa was not dead, but in a state of hibernation. Europe also, as the term "the Dark Ages" suggests, was culturally and scientifically little better off than Africa. "The whole world," Jerome wrote, "is sinking into ruin." Europe, however, imagined itself vastly superior to Africa in the sphere of the religious, but this was not so. European Christianity, at best, was but a thin veneer.

There were periods when the European ecclesiastical establishment fell on tough times. Malachi Martin reports that there were times when goats and sheep roamed though the Vatican itself, when Rome was almost a deserted city. Shrines to the old gods were never completely demolished. European Christianity, from the beginning, learned to disturb as little as possible the deepest cultural and spiritual springs of the people, preferring to absorb and embrace indigenous beliefs and cultural practices instead of insisting on radical change.

Once subjugated or Christianized, people were compelled to acknowledge the supremacy of the Pontiff of Rome, after which they were tolerated and accommodated. The old gods were made saints. The old feast days and holidays were baptized and given Christian names. Old Thor was never far from revival, from leaping onto the scene with all his ancient power.

"The worldviews prevalent in western Europe and in Black Africa in about 1500 had a great deal in common," writes Adrian Hastings.[29] He continues:

> "'No difference can be perceived between the practices of the Christians and those of the heathen,' said a Jesuit in Sierra Leone at the beginning of the seventeenth century. Religion was part of the continuum of life, not compartmentalized on its margins, and it was supernatural interventions that made rain fall, and determined the outcome of battle. The belief in witchcraft and magic was as characteristic of Europe as of Africa, and a study of seventeenth-century Brittany suggests 'that the majority of the inhabitants of medieval Europe were sunk in animist worship of trees, stones and springs and that Christianity was the thinnest of veneers on top of this.'
>
> "In Portugal, the dead were thought to return on All Souls' Day and the statues of saints were mutilated if they failed to provide expected benefits. In modern times, among the Kalabari of the Niger Delta, the same fate befell sculptures of dangerous spirits."[30]

The biblical Sabbath was preserved in Ethiopia, Central Africa, and Armenia during these centuries, and even in Europe there were pockets of resistance to the European ecclesiastical establishment. Groups such as the Anabaptists and the Waldenses defiantly and heroically clung to the faith and practice of the apostles. J. N. Andrews summarizes:

> "In consequence of their location in the interior of Africa, the Abyssinians ceased to be known to the rest of Christendom about the fifth century. At this point, the Sabbath and Sunday in the Catholic Church were counted sisters. One thousand years later, these African churches are visited, and though surrounded by the thick darkness of pagan and Mahometan superstition, and somewhat affected thereby, they are found at the end of this period holding the Sabbath and first-day substantially as held by the Catholic Church when they were lost sight of by it. The Catholics of Europe, on the contrary, had, in the meantime, trampled the ancient Sabbath in the dust.
>
> "Why was this great contrast? Simply because the pope ruled in Europe, while central Africa, whatever else it may have suffered, was not cursed with his presence nor with his influence. But so soon as the pope learned of the existence of the Abyssinian churches, he

sought to gain control of them, and when he had gained it, one of his first acts was to suppress the Sabbath! In the end, the Abyssinians regained their independence, and thenceforward till the present time have held fast the Sabbath of the Lord."[31]

End Notes

[1]Noble, p. 36.

[2]Edward W. Blyden, *Christianity, Islam, and the Negro Race* (Edinburgh, Scotland, 1969; reprint, Chesapeake, Va.: ECA Associates, 1993), pp. 9-24.

[3]Whitehouse.

[4]Blyden, p. 231.

[5]Koran, 2.136-138.

[6]*Ibid.*, 2.35, 36.

[7]*Ibid.*, 2.136-138.

[8]*Ibid.*, 15.155.

[9]*Ibid.*, 39.64-67.

[10]*Ibid.*, 39.63, 64.

[11]*Ibid.*, 25.3.

[12]*Ibid.*, 2.118.

[13]*Ibid.*, 6.101-104.

[14]*Ibid.*, 112.2-5.

[15]*Ibid.*, 1.174.

[16]White, *Great Controversy*, p. 577.

[17]Owusu-Mensa, p. 17.

[18]Joseph Williams, *Hebrewisms of West Africa: From Nile to Niger With the Jews* (Toronto, Canada: Longmans Green, 1930; reprint, Baltimore: BCP Books, 1998), p. 355.

[19]*Ibid.*

[20]*Ibid.*, p. 22.

[21]*Ibid.*, pp. 22, 23.

[22]*Ibid.*, p. 355.

[23]Quoted in Tudor Parfitt, *The Thirteenth Gate: Travels Among the Lost Tribes of Israel* (Bethesda, Md.: Adler and Adler, 1987), p. 154.

[24]*Ibid.*, p. 153.

[25]*Ibid.*, p. 154.

[26]*Ibid.*, pp. 151, 152.

[27]*Ibid.*, p. 153.

[28]*Ibid.*, p. 150.

[29]Hastings. P. 73.

[30]*Ibid.*, pp. 73-75.

[31]Andrews, p. 427.

CHAPTER EIGHT

REACHING OUT FOR LIGHT

> "In comparison with the Ethiopian and Coptic churches, the Christian communities established through Western, and especially Portuguese, influence during the middle years were fragile [like] exotic plants, which did not always thrive in African soil."[1]

Following the Middle Ages, the first Western attempts to evangelize the African continent, beginning about 1500, met with great difficulty and disappointment. Catholic missions had made forays into Angola, the Congo, and southwestern Africa even before 1500. But the work went slowly. Christian enclaves were established on the Coast, but did not spread into the interior. Africa seemed impervious to Christian mission.

Some reasons can be given. First, there was the harsh climate, with its accompanying health problems. West Africa especially was called the "White man's grave." Malaria was the dreaded killer. Second, there was the apathy and even antipathy of the African people. They were not particularly attracted to Christianity.

But missionaries kept coming, not in large numbers, but rather spasmodically over the years. In a few scattered areas Christianity held on stubbornly. With notable exceptions, it should be noted that Christian mission was almost identical with the imperial thrust of the great European powers.

Waves of merchants, adventurers, and explorers looking for riches brought to the continent goods and services, but also previously unknown diseases. European monarchs sent explorers and merchants out with royal charters to go up to "possess the land." They raised their national flags to the glory of their country and the honor of their king or queen. Portugal and Spain were foremost, but you can be sure that England and the Dutch were not far behind.

But Christianity, for some reason, did not take deep root in African soil during this long era stretching from 1500 to the times of strong leaders the likes of Livingstone, Moffatt, and others. This later group of selfless, dedicated missionaries made great contributions to missions by developing written forms of local languages, translating the Bible, and founding schools. While many of the great European missionaries were tied in some ways to the interests of their European sponsors, the Church of the Brethren (Moravians) and the Quakers were a breed apart. Thoroughly apolitical, free of ties to government, they dedicated themselves solely to the uplift of the people. Even then, converts were few.

This first group of missionaries were highly altruistic, fully committed servants of Christ who gave themselves without reserve to the work of evangelizing the continent. They identified with the people and treated the Africans as brothers and sisters in Christ. This did not sit well with the fortune hunters and chartered companies that looked on the missionary enterprise as meddling.

Nationally chartered companies, such as the Dutch Africa Company in Southern Africa, had power to act on behalf of their respective governments and, in most cases, were a government unto themselves. This made it difficult for missionaries who spoke out for human dignity and against the vices which were already wreaking havoc among the peoples of Africa, but from which the companies and their supporters were profiting.

So they often clashed, and more often than not, it was the mercantile and political forces that won. Later, new groups of missionaries were less likely to mount any serious challenge to the merchants and government agents. The ruling class seemed to be saying to the servants of Christ, "Stick to the gospel and don't meddle in political affairs." We have heard the same in our day.

Noble Example

One type of person seems to epitomize that first group of missionaries: Georg Schmid, of Bohemia. Schmid was determined to serve in Africa. He prepared well for what would be referred to in our day as cross-cultural ministry. Arriving in South Africa on July 1, 1737, he was received with laughter and scorn by the Dutch, who had protested that "their rule might tend to uphold righteousness and to plant and further pure Christian teaching among the natives."[2]

The Dutch had treated the indigenous peoples as beasts. The Boers regarded the Blacks as "creatures of the devil, and as the Canaanites, doomed to destruction. They were not to be treated as human beings. Christianity was intended only for White people."[3]

Schmid gave his life to the African people, working tirelessly to establish a model mission station about 50 miles east of Cape Town. Schmid introduced, among other modern agricultural improvements, the plow, which seemed to the African a magic instrument that caused the ground to produce a hundredfold.

Perry Noble, whose books on Africa were featured at the 1890 Chicago Columbian Exposition, had great admiration for the Khoi Koin (or Hottentots), the people among whom Schmid worked. Perry Noble described Schmid's work with apparent appreciation and described the Khoi Koin as a people who had developed a strong advanced culture, even by Western standards.

Mostly monogamous, they treated their women with respect; their moral code was, in some respects, superior to that of nominal Christians. They were skilled in metalwork and had developed a kind of simple alphabet, but they soon became ruined by the liquor traffic and other vices.

Schmid faced great opposition from the Dutch company and the Boer farmers in his attempts to improve the lot of the Kkoi Koin people. The Europeans felt threatened by Schmid's gospel, his powerful preaching against the sin of alcohol consumption and other vices and debilitating practices. It was, they concluded, bad for business.

After a time the Boer farmers and miners and the Dutch company people petitioned the government to deport him to Europe, which was done. Schmid left a broken man. After giving his best to Africa, he was forced to leave his beloved African brethren and the prosperous community he had founded after only seven years of labor.

Johannes Van der Kemp was another of this unique breed of missionary. Van der Kemp, an educated Dutchman, had been a dapper officer in the Dutch military. After losing his wife and daughter in a tragic boating accident, he returned to Christianity for comfort. His contact with the Moravians impressed him to forsake all and seek a mission appointment.

After some time Van der Kemp went to South Africa under the aegis of the newly founded London Missionary Society, arriving in the Cape in 1799.

Van der Kemp was singular in that he lived as a native, often going barefoot and shedding European dress. He was outspoken against social evils, slavery, liquor drinking, adultery. Because of this he was called a meddler in political affairs by the authorities.

Van der Kemp taught the absolute equality of the races, a position that brought discomfort to his missionary brethren. After a brief tenure of service at the Cape, he pushed on into Xhosa territory. A man of great imagination, he used every means of communicating with the people in their own idiom.

In 15 months among the Xhosa there was only one baptism, a Hottentot woman, the wife of a refugee. The Europeans had hoped that Van der Kemp would influence King Ngqika, and he did preach to the monarch. The king listened, but refused baptism. Van der Kemp wrote a grammar, did an extensive word list, and produced translations.

Ngqika was a Xhosa King. During these days of upheaval, brought on by the multiplication of land-hungry Boer settlers, many Khoi Koin, and even a few disgruntled Whites, had taken up residence at the great residence of the king. Here is a perfect illustration of the situation that existed before colonialism. The great chiefs and kings had to be reckoned with, so whether they liked it or not, Europeans had to deal with this kind of African authority if they wanted to live in peace and reap the benefits of the incredible riches of the continent.

If we are looking for spectacular results and dramatic breakthroughs of the Christian mission in the African culture during Van der Kemp's ministry and that of his contemporaries, we will be disappointed that is, if we take the short view. Future events proved, however, that his mission, in spite of apparently sparse results, was to bear fruit "after many days."

Years after Van der Kemp's death, King Ngqika, to whom he had preached unsuccessfully, confessed that he still thought of Van der Kemp often and regretted having scorned his preaching. Many African converts began to call themselves "Ma Yanka," the people of Van der Kemp.[4]

What made Van der Kemp so different? How has his influence after his death grown far beyond that which he exerted during his life? Hastings suggests several things.

First, he was regarded as a man of God. The Africans acknowledged him as a "rainmaker"; that is to say, his prayers were answered, he was in touch with the Most High God.

Second, he was a man of absolute poverty. His lifestyle was consistent with that of Messiah Jesus and the first disciples. He traveled as Christ's disciples did without purse or scrip, living with the people, accepting their hospitality, "living," as Paul said, "by the gospel."

Third, he was a man of high intelligence, willing to work hard to master the Xhosa language, to reduce it to writing.

Fourth, and perhaps most important, Africans remembered him most for his insistence upon the equality of the races. He married a young Malagasy woman, much to the consternation of the European brethren, who thought he was carrying this principle too far: "Color, race, the material level of culture and of living conditions meant absolutely nothing to him relative to the human personality, the rights of humanity, and the gospel of God."[5]

And along with this was Van der Kemp's continual and constant concern for justice. This man set a high benchmark for all who followed him.

Ntsikana

This is the place to say something about Nxele and Ntsikana, two promising young Xhosa, who, no doubt, heard Van der Kemp preach. Ntsikana was brought up to be a warrior and counselor to the king. Nxele, on the other hand, grew up on a mission station and became a spiritual leader among his people. However, over a period of time, Nxele's theological orientation became more and more radical, tending to violent revolution. Ntsikana, on the other hand, grew up in completely pagan surroundings, without the benefit of education at mission school. But he had talent innate ability.

Born in 1780, Ntsikana in 1815 experienced a dramatic conversion to Christianity in the manner of many African Christians who followed him. Plunging into the Ggorha River, he washed from his body every trace of red ochre, the red clay that the Xhosa used to identify themselves as proud pagans. Then he called his two wives and said to them, "The thing that has come into me tells me that I must send one of you away." And he did, giving the one that he sent away a liberal portion of his goods. He gave up traditional dancing and told his followers, "There are two Gods, Father and Son."

Ntsikana immediately began to write magnificent hymns. One of them has a beauty about it that appeals across racial and cultural lines:

"He is the one who brings together herds which oppose each other,
He is the leader who has led us,
He is the great blanket which we put on."[6]

Ntsikana gathered around him a group of disciples, including his own children. He composed for them a series of magnificent hymns, and he refused to participate in war when it came. His followers named themselves the "Poll-headed" people, cattle without horns, pacifists. Ntsikana held services twice daily in his hut or under a tree. Several of his hymns were soon taken over by the mission churches and printed during the 1820s to become forever a part of the Xhosa Christian worship tradition.

He told his people, "My children, something has commanded me to wash off the red ochre, therefore, do you also wash it off." A little later he declared: "The thing which has entered me, it says, 'Let there be prayer! Let everything bow the knee!'" Though this seems strange to Western Christians, there is something in Ntsikana's experience that reminds us of Yahweh's contacts with the pagans of Bible times. In that distant past Yahweh spoke to His children in a variety of ways.

It was this kind of powerful and direct encounter with the spiritual realm that led Ntsikana to reject the leadership of his contemporary, the Xhosa prophet Nxele, who had also come under Christian influence, but who was stirring up the nation to war against the British, promising that the ancestors would rise to assist them.

Ntsikana sent a message at once to Nxele, whom he had previously supported, which said that he was misleading the people:

"He who is our mantle of comfort,
The giver of life, ancient on high
He is the Creator of the heavens,
And the ever-burning stars:
God is mighty in the heavens,
And whirls the stars around in the sky.
We call on him in his dwelling place,
That he may be our mighty leader,
For he made the blind to see;
We adore him as the only good,
For he alone is a sure defense."[7]

Sources say that in his last address to his followers, delivered on the day of his death, Ntsikana said words to this effect:

> "I am going home to my Father. Do not, after I die, go back to live by the customs of the Xhosa. I want you to go to Bulineli (Brownlee) at Gwali. Have nothing to do with the feasts, but keep a firm hold of the word of God. Always stick together . . . should a rope be thrown around your neck, or a spear pierce your body, or you be beaten with sticks, or struck with stones, whatever persecution comes upon you on account of the word of God, don't give way, keep it and stick to it and to each other."[8]

Ntsikana's Christianity was developed quite apart from missionary influence or guidance. One might say that here is Christianity in an African idiom. God the Holy Spirit spoke directly to him. He, no doubt, had heard the missionaries preach; however, his hearing was a selective hearing, though not a misrepresentation of what he heard."[9]

Ntsikana had planned his funeral service and the manner of his burial. He insisted that it be a witness to his faith. He even turned the first spade of ground for his grave to impress his followers of his seriousness they must follow his instructions explicitly."[10]

Mission histories tend to ignore Ntsikana's work and mission, his place in the history of African Christianity. Many years after his death the Christian world did recognize Ntsikana by incorporating some of his hymns into their hymnals. He became a model for a free African church, a precursor of Ethiopianism to come. Ntsikana cannot be overlooked in the origins of Xhosa Christianity. His legacy is greater than usually acknowledged.

Partition: The Mad Scramble

> "I beg your attention to Africa; I know that in a few years I shall

be cut off in that country, which is now open: Do not let it be shut again! I go back to Africa to try to make an open path for commerce and Christianity; do you carry out the work which I have begun. *I leave it with you!*"[11]

In these words, David Livingstone spoke to England's elite in a Cambridge University address during one of his infrequent trips to his homeland. His European brethren did come to Africa, but with another "C" added to Livingstone's *commerce* and *Christianity*. This "C" was conquest. Pakenham summarizes what happened:

"Suddenly, in half a generation, the scramble gave Europe virtually the whole continent: including thirty new colonies and protectorates, ten million square miles of new territories and 110 million dazed new subjects, acquired by one method or another. Africa was sliced up like a cake, the pieces swallowed by five rival nations Germany, Italy, Portugal, France and Britain (with Spain taking some scraps) and Britain and France were at each other's throats."[12]

On the Way to Colonialism

For a long time various European nations would look with avaricious eyes toward the exploitation of the African peoples and the vast natural resources of the continent. But the Europeans, both secular and religious, were not complete masters of the situation. They were able to operate only by the sufferance of kings and paramount chiefs.

These wily African rulers were quick to see the benefits the White man could bring to them and their people. Clearly, the real power in Africa during this time was in the hands of these African leaders. They maintained a careful balance between their own interests and the interests of the Europeans.

The European powers were satisfied with this arrangement until they became alarmed that the British were poised to extend their rule over the entire continent as they had done in India. This led the major European powers to devise a plan whereby Africa would be partitioned, with a minimum of bloodshed that is, of European blood.

Berlin Congress

King Leopold of Belgium called a meeting of European powers, which took place in Berlin, Germany, and was called the Berlin Congress. It was really a series of meetings held over a period of several years, beginning in 1878 and running through 1885. One was called the Berlin Conference on West Africa. When the general act was signed in February 1885 and the congress adjourned, Africa was forever changed. The European powers could now concentrate on jointly possessing the riches of the continent instead of fighting each other for little patches of territory.

By acting as civilized nations, they could have the whole pie. From now on they could deal from a position of strength and work on the principle of divide and conquer. Colonialism could now proceed unimpeded by dissent of a single European superpower. "The spirit of Berlin" actuated European geopolitics for years to come."[13]

It is surprising to many that colonialism did not take root until the 1890s and that it was not until 1912 that the program reached its goal of total control of the continent.[14] Country after country and tribe after tribe were overwhelmed by the sheer force of superior firepower. Breech-loading rifles and maxim (machine) guns made European armies almost invincible.

There were, however, pockets of stubborn resistance. The Zulus in South Africa and the Ashanti in the West resisted stubbornly for a long time. The Ndebele, under their great king Lobengula, bear witness to the use of brute force in imposing European rule on the African peoples. In the great massacre at Bulawayo, 3,000 Ndebele warriors were cut down in one day by Rhodes's mercenaries, who had seven-pounder field guns and a number of machine guns, including five of the new Maxims. It was evident by now that there was an altogether new reality in Black Africa.

National and ethnic groups, including old enemies, were arbitrarily squeezed into geographical configurations without reference to ethnicity and blood ties, according to the whims and wishes of the colonial powers. Like modern freeways, which cut up and divide neighborhoods, separating families and friends, the partitioning of Africa caused untold suffering. On the entire continent only the Ethiopians and tiny Liberia and Sierra Leone were free.

"I have no intention of being an indifferent looker-on if the distant Powers have the idea of dividing up Africa," said Ethiopian emperor Menelik in an address to the European powers in 1891. "For Ethiopia has been for more than fourteen centuries an island of Christians in the middle of a sea of pagans."[15] Menelik's words were no empty threat, as we will see.

To the rest of Black Africa, the Ethiopians seemed invincible. When they repulsed the invading Italians at Adowa in 1891, the news moved like wildfire through the sub-Saharan area. Thus began a new period of political consciousness and religious awareness. We can trace the beginning of freedom movements in Africa to the Ethiopian experience.

Ethiopia's experience was not lost on the African diaspora. African-Americans were especially proud of their Ethiopian brethren. They maintained a keen and continued interest in Ethiopian resistance to the dominance of foreign powers. The struggle for freedom was fueled worldwide by the entire experience. African-American clergy looked again at the great prophetic word of Psalm 68 and took hope: "Princes shall come out of Egypt; Ethiopia shall soon stretch out her hands unto God" (verse 31).

There was a religious spinoff to the African independence movement. In Southern Africa the religious aspect of the independence movement went like wildfire in every part of the continent. The African Independent Churches are the most potent religious force on the continent. Their influence is felt even in African traditional religions and in the mainline Churches.

Ethiopia: The Struggle Continues

Europe has always been fascinated by Ethiopia the land of Prester John, the legendary African Christian King. The European ecclesiastical establishment found it difficult to believe that Ethiopian Christianity could be a valid expression of the faith, surrounded, as it is, by pagan nations.

The Jesuits viewed Ethiopian religion as a strange mixture of Hebrew, pagan, and bizarre elements. They were especially offended by the drums and sistrums used in the sacred liturgy. Of course, the Ethiopians believed their faith to be the one true faith, received from the apostles and unchanged since the Day of Pentecost. They had their own *Didascalia* purported to have come from the hand of the apostles and preserved by the Ehtiopian people. And Ethiopia was Zion, successor of Israel as God's chosen people.

During the sixteenth century, Portugal was flexing her expansionist muscles, eager to plant her flag in every part of the globe. Needless to say, she was determined to conquer and exploit Ethiopia, the beautiful hill country to present it as a gift to her monarch and to the pope, and, in the process, to find the fabled El Dorado (the gold mine), which the European Powers hoped to find on the continent.

The expansionist enterprise was driven by two factors: the economic and the religious. One explorer described his mission as being "to serve God and His majesty, to give light to those who are in darkness, and to grow rich, as all men desire to do."[16]

The Western Church blessed the explorers, whom it considered its agents for the enlargement of the kingdom of God. The pope cited Prince Henry the Navigator in a papal bull for his devotion to and "apostolic zeal in spreading the name of Christ." So the Portugese, who have taken Africa on as its special project, and the Vatican have made Ethiopia their special target. Portugal pursued her mission with dogged determination for 150 years, during which time, according to Lukas Malisha, the Portugese made three major efforts in Ethiopia.

The Jesuits, the spiritual leaders of the mission, recruited the best prospects for this extremely important and sensitive diplomatic mission. At one time Ignatius Loyola considered going to Ethiopia himself, but was prevented by poor health. Nevertheless, Loyola's interest in Ethiopia lasted throughout his life. His great counsel to those who were assigned to Ethiopia was to be wise and exercise *dolcezza*, the sweet voice, in dealing with the Ethiopians.

Europe attached much importance to Ethiopia; there developed an unusual, almost love-hate, relationship between Ethiopia and Portugal, which played out for a long period of time.

At the same time, Islamization of African countries was taking place at a rapid pace, and Ethiopia was the next target for takeover by her Muslim neighbors. All across North Africa, Christian states fell one after the other, like dominoes. The Ethiopian emperors looked to fellow Christians in Europe for help, but help came with at a huge price. When Portugal finally did come to the aid of the Ethiopians, with substantial military assistance in the struggle against the armies of Ahmed Gran, a great Muslim general, they immediately demanded an expensive *quid pro quo*—Ethiopia must pay homage to the pope, receive Portugese and Vatican diplomats at court, and establish the Catholic faith in the realm.

Ethiopia posed an enigma. The Ethiopian church developed early on, with little or no contact with the European ecclesiastical establishment, and created its own genre of faith and practice. Ethiopia was no pale expression of European Christianity. In theology, Ethiopia was not markedly different from the Latin Church, but its style of worship was African to the core.

We have already pointed out the Hebraic stamp on Ethiopian Christianity. To the Roman See, it was impertinence that the Ethiopian Church could go its own way, independent of any guidance from the successors of the apostles. The difference between the Ethiopian church and those Eastern churches that also kept the original Sabbath is that Ethiopia was never in the Vatican orbit. Ethiopian Christian antecedents go back beyond the origin of the Church of Rome. This made for potential conflict, and for many centuries the Catholic Church worked with all diligence to bring Ethiopia into greater conformity.

Ethiopia's motivation was not always as clean as the driven snow. Most of the emperors were willing to enter into some kind of military alliance with Portugal in order to defend themselves against the Muslim threat, which was always on the horizon. During these times Ethiopian Christianity was subjected to its greatest peril. The Portuguese saw this as an opportunity to gain a foothold, a vantage point, inside the kingdom.

The Portuguese breakthrough took place in the time of the Emperor Lebna Dengal (1508-1540), one of Ethiopia's most progressive rulers, who "was a pioneer in the modernizing efforts for Ethiopia. But military considerations were uppermost in his mind and in the minds of his successors. Ethiopia had been subjected to a Muslim military campaign intended to obliterate Christianity. Such was its ferocity that the material and spiritual heritage of medieval Ethiopia was destroyed."[17]

Dengal, brilliant but quite secular, was committed to the faith of his fathers, but he also was the emperor of Ethiopia and even more committed to preserving the integrity and independence of the nation. Faced with this threat, the Ethiopians invited the Portuguese to come as military allies, and in 1541 the Ethiopian-Portuguese Axis was formed.

Rome, Portugal, Ethiopia, and the Muslim World

The European ecclesiastical establishment was the greatest threat to the Ethiopian church and to Ethiopian national independence. But the Muslim world was always there, an ever-present and growing danger. However, the Ethiopian church faced dangers from within as well as without.

When Portugal helped Ethiopia to repel the armies of Ahmed Gran, she immediately demanded that Ethiopia pay homage to the pope and establish the Catholic faith. It was a long, bitter struggle, and extremely costly for Ethiopia to maintain her freedom. The ancient biblical Sabbath was always integral to the struggle. It can be seen that the Ethiopians looked upon the Sabbath as the sign of their allegiance to God. It was covenantal; it stood for independence and self-determination.

Ethiopia, the Nature of the Struggle, 1500-1896

Ethiopia's most striking religious characteristic is Sabbath observance. The Sabbath distinguishes the Ethiopian church and nation from all the rest. For more than 1,500 years the Sabbath has been central to Ethiopian theology and church life.

During the thirteenth century the leading monastery in the country was Sabbatarian the house of Ewostathians. Hastings refers to the Christianity of this era of Ethiopian history "as a religion whose most striking characteristic was Sabbath observance" when "even non-Ewostathians were moving toward Sabbath observance."[18]

The king of Ethiopia was a committed Sabbathkeeper and supported those monasteries which kept the Sabbath before the people. Sabbath is key to understanding Ethiopian history, to understanding the Ethiopian mind. The great monastic leaders, as teachers of the kingdom, kept emperor and people honest with reference to Sabbath observance. Hastings also observes:

> "The survival of Ethiopia's specific form of Christianity across much more than a thousand years, often in very adverse circumstances, appears to have depended above all upon its two greatest possessions the Ge'ez Bible and the Ge'ez musical repertoire, an essentially lay tradition, popular yet professional."[19]

In other words, the monastic leaders appealed to the emperors as defenders of the faith, exhorting them to maintain the ancient traditions. This was a unifying factor that "created a form of public religion which was absolutely Ethiopian only rather distantly related to its Mediterranean roots, while decidedly recognizable as African."[20]

Sabbath could also be a bone of contention for some. In the days of Zara Ya'iqob (1434-1468), the empire was torn apart by rival monasteries, some of which were Sabbath proponents and others opponents to the seventh-day Sabbath. (Reference has already been made to how the emperor addressed the issue by calling a church council to bring about a solution to the problem and took the political way out by issuing an edict that recognition should be given to both Sabbath and Sunday.)

It is remarkable, however, that these internal struggles did not destroy the national fabric nor prevent the Ethiopians from defending their national integrity and the faith of their fathers, especially when faced with an external threat to nation and religion.

This is all the more exceptional because differences between church leaders and monastic leaders were often very serious. Triangulation was a reality in the Ethiopian system of governance. There was the king, titular head of the church; there were the ecclesiastical leaders; and there were the monks. The king and the ruling clergy wielded organizational power, but the spiritual power was mostly in the hands of the monks. The common people and the local clergy usually followed the monks.

In spite of this "fragile box" alliance, when hostile external forces were introduced into the equation, Ethiopians usually united to face the crises. In such times the Ethiopians' universal regard for the Sabbath preserved their identity and purpose. The ancient faith, in most instances, won the day, as if doctrinal departures were only an exciting but temporary adventure, a passing fancy.

As the king went, so went the nation, except in the case of the Sabbath.

No Ethiopian king, not even the strongest monarch, could get away with tampering with the ancient day of worship.

In the days of Lebna Dengal (1508-1540) the empire was overrun by hostile Muslim forces. Somehow the goodwill that had existed between Ethiopians and their Muslim neighbors had dissipated. Ahmed Gran succeeded in subjugating most of the empire. The emperor was forced to take refuge in an inaccessible mountain monastery and found it necessary to call on the Roman Church to send help. Ahmed Gran continued his ruthless campaign of national and cultural genocide for 12 years.

At last the pope responded to Lebna Dengel's appeal and sent a contingent of Portuguese troops to assist the Ethiopians in the struggle against the Muslim forces. Ahmed Gran was defeated in 1543 and slain by Portuguese firepower. But the Portuguese immediately demanded that the emperor pledge allegiance to Rome. They insisted that the Ethiopians cease their *Judaizing,* that is, keeping the Sabbath, practicing circumcision, and abstaining from unclean foods.

Ethiopians have at times faced situations such as this in their past history. In several instances the emperor has temporized, attempting to save the empire by yielding to the demands of the Roman Church and the Portuguese nation. However, in every case, the people out in the countryside and the village priests and monks resisted any attempts to change the ancient faith.

Susenyos (1607-1632), one of Ethiopia's greatest rulers, was forced to abdicate when he agreed to the downgrading of Sabbath and the upgrading of Sunday at the suggestion (or, better stated, insistence) of the infamous Mendes. Susenyos was a man of great presence, physically imposing and intelligent. His military achievements were outstanding. But his fatal flaw was putting too much faith in the Portuguese alliance and miscalculating the depth of popular resistance to his Sabbath tampering.

Susenyos had already converted to Catholicism under Paez, Mendes's predecessor, in 1622. Paez, the personable Spanish Jesuit, headed the Ethiopian mission from 1603 to 1622. He had tremendous success in recruiting converts from the nobility and the elite, and he raised the level of Ethiopian-Portuguese relations to its highest. Paez was the model ecclesiastical diplomat, one of those "top university men . . . who had streamed into the Society of Jesus from Spain, Italy and France during the last quarter of the sixteenth century and volunteered for missionary work."[21]

After Paez's death, the Jesuits chose the heavy-handed Mendes as successor. He arrived in Ethiopia in 1625 with great fanfare and pomp and cannon salutes, full of self-confidence and determined to accelerate the process of "reforming" the Ethiopian church. The willing emperor, followed by high clergy and nobility, bowed before the patriarch and received Communion.

The king's subjects were angered at the sight of their monarch kneeling prostrate before the Roman emissary and pledging his fealty to the pope. However, it is only fair to point out that Susenyos' conversion had its political aspect: he was trying to save the kingdom. Hastings continues:

> "Mendes then issued his first proclamation, an irreparable blunder. No one in future was to offer mass or do anything else of an ecclesiastical kind until he had received faculties from the Patriarch. He had decided that all Ethiopian sacraments were of dubious validity and decreed that the faithful were to be rebaptized, the clergy reordained. This wholly undermined the basis of the Ethiopia-West relationship, for it impugned the very Christianity of the Ethiopians. Feasts and fasts were to be rearranged according to the Roman calendar. The mass, while it might be said in Ge'ez, must be according to the Roman rite. Saturday would become a fast day. Circumcision was prohibited. His only concessions were to allow the priests he reordained to remain married and to say their Roman mass in Ge'ez."[22]

Susenyos immediately realized that he had gone too far when he yielded to Mendes's radical changes in the ancient faith involving the Sabbath. Reaction was so strong that he tried to draw back, going so far as to grant religious liberty to both Catholics and the Ethiopian Orthodox ("Now therefore we restore to you the faith of your ancestors . . ."[23]), but the damage was done.

"Even the ignorant peasants of Lasta have died fighting against it," admitted the emperor. Hastings describes the sad spectacle of a king who overplayed his hand:

> "Tired and disillusioned, but not himself abandoning the Roman Church, Sosenyos handed over power to his son Fasiladas. Less than three months later he died, attended to the end by a Jesuit. He was buried in state as one of the greatest of emperors, but already his religious heritage had been overwhelmingly abandoned by his people. Men and women danced together, smashed their rosaries and chanted with joy:
>
> "'At length the sheep of Ethiopia freed
> From the bad lions of the West
> Securely in their pastures feed.
> St. Mark and Cyril's doctrine have overcome
> The follies of the Church of Rome.'"[24]

For 40 years there had been a Portuguese Catholic community of immigrants in Ethiopia. Most people who were attached to the Portuguese delegation—wives, servants, slaves, and their children—were converts to Catholicism. At times this community had actually thrived, but when the priest Belchior Da Silva arrived early in the seventeenth century, he found that many, while "still claiming to be Catholics, were already circumcising their children and observing the Sabbath."[25]

Fasaladas, the young monarch, demanded the withdrawal of Portuguese armed forces and the departure of the Jesuits. He did this with the zeal of an Old Testament reformer king, destroying images and hunting down Jesuits who tried to carry on their program of subversion in secret. Some priests were executed. The back of the Jesuit mission to Ethiopia was broken.

Here began a new period in Ethiopian history, a time of borders sealed to outside religious organizations. In order for foreigners to preach the gospel in Ethiopia, it was now necessary to obtain permission from the government. Catholics were especially suspect, but Protestant missions were also subjected to scrutiny and surveillance. The bitter pill of past history, the tendency of European Christians to treat all Ethiopians as rank heathens, and the refusal to recognize any redemptive features in the faith and practice of Ethiopian orthodoxy effectively dissolved the axis and soured the relationship for 200 years.

Breakthrough in the Nineteenth Century

Sheikh Zakaryas was a devout Amhara Muslim, born in 1845 in Bagemdir, the northwestern area of Ethiopia, which is Muslim territory. In the 1890s the sheikh began to have "a series of visions which led him to reconsider the figure of Jesus as it appears in the Koran. His movement began as one of Muslim reform but slowly turned to one of Christian conversion."[26]

In one of Sheikh Zakaryas's dreams, three elderly men appeared. They told him to purchase a Bible and read it and to keep the Sabbath day. After a period of intensive study of the Bible and the Koran, he announced that he was now a follower of Jesus. In 1910 Zaharyas was baptized along with 3,000 of his followers. He was given the name Newaya Krestos. Because the Orthodox Church leaders were skeptical of the sheikh's conversion, Zakaryas's community was not absorbed into the Orthodox Church. But the sheikh was not disobedient to the heavenly vision. He continued to teach his followers to be firm in their convictions.

Sheikh Zakaryas lived during the time of Emperor Menelik. The Orthodox religious authorities became unduly alarmed at Zakaryas's conversion. This must have been because they saw his movement as a challenge to their authority. There was no great theological difference here. Zakaryas was brought into court and charged with subversion. The case ultimately was brought to the emperor, who ruled against the clergy and gave Sheikh Zakaryas the privilege of preaching anywhere in the nation. Menelik also furnished Zakaryas with about 100 bodyguards.

Until this day the group remains outside of the mainstream of Islam and Orthodoxy. They still keep the Sabbath. They still worship in their own communities in the northwestern part of Ethiopia. The residents of Addis Ager, an entire village of more than 1,000, are descendants of the Sheikh's movement.

Through the years many of his followers chose to become members of the Seventh-day Adventist Church, because the angel had told their leader to "keep the Ten Commandments, including the Sabbath, and to prepare for the return of Jesus Christ." This seemed to them the teaching of the Seventh-day Adventists in a sentence.

By some accounts, neither Islam nor the Ethiopian Orthodox Church could accept the sheikh and his followers as Muslim or Christian, because they did not fit the mold. Hastings is right when he says: "Sheikh Zakaryas reminds us of the unexpectedness of religious history. He appears not wholly unlike prophets who were about to arise elsewhere in Africa, Harris in the west, Shembe in the south."[27]

Throughout Africa there have been unexpected revivals of religion, movements of the Spirit, at times which cannot be explained by human reasoning. It all seems to be dependent on the Holy Spirit. No human being or group of humans could program these events.

The Ethiopian Lesson

Ellen White's evaluation of the Ethiopian experience is succinct and at the same time surprisingly laudatory of African Christianity:

> "The history of the churches of Ethiopia and Abyssinia is especially significant. Amid the gloom of the Dark Ages, the Christians of Central Africa were lost sight of and forgotten by the world, and for many centuries they enjoyed freedom in the exercise of their faith. But at last Rome learned of their existence, and the emperor of Abyssinia was soon beguiled into an acknowledgment of the pope as the vicar of Christ. Other concessions followed. An edict was issued forbidding the observance of the Sabbath under the severest penalties. [See Michael Geddes, *Church History of Ethiopia*, pp. 311, 312.]
>
> "But papal tyranny soon became a yoke so galling that the Abyssinians determined to break it from their necks. After a terrible

struggle, the Romanists were banished from their dominions, and the ancient faith was restored. The churches rejoiced in their freedom, and they never forgot the lesson they had learned concerning the deception, the fanaticism, and the despotic power of Rome. Within their solitary realm they were content to remain, to the rest of Christendom.

"The churches of Africa held the Sabbath as it was held by the papal church before her complete apostasy. While they kept the seventh day in obedience to the commandment of God, they abstained from labor on Sunday in conformity to the custom of the church. Upon obtaining supreme power, Rome had trampled upon the Sabbath of God to exalt her own; but the churches of Africa, hidden for nearly a thousand years, did not share in this apostasy. When brought under the sway of Rome, they were forced to set aside the true and exalt the false sabbath; but no sooner had they regained their independence than they returned to obedience to the fourth commandment."[28]

Ellen White saw the seventh-day Sabbath as having something to do with national independence. Does Sabbath make an independence statement? Is Sabbath a biblical sign of freedom and human dignity? It is true that some of the African prophets see the Sabbath as the African day of worship? We do know that Sabbath is a code word for the faith of Ethiopia, and Africa looks to Ethiopia.

There is another lesson to the Ethiopian story. No monarch can afford to underestimate the power of the common people when galvanized by an issue of deep cultural and religious significance-matters of the heart and soul. For Ethiopia this issue was the Sabbath and the ancient faith. The people recognized a higher power, a more superior court. Though nameless and inexpressible, this conviction, this deep feeling, has toppled thrones and brought emperors to their knees.

End Notes

[1]Isichei, p. 52.

[2]Noble, p. 433.

[3]*Ibid.*

[4]Hastings, p. 200.

[5]*Ibid.*, p. 201.

[6]Isichei, p. 109.

[7]Hastings, p. 220.

[8]Quoted in *Ibid.*, p. 220.

[9]*Ibid.*, p. 221.

[10]*Ibid.*, p. 220.

[11]Thomas Pakenham, *The Scramble for Africa: The White Man's Conquest of the Dark Continent From 1876 to 1912* (New York: Avon Books, 1992), p. 1.

[12]*Ibid.*, p. xxi.

[13]*Ibid.*, p. 254, 255.

[14]*Ibid.*, p. 656-668.

[15]*Ibid.*, p. 470.

[16]Sanneh, p. 21.

[17]Malisha, p. 93.

[18]Hastings, pp. 32, 33.

[19]*Ibid.*, p. 132.

[20]*Ibid.*

[21]*Ibid.*, p. 148.

[22]*Ibid.*, p 154.

[23]Isichei, p. 51.

[24]Hastings, p. 156.

[25]*Ibid.*, p. 51.

[26]*Ibid.*, p. 240.

[27]*Ibid.*, p. 241.

[28]White, *Great Controversy*, pp. 577, 578.

PART THREE

RESTORATION AND RECOVERY

"The Mighty One, God, the LORD, speaks and summons the earth from the rising of the sun to the place where it sets" (Ps. 50:1, NIV).

"They will neither harm or destroy on all my holy mountain, for the earth will be full of the knowledge of the Lord as the waters cover the sea" (Isa. 11:9, NIV).

In Part Three we look to the end of the story and examine Yahwism and Christianity in the African setting. It is to the end of Israel's history that Africans on the continent and in diaspora must look rather than to the beginning. The biblical script reveals Yahweh as resolute and determined to recover all that has been lost. He reverses the stream that flows out that led to the fragmentation of the human family. He restores His people everywhere to the ideal community.

"This is the plan determined for the whole world; this is the hand stretched out over all nations. For the LORD Almighty has purposed, and who can thwart him? His hand is stretched out, and who can turn it back? (Isa 14:26, 27, NIV)"

CHAPTER NINE

NEW DAY DAWNING

"Yes, I will then give the people lips that are clean, so that all may invoke the name of Yahweh and serve him under the same yoke. From beyond the banks of the rivers of Ethiopia my suppliants will bring me offerings" (Zeph. 3:9, 10, JB).

"While every day in the West, roughly 7,500 people in effect stop being Christians every day in Africa, roughly double that number become Christians."[1]

A Continent Ready to Respond

It is as if in manifold ways the Spirit had all along been preparing the soil of Africa for its day. The New Testament writers would have used the word kairos, which means a set or proper time, an opportunity, due season, a signal juncture. A favorite phrase of the gospel writers was, "The time has come." A firmament of spiritual luminaries of every magnitude has burst on the Africa scene. In the power of the Spirit, it all has come together, it all has fallen into place. It is the movement of Yahweh, His Spirit poured out.

African Religious Revivals

At the beginning of the twentieth century, Christian awakenings took place in many places in Africa and continued for almost two decades. One of the striking characteristics of the awakening is that it was almost entirely led by laypersons. Hastings cites four examples of conversion movements, all taking place along the West African coast between 1912 and 1916

These conversion movements were independent of missionary control. Even as early as 1899 it was reported that Christianity was spreading "like a prairie fire" in many parts of Africa. "No White missionary was involved, and almost no African clergy." The movement was strictly led by laypeople."[2]

There had been a major Christian breakthrough in Buganda in the 1880s. This awakening also took place without foreign leadership. Thousands of conversions took place, and many thousands more, who were as yet unbaptized, professed allegiance to Messiah Jesus. Wherever these revivals took place, new Christians formed fellowship groups that met in house churches. These were always led in worship by the first adult male Christian in the village. In these new congregations the people would gather in front of the leader's home and burn their fetishes and religious symbols and statues of any sort while the new Christians danced around the flames, proclaiming the power of God and the impotence of the spirits of the past.

They would sing, "Destruction! The children of the church have destroyed the gods. Destruction! The children of Jehovah have destroyed the gods. Destruction! The children of Jesus Christ have destroyed the gods. Destruction!" This brought these new Christians into confrontation with the local guilds of image makers.[3]

Clearly, the spirit of revival was sweeping over Africa in separate places in much the same way. "What was happening in place after place was a spiritual revolution sparked by native evangelists in conditions created by the unsettlement of early colonial rule."[4] There were reports that the Igboes of West Africa converted themselves.[5]

But above and behind it all, the Holy Spirit was doing a new thing. It was as if divine agencies were assuming direct leadership of the work of God. We could call it the great African awakening. The mission churches were reluctant to baptize candidates until they had undergone long periods of instruction, extending, in some instances, to more than a year.

Missionaries required African candidates for the ministry to go through long periods of theological training and many years of internship and training before ordination. In some cases, ordination took place just before retirement.

But under the influence of this powerful conversion movement, scores of laypersons stepped forward to perform the work of ministry. Some of the missionaries, as Hastings observes, were neurotic about what was taking place. They could not believe that untrained persons could carry on the work.[6]

These great movements occurred before the emergence of the great African prophets. "Who hath heard such a thing? who hath seen such things? Shall the earth be made to bring forth in one day? or shall a nation be born at once? for as soon as Zion travailed, she brought forth her children" (Isa. 66:8).

So it is true that the church came first, and then the prophets came forth from the loins of the church.

Africa has been the place of great revivals in the past. The people of this continent have from time to time stretched forth their hands unto God in dramatic ways that go beyond anything seen before on the African continent. Actually, one is reminded of the experience of the early church.

Shall a Nation Be Born at Once?

On the eve of the twentieth century, the prospects for Christianity were not very encouraging. The Christian mission had failed to take root on the African continent. Livingstone, Moffat, Schmid, Van der Kemp, and other dedicated missionaries had established Christian communities or villages, and, by sheer dint of untiring labor, gathered a few converts. But in almost every instance, after their departure, their work unraveled, the missions deteriorated, the converts disappeared, and traditional religions returned like the undergrowth of the forest to reclaim the land.

We must not, however, disparage those faithful servants of the cross. The scriptural admonition is to not despise the day of small beginnings. Nevertheless, the fruits of their labors were not visible. As Messiah Jesus has said: "Other men have labored and ye have entered into their labors" (John 4:38).

If one is impressed with statistics and spectacular growth patterns, there was little here to crow over. There were Christian communities on both coasts, but very few believers in the interior. Much of the missionaries' labor was spent on the expatriate group the merchants, soldiers, governmental representatives, etc. The whole continent seemed one dense and impenetrable jungle--impervious to the claims of Messiah Jesus.

If anyone had predicted that during the first half of the new century Christianity would become the majority religion in Africa, he or she would have been seriously questioned. No responsible church historian or serious observer of the scene would venture to make such a prediction. What factors caused the Christian mission to explode on the African continent, making the twentieth century the century of African Christianity?

The suddenness of this turning to God is called by some the greatest miracle of modern missions. "The fourth great age of Christian expansion" is what Elizabeth Isichei calls it.[7] A manifestation of Revelation 14:6, that significant and timely word of Scripture.

This word comes with its greatest impact to those who live in earth's "twilight hour," to use Cornell West's phrase. The wording of the text suggests that it is a universal word, a word for the space age. With blinding speed and global impact, the word goes forth: "Fear God and give glory to him, for the hour of his judgment is come" (John 14:7). This text couples with another from the Old Testament: "But thou, O Daniel, shut up the words, and seal the book, even to the time of the end: many shall run to and fro, and knowledge shall be increased" (Dan. 12:4).

Revelation 14:6, 7 seems tailor-made for our time. At no other time in history could the phrase be employed with maximum force worldwide–"every nation, kindred, tongue and people." Yahweh's communication system with His planet and its people is more firmly in place than ever. Even skeptics must agree that the possibility for reaching the masses with the message of Messiah Jesus has never been as great. The means to this end, the technology, is not only in place; it is exploding.

At the beginning of the Christian mission, the Roman Empire enjoyed a time of peace and stability, the *pax Romana*, which facilitated the communication of the gospel. There was a common language, a system of roads, well-charted shipping lanes, a strong system of government, and a reliable postal system. Even in the first century there was a sense of modernity and sophistication that made for a confident and optimistic populace.

Kenneth Scott Latourette, in his day the foremost scholar of Christian missions, spoke of the gospel of Christ going into all the world in progressive waves of outreach, extending farther and farther, until the word of Messiah Jesus is fulfilled "to the uttermost parts of the earth."

Africa has been, in the view of the developed nations, the uttermost part of the earth. What a rude awakening has taken place in the Christian community! Africa today is no longer on the fringes it is the center of Christian mission. There has been, indeed, a radical shift, a sea change, "a complete change in the center of gravity of Christianity."[8]

The people of sub-Saharan Africa, who for many centuries seemed unmoved by the claims of Messiah Jesus, suddenly have become ardent seekers, reaching out, stretching their hands toward Christianity, an outworking of that master prophecy of Psalm 68:31: "Ethiopia shall soon stretch out her hands unto God."

The African continent has become the very center of the Christian New World. It is a force to be reckoned with. This is unprecedented in the history of the Christian church.

African Independent Churches and the Great Prophets

> "Now when this was noised abroad, the multitude came together, and were confounded, because that every man heard them speak in his own language. And they were all amazed and marvelled, saying one to another, Behold, are not all these which speak Galileans? And how hear we every man in our own tongue, wherein we were born?" (Acts 2:6-8).

Missiologists speak about the indigenization of the gospel, that is, the localization of the message, expressing the story of salvation through Messiah Jesus in terms understood by the culture. Some would say, "the church of what is happening now," where everyone hears the message in his or her own tongue. It is obvious that the messenger who speaks the language and has lived all of his or her lifetime in the culture can communicate more effectively than an expatriate.

People resonate more positively to one of their own. The idiom is familiar;

they can identify with the messenger; the "vibes" are positive. Barriers to communication are broken down, and the comfort zone is enlarged.

> "The formal preaching of missionaries seldom proved very convincing or even comprehensible (except to a more or less captive audience of house servants and ransomed slaves), but the Bible in its range of history, particularity, legal prescription, and deep mystery provided a compelling vision, and one seemingly more at home in traditional Africa than in 19th-century Europe."[9]

Africans longed to hear the gospel in their own tongue, body language and all. They were ready to respond with soul and mind to its claims. However, they wanted their response also to be expressed in their own way African–unfettered by foreign idioms and thought forms. The message is always the same, the packaging and delivery is local.

African Independent Churches

In the partition of Africa, Ethiopia was made the pawn of Italy, and the Italians moved quickly to establish control of the oldest Christian nation on the African continent. Much to the consternation of Europe and the humiliation of Italy, Menelik's troops drove the invading army into the sea. This decisive victory, which took place at Adwa in 1896, sent the whole sub-Saharan world into paroxysms of joy.

The shock waves from Adwa convulsed the continent and set into motion the African Independent Church movement, which made way for the rise of the "great African prophets." Hastings observes:

> "Ethiopia was to be preserved, not only as an independent political entity of considerable size but as a symbol for the whole continent of enormous power: independence from European control, Africanness, traditional culture, Christianity. Everywhere, in West and South Africa, Adwa was important and heartening news. The details of Ethiopian Christianity were understood no more than its secular polity. They did not matter. It was Black. It was free. It was Christian.
>
> "Even if Christianity elsewhere was brought by White missionaries linked with European colonialism, Christianity itself was not so linked. Ethiopia was proof of it and constituted both justification for being Christian despite White domination and a name to cover any African movement of protest within the church against perceived missionary errors. The combination of politics and Christianity which was crucial to the identity and survival of Ethiopia was no less crucial to its message for Africans elsewhere, to

> the 'Ethiopianism' which Europeans would soon be suspecting in every corner of continent and church."[10]

Thus, *Ethiopianism* is a code word for independence, freedom from foreign domination or rule in the political realm, and also for self-determination in matters of religion.

"In various parts of the continent," says M. L. Daneel in his book *Quest for Belonging*, "the last hundred years or so has seen a remarkable series of corporate autonomous religious initiatives, which for number, influence, expansion, creativity and originality have been described as a phenomenon unprecedented in the entire history of the expansion of Christianity."[11]

The proliferation of these religious movements continues unabated to this day. The academic community is fascinated with this phenomenon, and of course, there has been a rapid growth in the literature on the subject. An African theologian comments:

> "We find articles, reports, notes, essays, surveys, books, either concentrating on particular movements or on the general impact of the various movements on a continental scale. A bibliography compiled by R. C. Mitchell and H. W. Turner includes not less than 1,320 studies in different forms. Among these, 211 deal with the movements in South Africa, 175 in Nigeria, 150 in the former Congo (Zaire), 81 in Kenya, 62 in Ivory Coast. 55 in Ghana, and so on."[12]

The independent churches broke away from the foreign domination of the African church, and the great prophets ventured to take up the mantle of the Old Testament prophets with little reference to, or consultation with, the established religious authorities, which were powerless to stop them. The prophets were indeed trail-blazers.

The Legacy of Adwa

The years 1890 to 1925 may be termed the post-Adwa years, when churches and the prophets comprised a new African religious scene. A number of prophet-like figures appeared, singular preachers of simple religious faith, who took on the guise of the Old Testament prophets and traded their European dress for native African garb. Some carried a staff or a shepherd's crook, with Bible in hand. The preaching of these men had a tremendous effect on the entire continent from West Africa to South Africa and in between. (One or two women could be included in this group.)

The people were moved to call them prophets. And indeed, their appearance and their manner of speaking conjured up visions of Elijah and

John the Baptist. Their messages were simple and direct: "Repent." "Turn away from sin to the true and living God." "Put away your fetishes." "Keep God's commandments."

Johane Maranke (1912-1963), one of the Shona prophets, said that he heard a voice commanding him: "You are John the Baptist, an apostle. Go forth and do my work. Go to every country, preach and convert the people. Command them not to commit adultery, steal or become angry. Baptize people and observe the Sabbath."[13]

In her book *A History of Christianity in Africa*, Elizabeth Isichei says: "Many modern African prophetic churches keep the Sabbath holy and adopt dietary and other prohibitions similar to those laid down in Leviticus, as the Ethiopians do."[14]

Maranke's followers, known as the Vapostori, became the largest independent church in Central Africa. Eventually, they spread to the Belgian Congo and Kasai, where they were called Bapostolo and became known for their large, open-air Sabbath services. An American scholar, Benetta Jules-Rosette, came to Africa to study the apostles and joined them."[15]

John Masowe (1915-1973), or John of the desert, the other Shona, founded the Apostolic Sabbath Church of God, better known as the VaHossana. A strange and mysterious figure, John disappeared into the wilderness. His followers became pilgrims and strangers, migrating all over the southern part of Africa. From Bulawayo, they spread to South Africa and as far north as Nairobi, Kenya. "The apostles [Masowe's followers] worship Jehovah, follow Old Testament dietary rules, and keep the Sabbath."[16]

According to Pauw, three strands of indigenous churches "can be described as either Pentecostalist, Sabbatarian-Baptist or Zionist."[17] I prefer to group them: Ethiopian, Zionist, Sabbatarian Baptist, and Charismatic. What is important to our study is that there is a Sabbatarian strand that runs through each group.

The main prophetic movements and churches do, however, tend to share a number of characteristics which, placed together, create a new, rather African form of Christianity. Healing, visions and dreams, a holy city, certain kinds of rituals, food taboos (as in the Old Testament), and of course, with some of these prophets, an emphasis on keeping the seventh-day Sabbath.

That the movement had its Sabbatarian strand is undeniable, which should not be surprising because there has always been a favorable disposition toward the Bible Sabbath in Africa. The research of Mary Getui, Sammy Ngetich, and Josiah Okinda, three Seventh-day Adventist African scholars, points this out.

Mary Getui, Ph.D., a full lecturer at Kenyatta University, observes that the Abugasii of western Kenya have a concept of rest which is the essence of

Sabbath. They claim to have migrated from Egypt, which they call Misiri. Getui believes that the interaction of her people with the Egyptians can account for some of the Hebrewisms in their language and customs. Ngetich and Okinda agree to this sensitivity of Africans toward Sabbath on the basis of their research among the Kalinjin and Luo peoples.

Among the Abugassi, God, Engoro, was worshiped regularly. Time was observed by putting a mark on a stick, or by putting sticks aside to mark a day. Days of rest were set aside for family time, personal reflection, and response to crises, such as recovery from sickness and danger. These were regarded as holy days and not holidays. Getui concludes:

> "Their migrations, form of worship, system of sacrifice and occasions of rest provide clues that they may have had Jewish antecedents. . . . In particular they did not observe Sabbath systematically on the seventh day but the various occasions of rest and their significance are echo of the Sabbath."[18]

Sammy Ngetich writes about his people group, the Kalenjin. Ngetich finds that they have a Hebrew heritage, as evidenced by certain "loan words like *Sabaot,* meaning multitude, nation, *Yim,* meaning sky, or *Kokel* meaning star." There is a "Kalinjin midrash that is reminiscent of biblical narratives like the Exodus [Red Sea] and the Flood accounts."[19]

Kalenjin oral history recalls the same migration as the Abugasii—from Egypt (Misri) to their present home. Rest days were also occasioned by birth and death, and for thanksgiving and sacrifice. The practice of circumcision indicates a possible Semitic borrowing. The seventh day of the week was set aside to honor men, and the first day in honor of women. The number seven comes into greater play in the story that has man at the beginning descending from heaven in seven days. This was also reflected in the casting of lots, seven being the perfect lot.

"There are three possible hypotheses as far as our findings are concerned," says Ngetich:

"1. An issue of borrowing, or Jewish influence. . . .

"2. A case of reverse borrowing. The Bible is replete with instances where God [does this] in revealing Himself to our limited language, cultural norms and contemporary outlooks. Proverbs 22:17-24:34 is one example of 'African wisdom' in the Scriptures, while the Decalogue is God's eternal principles, which we find echoed in Hammurabi and ably articulated in the Egyptian (African) Amenhotep's negative confessions.

"3. Independent revelation. No people on the face of the earth have been without God, one who speaks their language; for the same universal God 'appeared many times to our ancestors in many forms' (Heb. 1:1; cf. Acts

14:16-17; 17:26-28). The Coptic and 'Hebrew' strands could therefore be independent of any Jewish influence."[20]

Ngetich concludes: "From the data collected so far, it seems safe to opt for the third hypothesis, namely, that of independent development of the two elements in the Kalenjin cosmology and religion."[21]

Josiah Okinda, a Luo whose research has been among his people group, cites Paul Mboya, who writes that the Luo were given 14 commandments; that God is Nyasaye Nyakalaga, of unlimited presence; that the Luo call themselves the commandment keeping people, and that counting of days was important to them. "At the family level, women were called upon to do the counting. Sticks were broken, starting with the first day of the week, Sunday. For five days each stick was preserved. On the sixth day, one stick with a Y-shape was placed to be counted for the sixth and seventh day. This end of the week was a special day of rest accompanied by celebrations and sacrifice."[22]

The ninth and the fourteenth commandments "are clearly relevant to the concept of rest day(s). . . . [Commandment 9 says] 'You shall love your brother and a stranger in your gates'; [commandment 14 says] 'You shall rest when someone has died in your community; a man four days and a woman three days.'"[22] (The Luo still have high regard for the number seven and count in multiples of seven.)

Okinda concludes: "Even in their state of lapse and departure from the commandments of God, there still remains a faint consciousness of Yahweh's Sabbath."[23]

The importance of having Scripture in the vernacular, the local languages, cannot be overstated: "The appearance of the sacred script in the vernacular languages of Africa is an event of unprecedented importance."[24] The effect was liberating. The Scriptures became to the African the highest authority, superseding that of the church and its hierarchies.

This has always been the Protestant principle. Of course, it was Yahweh who delivered His Word to Africans in their own tongue. He was speaking out of this Word directly to them. He knew their names. As in the case of the Old Testament prophets, they were overwhelmed by that Word and compelled to deliver it to their own people. The word in the hands of the prophets became a powerful sword, "mighty through God to the pulling down of strong holds" (2 Cor. 10:4).

They Called Them Prophets

> "And it shall come to pass afterward, that I will pour out my spirit upon all flesh; and your sons and your daughters shall prophesy, your old men shall dream dreams, your young men shall

see visions: and also upon the servants and upon the handmaids in those days will I pour out my spirit" (Joel 2:28, 29).

Lamin Sanneh believes that Garrick Braide (1882-1918) was an instrument particularly suited to respond to the situation. The events of the day, the times, made the appearance of the prophets and the rise of the independent churches seem almost a natural happening. Braide, born around 1882 at Bakana, a center of Christian missionary work, was baptized in 1910. According to Sanneh, two principal themes surface in Braide's preaching: "complete dependence on God," and "the requirement that his followers abandon idols, fetishes and the use of charms." Sanneh continues:

> "On the social side, he preached an uncompromising abhorrence of alcohol the scourge of the Niger Delta. For example, it is estimated that each year some 3 million gallons of gin were consumed in the Delta towns of Brass, Kalabari, Bonny and Opobo."[25]

Consumption of liquor fell drastically in the wake of Braide's fiery preaching. This also caused a dramatic drop in taxes collected by the colonial authorities on the alcohol trade. They brought Braide up on charges that he was responsible for this loss in revenue."[26]

Braide also assumed an Old Testament stance, drawing parallels between himself and Isaiah and Malachi. He once called himself Elijah II and gave Bakana, his hometown, the title Israel. At times he would spend whole nights in prayer, with his Bible in hand. One story that is used to support his miraculous powers is that his prayers caused a storm to break on a village that defied his ruling on keeping the Sabbath. It is reported that the rainstorm inundated the entire countryside."[27]

William Wade Harris (1865-1929), of Liberia, was probably the most outstanding of these major African prophets, as they were called. Harris walked all over West Africa, from country to country, preaching his message of obedience to the commandments of God.

His ministry was brief but spectacular, as he would baptize as many as 100,000 people in a single year. Because he would remain in a place for only a few days, Harris began the practice of baptizing people immediately. This would have never been the case among mainstream African Christians and missionaries, whose custom was to defer baptism for long periods of time, often longer than a year.

Harris did not build an organization. He did not leave any sacred places or shrines. However, he did leave "apostles" with each group of converts, who were responsible for holding the fellowship together, but they were often ill-prepared to serve as pastors. As he would hasten on to new fields, Harris would tell his converts to await teachers with Bibles. This put the Catholics in a dilemma, because they did not utilize the Bible very much in their mission work. However, those churches which gave prominence to the Bible were rewarded handsomely.

After a few years of nonstop ministry in the coastal areas of West Africa, Harris was deported back to Liberia, never to regain his position of power and influence. As his people gathered around him during his last illness, Harris pointed them to the sky and told them to look for Jesus' return:[28]

> "Harris [was] a Grebo schoolteacher of Methodist and Episcopal background. During a period of imprisonment he experienced visions of the angel Gabriel commanding him to become an evangelist like John the Baptist. His subsequent months of peregrinatory preaching during 1914 in southern Ivory Coast and Ghana produced tens of thousands of baptisms and permanently altered the religious character of the area he traversed. The decisive effect was fully recognized both by missionaries and by colonial officials. Harris had abandoned his European garb, his shoes, and his trousers; he had also abandoned any particular church affiliation. He preached a very simple Christian monotheism, expelled devils, carried the Bible wherever he went, and baptized all who rejected and destroyed their pagan 'fetishes.'"[29]

It should be pointed out that several of these great religious leaders accepted the seventh-day Sabbath as the Africans' day of worship.

Wherever Harris and Braide preached, tens of thousands of people abandoned their fetishes and were baptized, and from that day on endeavored to live as Christians. Once baptized, they were encouraged to worship in whichever church the missionaries provided for them. Christ was coming, and those, Black or White, who rejected His commandments or His prophets, did not observe the Sabbath, or otherwise despised His commandments would be punished. The fetishes went up in great bonfires.

The Place of the Bible

The Bible was central in the ministry of the African prophets and in the African Independent Churches. Harris made it a practice to lay his well-worn Bible on the convert's head at baptism. The Bible had great power in these communities and in the preaching of these prophets. The Ten Commandments figured prominently in their preaching, as they insisted that all of the commandments should be kept. They also preached the gospel of cleanliness that is, cleanliness is next to godliness.

The second coming of Jesus Christ was one of the keynotes of the prophets' preaching. They declared that the coming of Christ was imminent. And their people sang about it! The new Christian communities were characterized by their hymn singing. "Lo, He Comes With Clouds Descending" was the favorite hymn of both Harris and the Ndebele Zionist Elias Mhlangu.[30]

Where there were no hymnals, new hymnals would quickly be compiled Ntsikana's hymns spread all over the continent, and new hymns were written all the time. In some instances, singing provided the principal means of Christian instruction. This is quite Old Testament the Hebrews would sing their way through Israel's theological repertoire.

The African Independent Churches tended to be Hebraistic, with a strong orientation to the Old Testament. There was also a millennial note in the preaching of the African prophets, an emphasis on the last things eschatology. These are the last days, the time of judgment.

And this last-day theme was apocalyptic the sudden cataclysmic end of all things: "But the day of the Lord will come as a thief in the night; in the which the heavens shall pass away with a great noise, and the elements shall melt with fervent heat, the earth also and the works that are therein shall be burned up" (2 Peter 3:10). The African prophets identified with Father Abraham, who "looked for a city which hath foundations, whose builder and maker is God" (Heb. 11:10).

Many prophetic movements had their Zions or New Jerusalems, usually an actual geographical location, a place, a fortress, where the prophets and their followers could find shelter and relief from a hostile world. They not only believed in a city to come; some even built prototypes.

Hastings makes a plausible observation when he says the new converts' lives now revolved around a weekly cycle. The seven-day week was very important in African life after they had accepted the preaching of the prophets. The prophets placed great emphasis on the observance of a weekly day of rest. Central to their teaching was the idea of Sabbath (or Sunday) rest and preparation for the imminent return of Christ.[31]

The missionaries were surprised that so many of the converts remained Christian. The preaching ministry of most of these prophets spanned only a few years at most, and a few preached for only months. The usual waiting time for baptism was drastically reduced. Seasoned African Christians and missionaries complained about this "instant baptism." Small wonder that the missionaries were surprised that the majority of the converts, in spite of their immediate baptism, continued to live like Christians.

All of the churches benefitted from the evangelistic endeavors of Harris and

Braide. They did not begin their ministry with the idea of founding new churches, though in time this happened, usually upon the death of the prophet.

Shembe–Zulu Prophet King

Isaiah Shembe (c.1870-1935) was the greatest of the Zulu prophets. The most influential Zulu leader of his day, his power with the people was greater than that of any of the Zulu chiefs. Shembe was born in the Orange Free State in South Africa between 1867 and 1870. His father was a farm laborer who had a great love for Zulu culture and the traditions of the Zulu ancestors. This probably explains Shembe's burning zeal and desire for the uplift of the Zulu people.

When Shembe died on May 2, 1935, he left behind one of the most influential churches in Africa, totally separate from missionary and foreign control. The organization is in no way dependent on others for ideas or financial support.

Filled with a burning desire to restore the former glory and dignity of the Zulu people, Shembe chose to do so through religion rather than the political process. He saw himself as an agent, under God, for the accomplishment of these goals and sought to mobilize the masses to make it a reality.

Shembe's deepest self-understanding was that of a chief/king, a people's king, the ideal Old Testament ruler. Through diligent study of the Bible, he established a moral basis for his message and his actions. In this he was reminiscent of the Old Testament prophets, always lashing out against the sins of commoners and leaders, religious and political.

Recent scholarship shows that Shembe did not accept the traditional African veneration of ancestors. In fact, he taught that it was the sins of the ancestors that lay very heavily, in an adverse way, on the Zulu people. He totally rejected the idea of praying to the ancestors.[32]

Even though Shembe was thoroughly apolitical and urged his people to obey the established political authority, the government suspected him of preaching insurrection. Under almost all colonial administrations, the authorities were suspicious of any leader who had power with the people. This tendency on the part of colonial authorities to overreact to mass movements is seen repeatedly in the experience of the major African prophets.

This is the context in which Shembe's work and ministry is to be understood. His ultimate objective, his kingdom vision, was nothing less than the total revitalization of the Zulu people and, indeed, the whole of African society, but through peaceful and spiritual means.

Shembe's call to ministry was dramatic. As a young man he had serious moral conflicts, and in crisis situations he would experience dramatic spiritual encounters. One of these took place as he prayed during a lightning storm. In a later encounter "it was revealed to him that he should leave his four wives."[33] As difficult as this was–this almost drove him to suicide–Shembe obeyed.

Another decisive experience occurred when a lightning strike severely burned his leg. He refused medical help because he thought the voice told him to rely only on the power of prayer. He reported that he was healed because of his obedience to God.[34] Shembe soon developed a reputation as a master healer.

After his conversion to Christianity, Shembe connected with the Methodist Church for a time. Then he joined an independent African Baptist Church and received baptism by immersion. But he later severed his connection with the Baptists when he became convinced that the seventh day, or Saturday, was the Sabbath and his church refused to accept this Bible truth.

> "When he [Shembe] founded the iBandla lamanazaretha in 1911 he did so because he was fully convinced that the Christians had failed to obey God's law as laid down in the Hebrew Bible. In particular he emphasized that only through observation of the Sabbath could the Zulu nation be fully restored to its independence and former glory. In 1913 he selected a mountain in southern Natal, Nhlangkazi, as the 'holy mountain,' or Sinai, of his church and founded the holy city of Ekuphakemeni in 1914. Both places were to be the sites of pilgrimage and annual rejoicing. (Ways and means to survival in a hostile world.) . . . In 1913, two years after he founded the Church of the Nazarites, he had a vision which led him to declare that the church accepted the Sabbath as God's holy day instead of the Christian Sunday. As a result of this vision, he considered the Sabbath to be the key to Zulu fortunes because it was the test of true obedience to God."[35]

The Sabbath was also a matter of religioracial identity with Shembe. An African Sabbatarian, A.W.G. Champion, one of Shembe's contemporaries, makes the following observation to Sundkler: "From 1913 [the date of the infamous land act making it illegal to sell property to Black Africans in restricted areas] we knew one thing there is no God with the White man."[36]

Sundkler comments:

> "So Jehovah was chosen, the God of the wandering tribes. The use of Jehovah as the name of God has already had connotations attuned to the racial situation, which were to be powerfully increased in Natal and Zululand about the beginning of the 1920s. At this time Isaiah Shembe set Jesus aside, the Whites' Sunday-God, and chose the Sabbath-God, Jehovah. Behind the mighty shield of the name of the Jehovah of the Old Testament, his church sang:

"'There is no other name
By which we can be saved.
Only the name of Jehovah
By which we can be saved.'"[37]

I do not believe that Shembe rejected the Christ of the Bible. The fact is, many Africans were turned off by the representation of Jesus as someone entirely unintelligible to their concept of God and their own personhood. Someone with whom they could not identify, the Christ of a foreign culture, more of a European invention. But the real Jesus, as presented in the Gospels and foretold in the Hebrew Scriptures, was precious to the people who were themselves acquainted with oppression and sorrows. Here again is that universal longing for a deliverer who comes to us, meets us where we are, and identifies with us.

Shembe's reasons for accepting the Sabbath are several. First, it is biblical. He arrived at this understanding from his study of the Bible. Second, he came to see the Sabbath as being important to the cause of liberation and freedom. As has already been stated, he linked the Sabbath to the fortunes of the Zulu people, making it a test of obedience to God and a means of securing His blessing. Third, in Shembe's theology, the Sabbath is relevant to the wholeness and well-being of Africans and Africans in diaspora today. He provides us with a radical option. The Sabbath would be an affirmation of human worth, especially to the peoples of Africa and of African descent.

> "Isaiah Shembe began his religious pilgrimage as a Methodist: he gained an African Baptist background and ended up creating a dynamic indigenous church in which he proclaimed the Old Testament Sabbath as the 'key' to heaven. This holy day, with its ritual prohibitions, became the binding factor of the church."

Shembe s influence continued to grow with the Zulu chiefs until the day of his death. Dube says that not even the tribal chiefs were ever shown such respect as that bestowed upon Shembe. A young non-Christian chief came to visit the prophet's place, "not in order to become a Nazarite, but to study the ways of imposing *inhlonipho* (Zulu word for respect) on his people."[39]

> "When Shembe died he was buried with great honors. One minister called out *'Uyingcwele!'*(He is holy), and the great mass of Nazarites, in their white uniforms, responded with a cry which no one who was there will ever forget: 'He is holy.' Over his grave at Ekuphakameni there was built a mausoleum which is regarded as sacred by the people of his church."[40]

Shembe's Legacy

Isaiah Shembe's experiences during lightning storms made a deep impression on him which he understood in terms of the Mount Sinai experience of Moses, with the giving of the law accompanied by thunder and lightning. This deepened his appreciation for the law, and through this key of the law, he continued to lead his people out of the land of bondage.

"The liberation of the Jews from Egyptian bondage was a theme which Isaiah Shembe associated with his people. Just as the Jewish liberation was based on religious grounds, so too would be the liberation of the Zulu people. In Hymn 17:3, Isaiah Shembe stated: 'The enemies of Jehovah rise up against thee, wake up, wake up, ye Africans.'"

Zulu Zionists seem to have had similar dream experiences which historians call stereotypical dreams, in which certain elements recur. Lazarus M., about 50 years old, earlier a Methodist and now a Zionist Sabbath Church member, tells his story:

> "'I came to a beautiful place with green grass. I first passed a small stream, and then came to a wide river. I saw many people on this side of the river, and another group on the other side. When those people saw me coming they laughed and said: "We would like to see how that one is going to cross the river." But when I arrived at the river, I suddenly saw myself already on the other side. There I saw a very steep mountain (which is called Zion) and people climbing the mountain. At the foot of the mountain I saw an old woman praying. When I started to climb, people laughed, saying: "We would like to see how that one is going to climb that steep mountain." When I tried the second time I was quite surprised that whip! I was on the top of the mountain. There I saw a big city, so big that one could not see where it ended, and right through that city there passed a road. Over the city were morning mist and rays of the dawn. When I came near, there arose three men in white clothes. Two of them were half-hidden, but the third spoke to me and said: "It is not permitted to enter here without repenting." I heard a fine choir singing, and they were all in lovely white robes (but I don t remember what song it was). Then the man in white said: "I will send you to Evangelist Makhaye; you must ask him why he has turned the day of the Lord into a working day. If they do not repent and honor the Sabbath [Saturday], the Lord will send cold winds and hail and storm to destroy all that they have planted."'
>
> "He awoke. The following Sunday, when he came to the mission church, he remembered the dream and the choir whose song he had

listened to. He started to cry on remembering this. People were startled, and asked what was the matter. When he had narrated his dream, some people made a laughingstock of him."[41]

Chiding him for dreaming about the Sabbath day, people wanted to know why he interpreted the dream as meaning he should become a Sabbathkeeper. Later he met a Sabbatarian Zionist who brought him to a Zionist church, where he learned more about the true Sabbath. This kind of dream experience is rather common among the Zionists.[42]

The Connection in Diaspora

"God sent a man, his name was Crowdy.
He came to bring back the ancient of days.
He said he just got down in time
To save Israel from seventy years bondage.

Because he came, we keep the Sabbath Day.
Because he came we know the truth.
Because he came, we keep the Passover.
Our lives will never be the same because he came."

So wrote Evangelist C. C. Farrar of the Church of God and Saints of Christ in 1987, more than 80 years after the death of the founder, William Saunders Crowdy.

The ministry of William Saunders Crowdy has been strangely neglected by church historians. This remarkable man was born a slave in 1847 in the state of Maryland and died in the year 1906. After going through a series of profound spiritual experiences, including receiving visions and dreams similar to the experiences of the great African prophets, Crowdy founded the Church of God and Saints of Christ in Lawrence, Kansas, in 1896.

On one occasion Crowdy was clearing a field for planting when he fell into a deep sleep. He dreamed he was in a large room and saw a number of tables descending. They were of various sizes, but were all covered with filth, as in Isaiah's vision (see Isa. 28:8). He interpreted this to represent the spiritual condition of the various denominations.

Then he saw another table descending that was completely clean. This table was labeled "Church of God and Saints of Christ." The table grew to such proportions that the other tables were displaced. He took this to be a representation of the true church and decided that he was God's agent to establish it.

During the same vision Crowdy was given a set of keys, rules and guidelines for the church, later to be known as the "Seven Keys." The dream ended after a Bible was placed in his hands and he was commanded to eat it. He did and then awakened. This spectacular dream, Crowdy believed, prepared him for his ministry. He was totally committed from that day on to the spread of the message of Messiah Jesus to the whole world, but particularly to his brethren according to the flesh.[43]

By the time of his death the Church of God and Saints of Christ was established in the United States of America, the island of Jamaica, and South Africa. There were more than 200 churches and 37,000 members in the United States alone.[44]

The Church of God and Saints of Christ has been called the first Black Jewish movement in America.[45] (Today there are a number of Israelite/Hebrew Christian organizations in the United States and the Caribbean that observe the ancient Sabbath.)

In her book *My Lord What a Morning,* the celebrated concert artist Marian Anderson reports that her grandfather's "religion was of tremendous importance to him. . . . In his religion he observed Saturday as his Sabbath, spent the whole day at the temple, and referred to himself as a Black Jew. The words 'Passover' and 'unleavened bread' I heard first from his lips."[46] This man could well have been a member of the Church of God and Saints of Christ or a similar denomination. But it would be a mistake to categorize Crowdy as Jewish. He was a thoroughgoing Christian who acknowledged Christianity's Jewish roots.

A man of great determination and stamina, Crowdy's preaching mission took him to many parts of the United States. Large crowds of Blacks and Whites flocked to hear the "Black Elijah." Convinced that he was God's agent and that his church had a worldwide mission, Crowdy preached with power and baptized many converts.

Croudy was arrested 23 times for preaching. Two Philadelphia pastors petitioned the mayor to order Crowdy out of town because he was preaching that Saturday was the Sabbath. When the mayor came to hear Crowdy preach, he was impressed with his sincerity and said the city needed more of his kind.[47]

Early in his ministry Crowdy observed that the traditional church was confused about its relationship to Judaism. There was a continuity, in Crowdy's thinking, between Judaism and Christianity. His movement sought to restore the authentic Hebrew roots of Christianity.

All African-American preachers have emphasized the Exodus and the emancipation of the Hebrews as the major salvation paradigm in the old Testament and, indeed, in all of salvation history. But Crowdy is the first African-American to preach that the seventh-day Sabbath is particularly meaningful to Black people around the world. He saw his role as reaching out to the lost sheep of the house of Israel, Black people, who are the true Israelites. Crowdy's biographer, Elly M. Wynia, says: "The combination of Judaism and Christianity that provides the theological foundation of this movement is distinctive, even unique."[48]

Crowdy did not, however, reject the person of Jesus. In Crowdy's theological system, Jesus is the Messiah, the Christ. Messiah Jesus is exalted as the advocate of racial equality, a subjective role model for establishing a truly nondiscriminatory existence. The established churches have misrepresented this aspect of Jesus' ministry. Crowdy taught that it was the first and highest duty of every person to treat others with dignity and respect. His great concern was the empowering of the disfranchised and oppressed, equipping them for survival and even for success in the struggle for dignity.

Crowdy developed a core of basic doctrines fundamental to his theological system, which he called "the Seven Keys":

1. The church of God and of the saints of Christ.
2. Wine forbidden to be drunk in the church of God forever.
3. Unleavened bread and water for Christ's body and blood.
4. Foot washing is a commandment.
5. The disciples' prayer.
6. You must be breathed upon with a Holy kiss
7. The Ten Commandments.

Crowdy was determined to return to the Jewish roots of the Christian faith, because Jewish scenes of bondage and liberation were appropriate to the condition of Blacks at that time: "It is worth noting here that Crowdy seemed to have a rather acute understanding of the pivotal point in history that Blacks occupied. He knew that if something weren't done soon that it might be too late for the Blacks of his time."[49]

Crowdy believed that Blacks were the true descendants of Abraham and thus were the true Hebrews. His vision foresaw the spreading of his message to Black people all over the world. He organized an overseas ministry or missionary force and sent agents to the West Indies, who established churches in Jamaica.

Crowdy's influence in Africa, an amazing story, must be noted: "The work of the Church of God and Saints of Christ in South Africa was begun by a Xhosa, Albert Christian, a sailor and former Baptist missionary based in Port Elizabeth. While in Port Elizabeth, Christian had a dream in which he purportedly received instructions to go to America and seek out Crowdy. He did so, and returned to Africa in 1903 as a minister under Crowdy's charge."[50]

Christian founded churches in several places in South Africa. At least one African preacher, John Msikinya, was sponsored to Lincoln University, a Black institution in Pennsylvania, for theological training. He was Christian's successor. After Msikinya's death, Enoch Mgijima became the leader of the church in South Africa, where he emphasized the Israelite nature of the community. In 1921 he and his followers set up a squatters' village of 300 huts and refused the authorities' orders to vacate. After a standoff of some weeks, the soldiers suddenly opened fire and 117 followers were killed.

Crowdy saw the Sabbath as being important to Black liberation. Along with some of the African prophets, he recognized the Sabbath as being of great significance to the deepest concerns of Black people wholeness, happiness, well-being, progress, and a healthy self-image.

In Crowdy's church, Sabbath worship begins on Friday evening. The Sabbath is a day of fellowship and learning, a time for renewal of vision. The Sabbath school is the time for broadening the knowledge of the members not only about the Bible but also about Black history. Youth leaders have developed a manual of 85 Black-history questions to teach the youth about their past. The activities of the Sabbath and its worship services focus on the corporate mission of the church. The members are encouraged to maintain the spiritual unity achieved during Sabbath services.

Crowdy preached the gospel of self-help and strength to overcome against odds. At the center of his message is a gospel that produces visible results in the uplifting and empowerment of people. One of the seven or eight departments of the church was the "M & W. D. A," which "services the Tabernacle by fostering literary programs and finances for cultural development."[51]

Crowdy was very successful in attracting strong people with leadership qualities to his organization and in bringing out the best in his young associates. He educated and sent several preachers to Africa. His successors were achievers. Howard Z. Plummer, one of Crowdy's successors, became president of the famous Interdenomination Interracial Hampton Ministers' Conference. Plummer established a number of enterprises to provide employment for his people. In addition, the church founded and operated for a number of years a widows' and orphans' home, an industrial school in Belleville, Virginia, and a printing press.

This visionary preacher forged a connection between Africans in the United States and Africans on the continent through his adherence to the ancient Bible Sabbath. This immediately identified him with African thinking and differentiated his movement from the European mission in Africa which was so committed to Sunday worship.

A typical worship service of the Church of God and Saints of Christ in South Africa would be much like the typical meeting in the United States. Pauw describes his visit to an Israelite gathering in South Africa:

"The attendance is good, some sixty to seventy people are gathered. The women wear black shirts and black ties and white coats, and the men frock-coats. The Israelites are deservedly famous for their fine singing; the choir has a prominent place in the church. After a hymn the minister gives a short address: 'The right day on which to worship God is the Sabbath, as it is written in the Book. To worship God on Sunday is not written in the Book. People who worship God on Sunday are hypocrites, for if they study the Scriptures they would find that they ought to worship on Saturday. The calendars show that this is true, because there the first day is Sunday and the seventh is Saturday. Our church is the Church of God and Saints of Christ. We do as the first Church of Christ did.'

"After an anthem by the choir, the minister reads a Bible text and 'Our Father' is sung by all. . . . A deacon addresses the congregation with a few thoughts about the creed of their church: 'I thank God who has sent us the Prophet William T. Crowdy, who came with the plan of salvation, the Ten Commandments and the Seven Keys.' (Amen.)

"He deals above all with 'Grandfather Abraham,' H. Z. Plummer, and the blessings they have received through him. The main thought in his address is the necessity of worshiping on Saturday. No less than twenty-one people follow him with short testimonies, all beginning with the formula of their creed: 'I thank God who has sent the Prophet William T. Crowdy. who came, etc."[52]

Simon Kimbangu, in some respects the most remarkable of the African prophets, was born in the lower Congo in 1889. As a young man he married Mivilu Marie, with whom he sustained a monogamous relationship for the rest of his life. After accepting Christianity, Kimbangu and his wife were baptized in 1915. Almost immediately he felt called to preach. He resisted the impression and tried other occupations and callings, but without success.

Finally, in March of 1921, on a Friday, Kimbangu yielded to the vision, or, as he put it, to the voice. He then launched an amazing preaching and healing ministry that shook Zaire. Such large crowds attended his meetings that both Catholics and Protestants were alarmed. They keenly felt the sudden loss of influence. All of their members, they reported, were rushing after Kimbangu.

The frightened prelates and pastors appealed to the civil authorities to stop Kimbangu. He was able to escape arrest for some time, but finally gave himself up to the authorities, who tried him, found him guilty, and sentenced him to death. However, some Protestant clergy petitioned the government and even the king of Belgium to pardon Kimbangu. The death sentence was commuted to life imprisonment. Kimbangu spent more than 30 years in confinement until his death in 1951.

Kimbangu was no threat to the Belgian government, nor was he working at cross purposes with the mission churches. In fact, some of the missionaries came to see this. The overreaction of both Protestant and Catholic missionaries so alarmed the Belgian government that the matter was taken out of the missionaries' hands. The Belgians, as is the case of all colonial powers, was implacable and absolutely ruthless when challenged by the slightest show of African power. No one could now effect Kimbangu's release.

Kimbangu's active field ministry lasted only six months, and during much of that time he was in hiding from the authorities. In spite of these severe time restrictions on Kimbangu's public ministry, his movement is still today, without question, the leading African Independent Church in Zaire and ranks very high among all the indigenous churches of Africa.

Kimbangu's imprisonment did not mean the end of his movement. From his prison cell he was able to smuggle out messages to followers. His wife was appointed mother of the churches, and in due time his sons were made leaders of the movement. Prisoners who were confined with Kimbangu spoke of him almost with reverence and testified that he was a model prisoner. Though behind bars and under the administration of hard prison officials, he maintained his dignity and Christian demeanor. Everyone in the prison respected him, even those who hated him.

There is no record that Kimbangu was a Sabbathkeeper. However, the articles of faith of his movement are very explicit in their requirement for keeping all the commandments of God. The "foundation stone is the law" and the prophets.

Jonas Mybirukira, a highly respected Seventh-day Adventist senior church leader, told me that Kimbangu had a vision during his time of imprisonment in which it was revealed to him that a great new light would come to Zaire, and he urged his followers to accept it.

Most of the African prophets instructed their converts to wait for teachers with Bibles, be they Black or White. Pastor Jonas believed that this great light was the biblical witness about the Creation Sabbath. The African prophets were aware that their theological systems were still developing. They were not hidebound by restrictive creeds and theological formulas. They wanted the body of doctrines, the deposit of truth to remain open-ended and dynamic. In other words, there was more and greater light to come (see Prov. 4:18).

Harris also told his people to receive missionaries who would come with Bibles including White missionaries. The African prophets were not racist, nor were they sectarian. They would like to have served in mainstream Christianity, but on terms of equality and dignity.

Kimbangu's church grew rapidly until the membership reached more than 500,000. The authorities were determined to stamp out this new religion, but it was impossible. At first all Kimbanguist church leaders were jailed and terribly mistreated. Public meetings were banned, but Kimbangu's people met from midnight until 4:00 a.m. and whispered their prayers and exhortations so that they would not be heard by the soldiers.

Gradually the movement gained acceptance and even admiration. The ban was lifted in 1957, and congregations could meet and worship regularly as they wished. The EJCSK (Kimbanguist) Church is the only indigenous African church that has been admitted to membership in the World Council of Churches.

Following is a brief description of the EJCSK Church:

1. The church was founded by Simon Kimbangu.

2. It is based on the Christian religion.

3. It has no restriction with regard to regional boundaries.

4. The foundation stone is the Law and the Prophets enlightened by the Holy Spirit. Thus they promote love, peace, fear of evil, and moral purity.

5. It limits its activities to the relationship between man and God.

6. It refrains from political activities.

7. It worships God the Creator and practices no discrimination.

8. It follows the Ten Commandments, and, in addition, its adherents must (a) respect authorities, (b) love one another, (c) abstain from alcoholic drink, (d) abstain from dancing, (e) abstain from bathing or sleeping in the nude, (f) keep out of quarrels, (g) abstain from smoking, (h) abstain from fetishism, (i) pay taxes, (j) avoid rancor against their neighbors, (k) confess their transgressions before the appropriate body, and (l) abstain from eating pork and monkeys.

9. It is a church of the Holy Spirit. For this reason, all Kimbanguist Christians must live according to the Spirit.[53]

I believe that Kimbangu and other African prophets were Yahweh's instruments to prepare the way on the African continent for the biblical witness to the Creation Sabbath, which has been received with such great joy and enthusiasm among the African people.

Sabbatarian Churches in South Africa

The name of W. W. Oliphant comes up often in the discussion of Sabbathkeeping groups in South Africa. Oliphant was a leader in an African Independent Church and at first tried to convert the Church of God and Saints of Christ, or Israelites, as they came to be known in South Africa, from their custom of Saturday worship. But Oliphant was himself influenced by the Israelites and, in fact, became a Sabbatarian.

When he returned to his church in 1914, he was "excommunicated" from the movement he had started because of his Israelite views. He then formed the Baptist Church of the Seventh Day Adventists of Africa. A number of Sabbatarian groups are designated by variations of the name Seventh Day Baptist Church of Christ. The best known is the (Bantu) Church of Christ, which gained prominence under Bishop James L. Limba.[54] Limba's organization was strong in the Cape area, and at one time was the largest indigenous African church in the area.

The name *Baptist*, as used in the South African setting, indicates preference for baptism by immersion rather than denominational affiliation. Pauw explains:

> "Some of these groups believed that because of their emphasis on Jewishness and their fidelity to the Sabbath, they were not only more biblical than the Ethiopians, but even more Ethiopian! Oliphant produced an 'Expose of the Faith and Practice of the Church of Christ,' in which he linked the two emphases with Christ and the apostles, with one Peter Wolds 'in the Wilderness,' and with Cromwell, 'who was a most zealous Sabbath observer.' 'Baptism in Ethiopia,' he continues, 'was through the Eunuch of Ethiopian queen Candace, baptized by Philip, Read Acts 8:36. Sabbath in Ethiopia [has] been kept from the days of Nimrod, about 2140 B.C, Read Gen. 10:8, 9, that is 700 years before the birth of Moses.'
> . . . Africans or Ethiopians had been Sabbath observers from the days of Nimrod, the son of Cush. . . . Report, then, the membership in the Ethiopian Empire: Addis Abbaba, 3,000,000, Uganda, 350,000, and in Nigeria, 1,000,000."[55]

Sandier points out that the association with Cush provides "a charter and the assurance of a link with our first ancestors mentioned on the first pages of the Bible."[56]

Pauw sums up the situation as he sees it in South Africa:

> "The orthodox churches, with which most of the Ethiopian type of independent churches are grouped in the study, account for the great majority of members and adherents of churches in the rural areas. In the towns they also predominate, but a substantial minority of the people belong or adhere to other types of churches, most of which can be described as either Pentecostalist, Sabbatarian-Baptist or Zionist. The latter represent an independent syncretistic development of Pentecostalism, while most of the Sabbatarian Baptists are independent Bantu groups deriving from mission work of American Negro churches of this type. Some Bantu Pentecostal groups are

> associated with non-Banutu groups of the same church, but there are also some independent Bantu Pentecostal churches that are not distinctly syncretistic like the Zionists. There are also Seventh-day Adventist congregations among the Xhosa."[57]

Summary

Scholars identify several waves of African Independent Churches. The first is the Ethiopian. The second is the cluster of Sabbatarian-Baptist Independent Churches. The third group is the Zionist, which appeared sometime later.

> "Within the Sabbatarian Baptist cluster one could further distinguish two subclusters, namely, the 'Israelite' groups and the 'Church of Christ' groups. In the wider South African context this second wave may not appear very significant, but among the Xhosa it should certainly be distinguished as representing a type apart from the Ethiopians and the Zionists. There is the more reason for this since the Zionist groups are fairly recent in many parts of the Xhosa-speaking area, so that the Sabbatarian-Baptist type was for a long time more in evidence than the Zionists."[58]

Most of the independent movements look on themselves as possessing a "mythical charter," linking them, the indigenous churches, by means of the Bible, with the ancient Christian traditions of North Africa and with all of those old Testament references to the peoples of Africa. Thus they claim to be part of a heritage that is more ancient than any European tradition.

Several general observations can be made about the Independent Church movement:

1. Almost every aspect of the African Independent Church movement is unique to the African continent. The first Independent Churches were founded in South Africa. The first genuine African Independent Church was that of the Methodist preacher Nehemiah Tile, who disagreed with his White supervisors in 1833 and founded his own church in 1834. They called themselves Ethiopian. The movement spread throughout Africa. The contributing factors seem to be colonialism, the severity of which shocked the African people out of sleep and stirred their thirst for independence. Before that time African states and people groups lived by agreements made by their chiefs and kings with Europeans. "Uhuru," the Swahili cry for freedom, became the slogan, the burning watchword that galvanized a continent. The realities of the situation were recognized by British prime minister Harold Macmillan, in his "Winds of Change" speech. Those freedom cries were a

harbinger of the new day dawning in colonial Africa.

2. There is concrete evidence in the African Independent Church movement of the connection between African-Americans and Africans on the continent and of the influence that each exerts on the other. A number of African-Americans went to the continent to share their faith in Christ. African Christians were impressed that those sons and daughters of slaves had, in spite of great difficulties, progressed to the point where they were able to make a major contribution to their brothers and sisters on the continent. They also discovered that African-Americans generally administered their own churches. These contacts awakened the desire for indigenous leadership on the part of clergy and laity. African-Americans also were cheered by the good reports from the homeland. The feeling was mutual and the response reciprocal.

Good examples of this mutual exchange are the influence of Crowdy and Oliphant. The Church of God and Saints of Christ was founded by William Saunders Crowdy, an African-American born a slave. Crowdy taught that Africans were the true inheritors of Yahweh's covenant with Israel. W. W. Oliphant and James L. Limba became leaders of Sabbathkeeping Baptist groups in South Africa. Limba named his group the Church of Christ Mission. In this instance, we have a pastor from South Africa, Oliphant, who went to North America, received his training through African-Americans, and returned to Africa, where he took up his work.

My father was acquainted with Thomas Branch, an American Black from Colorado, who accepted an appointment from the Seventh-day Adventist Church to go to Nyasaland as director of a former Seventh Day Baptist mission station. Branch renamed the station Malamulo, the Ten Commandment mission. Branch was a hard-driving taskmaster whom his young African students called Pharaoh because he rang the rising bell at 5:00 a.m. But the nickname Pharaoh was not derisive most parents for a decade or two at Malamulo named their firstborn sons Thomas! There were many other African-Americans who helped forge the African connection.

3. The African Independent Church movement has not been entirely without its faults. One could point out the theological deficiencies of the great prophets. The African prophets were human and made grave blunders and mistakes. We will have to leave their final judgment to Yahweh. And His jury is still out.

What is remarkable is the response throughout the African world to the biblical witness regarding the ancient Sabbath. The scenario seems almost to derive from Old Testament times. A sovereign God visits His flawed and benighted earthborn children using earthen vessels both foreign missionaries and indigenous people. After "many days" the seed of the pioneers germinates; it all comes together, comes alive, when the people hear the message of Messiah Jesus in their own language.

Under the impetus of the Independent Churches, Christianity has become the majority religion on the African continent. It is to Yahweh's glory.

Two Western Scholars Look at the African Prophets

A number of scholarly observers of the African religious scene have made interesting comments on the work of the African prophets. One of these, G. C. Oosthuisen, writes:

> "These prophets are not only founders of new religions but are charismatic leaders, the mediators between God and His people, who have a concrete historical task in time of crisis, as had Moses. . . . Anyone who has attended their meetings and also reads the book of Acts with an open mind can have little doubt that he is reading about something he has seen."[59]

Another, D. B. Barrett, states:

> "Any comparison is, in fact, somewhat flattering to African independency, which emerges as a far more staid and orthodox movement than many of the early, medieval or Commonwealth sects. Contemporary Africa has little to compare with the murderous craving for martyrdom of the Donatus Church's Circumcelions, the Lombardy Apostolics' dressing in swaddling clothes to honor the infancy of Christ, the Anabaptists running naked through the streets of Amsterdam, the Quaker abolition of all sacraments, or the Cammisard's addiction to child prophecy."[60]

It has been said that Kimbangu and Shembe were more orthodox than Albert Schweitzer, the selfless theologian/physician who gave himself unreservedly to the people of the Cameroons.

Above all, the Israelite churches wanted to distinguish themselves from the "world." These various bodies or movements selected biblical metaphors which would emphasize their position over and against nominally Christian or "worldly" churches. They wanted to be known as small remnant communities, a counterculture that the world chose to ignore. Messiah Jesus also told His disciples that the world would hate them.

The Israelite churches considered themselves a hidden kingdom. So they gave themselves names like the Church of the Lost Christians in Zimbabwe, the Lost Israelites of Kenya, the African Remnant of Israel Church, and the African Israel Church in Western Kenya. Another group simply called themselves the Israelite colony. Always the identification with Israel is underscored, because Israel was Jehovah's chosen, Jehovah's elect.

In African cultures the name is exceedingly significant. A child is not counted as an individual until named. It is understandable, therefore, that those churches who observed the seventh day as Sabbath would want this belief reflected in their name. Also, the fact that Sabbath is included in the name indicates how seriously they view the matter.

Below is a list of Sabbatarian churches existing in September 1945 from the list of separatist churches compiled by B.G.M. Sundkler in Bantu Prophets in South Africa:

African Apostolic Church in Sabbath
African Apostolic Church in Sabbath South Africa
African Sabbath Mission Church
African Seventh Church of God
African Seventh Church of God Laodicean Mission
African Seventh-Day Adventists
African Seventh Day Zulu Shaka Church of Christ
Apostolic Jerusalem Church in Sabbath
Baptist Church of the Seventh-day Adventists of Africa
Baptist of the Seventh-day Adventists
Christian Church Saturday
Free Sabbatarian Mission of the Seventh-Day Observers Church of the United States of America in Southern Africa
Nazareth Baptist Church of South Africa in Sabbath
The New Jerusalem Sabbath Apostolic Church in Zion South Africa
Sabbath Church in Zion Message of God to African and Zulu Man
Sabbath Church in Zion of South Africa
The Sabbath Christian Church Apostolic Church in Zion
Seventh Day Adventists
Seventh Day Church of God
Seventh Day Baptist Church of Christ
Seventh Day Baptist Church of London
South African Seventh Church of God.[60]

One church took the name "abaNyulwa bakaYesu Kristu, abaLindi bomGqibelo" (the Elect of Jesus Christ, the Watchmen [or Expecters] of Saturday)! By the choice of names is seen the sense of connectedness with the Sabbatarian and Second-Coming nature of their fellowship.

It is impressive that the African people have internalized the biblical narrative and have formed it in their own way their own idiom. During one of my travels in Africa, a missionary friend repeated a story told by a young lad that graphically illustrates how the original Sabbath was changed by the European ecclesiastical establishment. The story shows the keen perception of the young fellow and his ability to articulate the salient points of the story in African terms.

> "Once upon a time there was a great king who had ten sons. Then one day the king decided to go on a journey. He called his ten sons before him. He also called for the prime minister. He embraced each of his sons, one by one, saying 'Oh, my son.' The king then turned to the prime minister and said, 'While I am away, take care of my sons.'
>
> "Soon after the king was gone, the prime minister called the sons and lined them up before him for inspection. When he came to son number four, the prime minister said, 'You do not look like a royal son.' He took him out of the lineup and sent the boy into the fields to work with the slaves. Then the prime minister took his own son and put him in the place of the king's son.
>
> "But the king came back one day, and called the prime minister to give an account of how he had taken care of his sons. The prime minister said, 'O king live forever. I have done as you have commanded.' He told the king that his sons were well.
>
> "Then the king said, 'Bring in my sons.' As he had done at the first, he embraced them all until he came to the fourth son. Then he said, 'You are not my son. You must be an imposter.' The king turned to the prime minister and said, 'Who is this?'
>
> "The prime minister replied, 'Your Majesty, your son did not look like a royal son, and so I removed him from the lineup and put my son in his place.'
>
> "'Who gave you permission to do that?' the king demanded. The prime minister was speechless. 'But where is my son?'
>
> "The prime minister responded, 'He is in the fields, Your Majesty, working with the slaves.' This made the king very angry. He banished the prime minister and his son from the realm and restored his own son to his proper place in the lineup."

When the story was over, the usual response from an African audience was, "Tell us, what is the meaning of the story? The story must have some teaching value." Well, the little fellow would answer:

"The king is God, and the ten sons are the Ten Commandments. The fourth commandment is the commandment that says 'Remember the Sabbath day to keep it holy.' The prime minister is the church, the one He left the commandments in charge of. But the church changed God's day of rest and put another day in its place, a day it chose. But the King is coming back!"

How skillfully this lad places the biblical text into an African setting that speaks powerfully to the African mind. And to all who have ears to hear.

End Notes

[1]Isichei, p. 1

[2]Hasting, pp. 443, 449.

[3]*Ibid.*, p. 448.

[4]*Ibid.*, p. 453.

[5]*Ibid.*, p. 451.

[6]*Ibid.*, P. 445.

[7]Isichei, p. 1.

[8]A. F. Wallis, quoted in *Ibid.*, p. 354.

[9]Barrett, quoted in Mircea Eliade, ed., *Encyclopedia of Religion* (New York: Macmillan, 1986), p. 413.

[10]Hastings, p. 237.

[11]M. L. Daneel, "Quest for Belonging," in *Old and New in Southern Shona: Independent Churches* (Hawthorne, N.Y.: Mouton, 1971), vol. 1, p. 36.

[12]Daneel, p. xiii.

[13]*Ibid.*, p. 36.

[14]Isichei, p. 49.

[15]*Ibid.*, pp. 256, 257.

[16]*Ibid.*, p. 256.

[17]Pauw, p. 292.

[18]Getui, p. 12.

[19]Sammy Ngetich, "Possible Sabbath Traditions in Africa: The Case of the Kalenjin People" (paper presented to the Sabbath in Africa Project, Jan. 1995), pp. 11-13.

[20]*Ibid.*, p. 13.

[21]Josiah Okinda, "Possible Sabbathkeeping Traditions in Precolonist Africa: A Study of the Luo People in Kenya" (paper presented to the Sabbath in Africa Project, Jan. 1995), p. 8.

[22]*Ibid.*, p. 10.

[23]*Ibid.*, pp. 8-11.

[24]F. Duane McKey, "History and Analysis of the Relationship Between the Seventh-Day Adventist Church and Several Independent Churches in the Kasai Province of Zaire, 1972-1985" (dissertation, Andrews University, 1989), p. 26.

[25]Sanneh, p. 181.

[26]*Ibid.*, p. 183.

[27]*Ibid.*, pp. 182, 183.

[28]Shaw, p. 248.

[29]Hastings, in Eliade, p. 415.

[30]*Ibid.*, p. 436.

[31]*Ibid.*, pp. 458, 459.

[32]Irving Hexham, ed., *The Scriptures of amaNazaretha of EkuphaKameni* (Queenstown, Ontario: Mellon, 1993), pp. 43-49.

[33]Sundkler, p. 110.

[34]*Ibid.*

[35]*Ibid.*

[36]*Ibid.*, p. 331.

[37]*Ibid.*

[38]Hexham, p. xviii.

[39]Sundkler, p. iii.

[40]*Ibid.*

[41]*Ibid.*, p. 269.

[42]*Ibid.*

[43]Elly M. Wynia, *The Church of God and the Saints of Christ: The Rise of Black Jews* (New York: Garland Publishing, 1990), pp. 20, 21.

[44]*Ibid.*, p. 26.

[45]James S. Tinney, "Black Jews: A House Divided," *Christianity Today*, Dec. 1973, pp. 52, 53.

[46]Marian Anderson, *My Lord, What a Morning*, reprint (Madison, Wisc.: University of Wisconsin Press, 1992), p. 16.

[47]Wynia, p. 31.

[48]*Ibid.*

[49]I*Ibid.*, p. 55.

[50]*Ibid.*, p. 40.

[51]*Ibid.*, p. 110.

[52]Pauw, p. 118.

[53]Martin, quoted in McKey, pp. 30, 31.

[54]Pauw, p. 31.

[55]*Ibid.*, p. 292.

[56]*Ibid.*

[57]*Ibid.*, p. 31.

[58]Prophecy 258.

[59]Prophecy 259.

[60]Sundkler, pp. 354-374.

CHAPTER TEN

SABBATH IN AFRICA TODAY

There is a remarkable response throughout the African world to the biblical witness regarding the ancient Sabbath. The question needs to be restated in terms of today: "Does this response still continue? Has it abated, or has it grown? What is the status of the ancient biblical Sabbath in present day Africa?"

M. L. Daneel points out that a significant number of Hebraic or Judaistic movements may be found in many parts of Africa "that have radically departed from paganism and have made faith in one God, as defined in the Old Testament, a key tenet. . . . There are striking parallels with the Old Testament people of God."[1]

There is an abundance of anecdotal evidence here. In my contacts and conversations with a variety of people on the African continent, this comes up. Someone will casually mention that their parents or people group would not travel on the Sabbath, Saturday. Or they may say that the people of a certain village keep Sabbath. A European missionary told me of a group of white-robed worshipers that she observed near her compound on a Saturday afternoon (as already stated, the word for Saturday in many languages is, in essence, "no work today"). We have reason to believe, as Daneel says, that scattered throughout Africa there are a number of these Hebrew or Judaic cults that observe the Sabbath.

The Abayudaya of Uganda

One of the most fascinating of these scattered Sabbatarian people groups is the Abayudaya of Uganda: "Nestled within the rolling hills of eastern Uganda lives a community of 500 Black Ugandans who practice Judaism, observing Jewish holidays, singing Hebrew songs, dining under the Laws of Kashrut, and keeping the Shabbat holy, as they have for qenerations."[2]

Mbiti makes extensive comments on the Abayudaya:

> "Another community of African Judaism is found in eastern Uganda. Members of this congregation speak of themselves as Bayudaya (Jews, of Judah). This is a unique community in that it came into existence at the start of this century, and is made up of Africans from the local inhabitants around Mbale. It was started by

> an African, Semei Kakungulu, who was a leading personality in the history of Uganda at the turn of the century."[3]

Kakungulu took part in the religious wars and later assisted the British in establishing administrative control of eastern Uganda. Kakungulu, disenchanted with the Anglican Church and the British government, joined an independent church, the fast-growing Bamalaki group, in 1913. Kakungulu had always been a serious Bible student.

During this time his attention was drawn to the seventh-day Sabbath, and he began to take a particular interest in Judaism. His contact with Jews led him to accept the Jewish faith. By 1919 he and his sons were circumcised. And by the time of his death, in 1928, the number of his followers had grown to several thousand.

Like their founder, Kakungulu's followers are also diligent Bible students. Visitors to the community are impressed with their grasp of Scripture, that is, the Old Testament (Abayudaya do not accept the New Testament Scriptures as equal to the Old Testament). They have remained true to their convictions in spite of tremendous opposition from Christians and traditional religious groups.

Recently their contacts with Judaism have been strengthened. The Abayudaya have become missionary-oriented; after a period of slow decline in membership, the movement seems to be growing. What they want, above all else, is acceptance in the world Jewish community.

Mbiti reminds us that Judaism established itself in northern and northeastern Africa centuries before Christianity was born:

> "Furthermore, religious and social life of the ancient Jews is similar to that of many African societies whose religious thought we have surveyed here. Some of the obvious differences lie in the fact that Judaism developed a prophetic movement and a messianic expectation, neither of which has any parallels in African traditional background. The ancient Jews were more African than Asian in many respects.
>
> "Africans feel closer to the Jews than to the Arabs who migrated into Africa, took away land from the indigenous people and over many centuries enslaved them. Even today they deny Africans full rights in their own countries such as the Sudan. Israel, though so small, has involved itself tremendously in development projects and commercial enterprises in many African countries, and is thereby contributing far more than many and bigger nations of the industrial, socialist and oil-rich countries.
>
> "In modern times we find Jewish congregations in southern Africa, Kenya and other areas occupying themselves with commercial transactions. Jews of Egypt and north African states have deep

historical roots in Africa; and formerly there were conversions among African peoples, like the Saharan Berbers, to Judaism."[4]

Sabbath Keepers in the Sudan

I have recently been made aware of three groups of people in the Sudan who are longtime Sabbathkeepers. Gerry Karst, a Seventh-day Adventist minister, was in Khartoum, Sudan, on church business. At this meeting, workers from the Adventist Development and Relief Agency (ADRA) reported on their discovery of a group of Sabbathkeepers. One of ADRA's national workers had come into contact with a group of people that claimed to be Sabbathkeepers in the village of Wad Medani, approximately three hours' drive south of Khartoum, along the Blue Nile River.

The ADRA worker's name was Zacki Assad. His family originally came from Egypt, and some of his Egyptian relatives were Seventh day Adventists. Assad himself was a fairly devout Christian of an Evangelical Protestant heritage. He, as well as other Christians in the area, did not know what to make of people who kept the Sabbath. But since Zacki was acquainted with Sabbathkeepers, both because of his relatives and because he worked for ADRA, he reported the information to Adventist leaders in Khartoum. Karst set up a meeting with the group.

Two students attending the University of Sudan in Khartoum were from the Sabbathkeeping group in Wad Medani. It was arranged for them to show the Adventist party to the home of Mousa Abdulla, the leader of the Sabbathkeeping community, which Karst describes as "a well-maintained compound surrounded by a picket fence made of poles, sticks, and thatch":

> "Inside were four family houses and a separate building used for worship. We were escorted to the worship building and there waited for Mousa Abdulla to come and visit with us. He was at that time a man about 58 years of age. Tall and dignified, educated and well spoken, he received us graciously and took his place in a chair reserved for him during the times he gave religious instruction to the members of his group.
>
> "He sat in a straight-backed chair against the main wall. There was room for about 30 40 people to meet. There was a small, low table in front of him on which he had several books. On the wall behind him was a white paper chart with a handwritten genealogy which traced the lineage of Mousa Abdulla back to Solomon through the Queen of Sheba.
>
> "Mousa Abdulla began by giving us a history of his people. While they were brown skinned, they were not Black Sudanese. Their

features were more characteristic of Arabs, and he spoke Arabic. He indicated that during the time that Islam was conquering the Middle East, and either subduing or destroying the nations they conquered, his ancestors chose to flee from Yemen across the Gulf of Aden and/or the Red Sea into Africa. There were several groups in this migration, and they headed in different directions.

"One group apparently headed north along the Mediterranean Sea and settled in the region of Libya. Two other groups ended up in the Sudan. The group in Libya apparently disintegrated, and the Sudanese group no longer had any contact with them or information about them. We were informed that Mousa Abdulla's group numbered somewhere in the range of 150 200 people. And that a little further south and west of the White Nile, in the village of Ruwaba, was a larger group of Sabbathkeepers, numbering more like 400. Occasionally, these two groups had some contact with each other. . . .

"These were basically Israelite Sabbathkeepers who follow the Old Testament Scriptures and are still looking for the Messiah. Mousa Abdulla told me of two providential dreams. The first dream came to his great great-grandfather four generations back. In this dream his great great-grandfather was instructed to go to another village and there meet another man. And in the dream he was given the name of this man, whom he had never met before. In obedience to the dream, he went to the other village and inquired for a man by the name given in the dream, and was directed to that man's house. They visited, became friends, and entered into a friendship covenant of protection for the Sabbathkeepers. This other man apparently was from a family with considerable power and influence in the country.

"The dream went on to indicate that in the fourth generation there would arise in each family, a leader. In the Sabbathkeepers' family there would come a religious leader. Mousa Abdulla saw himself as the fulfillment of that dream. And in the political man's family, according to the dream, there would arise a man who would be a leader in the country. I was told that (at the time I was there) the prime minister or president of Sudan was the fourth-generation descendent of the political man mentioned in the dream. And that there was to be an understanding that Sabbathkeepers in the Sudan would be protected. It is providential that since 1980, when Seventh day Adventism began in an organized way in Sudan, our membership has now surpassed 5,000 and that Sabbathkeepers have not been unduly persecuted.

"The second dream actually came to Mousa Abdulla. In his dream he was standing in the doorway of his house looking out. There was a table in the yard just ahead of him which had both the Bible and the Koran on it. While he was contemplating what this meant, a whirlwind arose, came over the table, and lifted away the Koran, leaving only the Bible. Mousa Abdulla took this as a sign from God that the Bible was the true Word of God, and this was the book he should study and teach to his people."[5]

Mousa Abdulla was astounded to hear that Karst represented a group of Sabbathkeepers that numbered close to 10 million and were found in nearly every country of the world. "They had been isolated for so many generations there in the Sudan," says Karst, "they thought they were the only Sabbathkeeping people left in the world."

Karst asked Mousa Abdulla how they kept the Sabbath, what was their attitude to the Ten Commandments, what they believed about salvation and the forgiveness of sin, and what was their conception of the Messiah. He continues:

"In many respects, his understanding of salvation, the role of the law, the value of the Sabbath, and so on are very close to what we believe. I then pressed him on the topic of progressive truth, and asked him a direct question. Since he believed the Bible was the Word of God, and since he believed that God was leading him, if he was shown additional truth from the Bible which he did not now know, would he be willing to follow it?

"He pondered the question for some time, and then indicated that if it was truth from the Bible, he would be willing to follow."[6]

His answer is typical, for the African prophets recognize that they do not have the total truth, and they encourage their followers to be ready to receive teachers who come with Bibles.

Mousa Abdulla believes that the prophecy of Daniel 12:1—"And in that day shall Michael stand up . . ."—refers to the Messiah, who is yet to come. According to Karst, the leader was reluctant to fully accept Jesus Christ as Messiah because "Messiah comes in the manner of David, and David was married. Jesus never married."

The Seventh-day Adventist Message and Mission in Africa: The Story Less Told

Seventh-day Adventists and Seventh Day Baptists were the only mission churches that insisted on the observance of the Seventh-day Sabbath as a day of rest binding on all Christians in perpetuity. But the Seventh Day Baptist mission to Africa did not continue for very long. They turned over to the Seventh-day Adventists at least one of their mission stations, Malamulo, or Ten Commandments, mission station in Nyasaland. So the Seventh-day Adventists are the only Euro-American-based Sabbathkeeping church in Africa.

Seventh-day Adventists have pursued their mission in Africa aggressively. They have founded schools, hospitals, and clinics in many places. There are at least 3 million Seventh-day Adventists on the African continent. Church statistics, however, do not take into account the number of adherents who are not yet baptized, nor do they take into account the large number of people in various parts of Africa who claim to be Seventh-day Adventists but are unknown to the church.

In some countries when census is taken, a much larger number of people declare themselves to be Adventists than the number of baptized persons on the church records. In fact, in some areas the concentration of Sabbathkeepers is so strong, as in the Kisii District of Kenya, that the government cannot hold elections on Saturdays. Adventists who are involved in governmental affairs at the highest level in many countries do not feel it proper to vote on Saturdays.

Early on in their African mission the Seventh-day Adventists recognized the need for preparing national leadership. This is not to say that there was not a period of time when the European and American missionaries were reluctant to turn over the reins of church governance to Africans. But since the leadership of the church has become predominantly indigenous, membership rolls have increased dramatically.

It has been thoroughly demonstrated that Christianity is not a commodity to be exported. It is a faith to be planted and transplanted. The local churches must take root in the faith–buy into it–and themselves become responsible witnesses for Christ.

The Kasai Story

One of the great stories of modern missions comes out of the Kasai, a province in the Democratic Republic of Congo (formerly Zaire). Rich in mineral deposits, especially copper, second only to South Africa in diamonds, Congo is one of the largest countries in Africa, and its capital city, Kinshaha, is exploding in population and will reach 20 million people early in the twenty-first century. Congo is rapidly becoming Africa's geopolitical center.

Some historical overview is necessary. Christianity first came to Zaire (Congo) in the fifteenth century and was established around trading posts and castles by the Portuguese.

Zaire (Congo) even had its Joan of Arc, one Beatrice, "who claimed to be the medium of St. Antony. A member of the nobility, she had been an nganga, and absorbed the idea of spirit possession from traditional religion. She destroyed both crucifixes and traditional nkisi as powerless to save, and taught that Jesus was Black, born in the [Congo] capital. Both nobles and the poor responded to her teaching; the capital city that had been sacked by the Portugese was reoccupied. She was burned at the stake for heresy in 1706, at the age of 20, her baby son narrowly escaping the same fate."[7]

Beatrice was murdered because of her opposition to tyranny, whether European or African. But by the sixteenth century almost every vestige of the faith had disappeared. The Christian mission in Zaire (Congo) was revived by Protestants in the nineteenth century, after which Catholics began to assign priests and members of religious orders. The African Independent Churches also came to Zaire (Congo) in the first decades of the twentieth century. Simon Kimbangu was the movement's leading light.

The African Independence Movement and the Congo/Zaire

The growth and spread of the Vapostori movement, the Church of the Apostles, illustrates the connection that exists between and among the African nations. In July 1932 Johan Maranke, a Shona living at the time in Rhodesia, heard a voice speaking to him, saying, "You are John the Baptist, an apostle. Now go and do my work. Go to every country and preach and convert people! Tell them not to commit adultery, not to steal, not to become angry. Baptize people and keep the Sabbath day." This was the beginning of the Church of the Apostles, or the Vapostori.

The movement spread through the Belgian Congo in 1952 and reached Kasai Occidental in 1956. In Zaire (Congo) the church came to be known as the Bapostolo, which is the Tshiluba translation of apostles. The movement grew rapidly in spite of being outlawed by the colonial authorities. In 1968 there were 40,000 Bapostolo in Zaire. They oppose medicine and hospitals, stress baptism, and worship in the open air on Saturdays, the Sabbath. They believe in a literal interpretation of the Bible, as in keeping the Ten Commandments, not eating pork, praying barefoot, not shaving their beards, and practicing polygamy. Water baptism is a basic belief.

Seventh-day Adventists and Vapostori in the Kasai hold a number of beliefs in common, such as the literal interpretation of the Bible and the Sabbath. The Vapostoli correspond a great deal to the Apostolic Sabbath Church of God, also known as the VaHossana, noted for their powerful rituals carried out in Sabbath worship services. They too may well have contributed to the religious situation in Zaire (Congo) prior to independence.

Independent Churches in Crisis

Independence from Belgium contributed to the growth of the Independent Church movement. Though powerless to stop them, the Belgian government ruthlessly repressed the Independent Churches. Kimbanguists suffered greatly in the 1920s. When independence came, men and women could teach and preach and organize their followers.

In 1971 and 1972, Prime Minister Mobuto became disturbed with the proliferation of Independent Churches in Zaire and introduced legislation into Parliament to outlaw all unregistered churches. To him, this multiplication and splintering of churches was a scandal. Some observers of the scene, however, believe that the prime minister was threatened by the burgeoning movement, over which he had so little control. The strength of the Independent Churches had taken him completely by surprise.

The government began regulating the practice of religion in Zaire. At the outset, only a few Christian denominations qualified for legalization; for example, the Catholic Church and the Kimbanguist Church. Representatives of churches had to fulfill the following conditions: be a Zairean at least 40 years old; have good conduct and a sane mind; hold a master's or doctoral degree in theology, or a degree from a four-year theological school; have not spent five months in prison; and have 100,000 Zaires (US$200,000) in a local Zaire bank. In order for a religious group to function as a church, its leader must meet the above requirements and be granted "juridical personality" from the minister of justice. (The term "juridical personality" had been suggested by DeWitt Williams, an American missionary)."

By 1973, seven religious bodies had been accorded juridical personality in Zaire (Congo). The Seventh-day Adventist Church came to be known as the "forty-second community," because it was the forty-second to receive juridical personality.

What happened immediately is that a large number of Independent Church leaders and their groups came to the Adventists for cover. At the mercy of the government, they did not want to be driven completely underground. Also, they were determined not to go back to the mission churches from which they had withdrawn (in most cases, on account of biblical and theological disputes; however, there were also leadership differences).

Seventh-day Adventist Church leaders report that many of these groups were Sabbatarian, especially in the Kasai. About 100,000 people were involved (some estimates were as high as 300,000). Adventists were hard pressed to care for this great throng of people. Discussion groups were set up around the country involving Adventist leaders and the leaders of the various Independent Churches. Some of these groups decided to identify with the Seventh-day Adventist Church, while others were not quite prepared to become a part of this union.

European missionaries are credited with having translated the Bible into Tshiluba, official language of the Kasai, in 1927. But problems connected with the translation affected the work of the Seventh-day Adventists in the region. It was discovered that, when translating the Bible from French into Tshiluba, the translators had substituted the word *Sunday* for *Sabbath*. In the 1970s many ministers and young seminarians learned French and saw this mistake. Their confidence in their church leadership was shaken. They felt that the European brethren had deceived them, taken them for being stupid and gullible. Some actually severed their connections with their former churches and became Seventh-day Adventists.

According to a legend, one of Kimbangu's sons, Diangienda, "went to Jerusalem. There he opened a box, which had another box inside it. When seven boxes had been opened, he found the 'true Bible' concealed from Africans by the missionaries."[8] Certainly, Zairean Christians remembered this legend when the inaccurate Bible translation was discovered.

We should remember that Zaire (Congo) is the country of Simon Kimbangu, who functioned in the tradition of the major African prophets. Before his death Kimbangu prophesied that a great new light would spring from the Bible after his death. There are those who believe that Kimbangu foresaw the day when the people of Zaire (Congo) would take hold of the biblical Sabbath. (Of course, African Seventh-day Adventists would say that this prophecy was fulfilled in the experience of the 1970s, when multiplied thousands of Zaireans reached out to their Sabbathkeeping brethren for fellowship and mutual support.)

In the minds of the people, the Seventh-day Adventists and the Kimbanguists were the same. Adventists were taken for Kimbanguists, and vice versa. Both Seventh-day Adventists and Kimbanguists are Bible-oriented and believe in the Ten Commandments. Another commonality in the belief system of Kimbangu and the Seventh-day Adventists is that both oppose polygamy: Kimbangu sustained a monogamous relationship for life.

The "African connection" the Sabbath in the African culture can be seen in microcosm in Zaire (Congo), and especially in the Kasai Province.

Duane McKee points out the doctrinal beliefs some of the Independent Churches hold in common with the Seventh-day Adventists. These include: "the gifts of the Holy Spirit–specifically, the gift of prophecy; the authenticity of the Bible; baptism by immersion; clean and unclean meats; the second coming of Christ; and in some cases, the seventh-day Sabbath."[9] He also mentions healing in response to intercessory prayer. African Christians exhibit great faith in healing, evidence again of their strong inclination toward a literal interpretation of the Bible.

Phil Lemon, president of the Seventh-day Adventist Church in Zaire

(Congo) when this large number of people turned to the church for assistance in the crisis, fills in some of the details:

> "When their leaders came to the minister of justice for counsel, he said, 'Look, you join a church that is being recognized and that teaches the way you believe, that teaches the Bible the way you understand.' Their question, then, was, 'How can we find that out?' The minister said, 'Well, we have here all of the doctrines of the different organizations that are recognized.'
>
> "Fourteen or fifteen different independent churches were represented. These leaders sat down at the tables and read the many beliefs and doctrines of the various recognized churches, including those of the Seventh-day Adventist Church. This was a formidable task, and they became somewhat confused. Finally they returned to the secretary of the minister of justice and asked him, 'Who does teach the Bible among all of these? Who keeps the commandments and believes the way the Bible teaches?'
>
> "The secretary to the minister of justice answered, 'The Seventh-day Adventists teach the Bible; they are the ones that really know what the Bible teaches and live the way the Bible teaches it.' This young man was the son of a Seventh-day Adventist minister who was no longer a practicing member of the church, but still remembered his father's teaching."[10]

"Very shortly after this meeting," Lemon continues, "I began to receive registered letters from them. . . . There were 12 altogether." Seventh-day Adventist Church journals report that between 1972 and 1975, 75,000 to 300,000 members of Independent and other churches requested affiliation with the Adventist Church in the Kasai. By 1985, some 44,000 had actually joined the Seventh-day Adventist Church in the Kasai. Before 1972 the Adventist work in the Kasai was very small, but at the present time there are 117,176 baptized adherents.[11]

> "Basically, one can say, in summary, that the African Independent movement was a quest for a realized religious community in and through which immediate human needs social, psychological, and physical could be met. Therefore, the Independent Religious movement was a reaction against colonialism and racism, a move toward nationalism, and an effort by the African to understand his own faith in his own setting/society. The movement also arose for selfish reasons when a leader wanted personal recognition to be known as the prophet and founder of his church."[12]

In the words of Taylor: "The Africans themselves see their movement as the reformation of an over-Europeanized, over- Americanized, and over-materialized Christianity. They want to, indeed, indigenize the faith, interpret, and apply it to give it practical meaning in their setting/society."[13]

The happenings in Kasai in the 1970s constituted a veritable sea change in the fortunes of the ancient biblical Sabbath in Africa and were indicative of a larger harvest to come.

Independent Sabbathkeeping Churches in Ghana

Jacob Nortey, a Seventh-day Adventist minister, has made a special study of two large Sabbathkeeping denominations in Ghana. The first is the Memenada Gyidifo Church, founded by Samuel Brako. Brako was a member of the Methodist Church who claimed that he had been taught the Sabbath through a series of dreams in 1924. During his dreams he heard drums which pointed out the errors of the Christian churches in respect to adultery and drunkeness.

Brako died in 1946 and was succeeded by his nephew. By this time, the church had grown to 7,000 members. The Memenada believe in baptism by immersion three times in running water. They meet for worship on Saturday mornings, and during the main worship service no foreign hymns are sung.

Nortey gives more time to the Sabbathkeeping Kristo Asafo Mission, founded by 0panin Samuel Kwadjo Safo. Early in 1969 Safo felt the need for a closer walk with God. He began to read his Bible and also to fast and pray for greater light from the book. It was not until 1971 that his prayer was completely answered. He saw clearly for the first time that the seventh day was the Sabbath. From that day forward, his small group of followers grew rapidly, until today there are more than 350 churches of the Kristo Asafo Mission throughout Ghana.

The Kristo Asafo Mission teaches that the Sabbath begins at 6:00 p.m. on Friday and continues until 6:00 p.m. on Saturday. Worship services on Saturday begin at 3:00 p.m.(the morning hours of the Sabbath are devoted to prayer, Bible study, and meditation). The teaching of the church is that no secular work should be done on the Sabbath; no unnecessarily long travels should take place.

The Asafo believe in the literal return of Jesus Christ to this earth. In support of this teaching, the church uses Matthew 25:31 and John 14:1-3. When Christ returns, there will be two distinct groups or classes of people: the righteous and the wicked. The righteous will be taken by Christ to mansions that He has prepared for them, while the wicked will be totally destroyed by the fire of God. The Kristo Asafo teach monogamy as the will of God, but are tolerant toward polygamy.[14]

Nortey poses another, very serious question: "Are African Independent Churches really Christian?" Nortey draws his answer from his longtime observation and concludes that African Independent Churches have been important in Africa and are beginning to have an impact globally. Are these churches making a contribution that is worthwhile, and are they effective in their witness for Christ?

"The appearance of the African Independent Churches has been timely to meet political needs. Independence gave the Ghanaian people an opportunity to develop their own style of worship. . . . For many years, thousands went to church in order to please the officials or to get or keep a job. To most Africans, Christianity came with, or under, the protection of one colonizing power or another."[15]

This troubled many people, and they wondered if being a Christian meant that they had to be English, or Dutch, or French. Now people began to say, "We can be Christians and also be African."

The African Independent Churches have met needs that the missionary churches ignored. The converts into the missionary-church Christianity soon realized that their newly adopted religion dealt with only part of their life's needs—only for a few hours each week. Nortey goes on to say:

> "The missionary churches dismissed issues like ghosts, witchcraft, and taboos. But to the African, these things were very real. The bonds with the spirit world could not easily be broken. They heard the spirits speak to them, they suffered the effects of spells of witchcraft, and mysterious things happened to them as a result of neglect or disobedience of the old-time rules of the tribe. So when a convert became sick and could not find healing from the hospital run by the missionary's cousin, he would secretly go anywhere for help.
>
> "By and large, the African Independent Churches have squarely addressed these neglected issues. . . . In my estimation, these constitute real contributions to Christianity. In this way, Christians can confront such issues right in their own church, without resorting to diviners."[16]

Another accomplishment of the African Independent Churches is the indigenization of Christianity. "To make Christianity belong here in Africa . . . for people to worship in their own language, and in the way that appeals to them, is definitely a plus."[17]

Nortey sees this as paying off great dividends. He commends African Independent Churches for preaching the second coming of Jesus Christ and the Ten Commandments. At the same time, he recognizes that they do not preach these major doctrines just as his church, the Seventh-day Adventists. Nortey concludes: "It is evident that the Lord is using them to do His work."[18]

Sabbath in the U.S.A. and the Caribbean

What is the status of the Sabbath in the Western world? What is the response of Africans in the diaspora? Do we find Sabbath roots among African-American Hebrew Christian groups in the New World?

C. Eric Lincoln has researched African Hebrew groups in the United States and the Caribbean. He and the scholars whose work he collects remind us that Africans and African-Americans have always had an affinity for the Old Testament and its stories of the election of the Jewish people and their covenant relationship with Yahweh. This attitude was sometimes manifested in observance of the Sabbath.

Africans in the New World, especially the English-speaking areas, were not allowed to worship God as Africans. A new religion was forced upon them. However, since the turn of the century, a number of Sabbatarian Hebraic African-American churches, temples, and synagogues have emerged along the example set by the aforementioned Church of God and Saints of Christ.

There is a "traditional sympathy within Black religion for the Old Testament" observes Deanne Shapiro, "particularly its account of the persecution and election of the Jewish people." At the turn of the century, she reports, Black preachers traveled through the South affirming that "so-called Negroes were actually the lost sheep of the house of Israel."[19]

Shapiro adds: "This tradition of sympathy for the Old Testament and antipathy toward society provided a New World for Blacks."[20] It was, she says, quoting Howard Brotz, "a world centered upon veneration for the Bible as the literal word of God [in which] lay both the contents of and the freedom for . . . innovation by Negroes in America . . . specifically the freedom to move from an admiration of the Old Testament patriarchs to the view that they were one's very own ancestors."[21]

Ethiopia and its religious practices were very Hebraist. It follows, then, that Ethiopian influence is also a Hebrew influence. This is why the Black Jews, or Israelites, of America also became Sabbathkeepers and at the same time maintained their Ethiopian and Hebrew identity. Ethiopianism (spiritual and cultural identity with Ethiopia) and Ethiopian influence have always been strong among African-Americans and Africans on the continent as well. Ethiopia became a symbolic representation of African nationalism as it came to expression in the African Independent Churches. Ethiopian-type churches were established in South Africa in the 1870s.

Shapiro points out also that there is "a growing body of Black literature including works which claimed that all Near Eastern peoples of ancient and biblical history were in fact of Black origin."[22] She references the work of Arnold Ford, who, in the 1920s, traced the development of these Hebrew movements or groups that sprang up in the United States and in the West Indies:

> "Ford offered various evidences of the African origin of the Jews. He noted the persistence of elements of Hebrew culture in Africa, such as the motif of the shield of David which was used in West Africa and facial markings upon tribal Nigerians of the Ten Commandments. . . . Ford found the roots of Judaism to be an African concept of Sinye, the native law of the Sudan which his Mende mother had identified with the Arabic word for Sinai, and thus was the law of the Torah."[23]

Some African-American religious leaders insisted that many of the slaves were converts to Judaism before coming to the New World. This is given as the reason for the emergence of Israelite groups among African-Americans. Consciousness of these Hebrew roots gave impetus to the development of Black self-awareness and pride and provided nourishment for the Black cultural renaissance at the turn of the twentieth century.

It would be a mistake, however, to say that Black religion in the Americas was driven only by cultural and political concerns. This element in Black religion, vigorous protest for civil rights and equality, "has seeped through the soil of slavery and watered the hopes and aspirations of those who would be free." The people of the African diaspora looked for a better place where every day will be Sunday, and Sabbaths would have no end.

The *Howard University Directory of African-American Religious Bodies* reviews the following African-American Hebrew communities:

One of the oldest African-American Hebrew communities is the Church of God (Black Jews), founded by Prophet Cherry in the 1890s. The church considers Saturday to be the true Sabbath. Church teachings prohibit the consumption of pork. Passover and other Jewish feasts are observed, but the celebration of Christian holidays is forbidden.

The aforementioned Church of God and Saints of Christ, founded by William S. Crowdy, celebrates all Jewish holidays and feast days. The Sabbath is observed on the seventh day (Saturday). The Ten Commandments are accepted as the standard of conduct for all mankind.

The African Hebrew Israelite Community of Jerusalem, organized in the 1960s, is the result of the vision of Ben Ammi Ben Israel (formerly Ben Carter), who was born in Chicago. In 1967 about 400 of the group were led by Ben Ammi in migration to Liberia, but their ultimate goal was Israel, which they believed to be their true African homeland.

In 1969 Carter and 38 of his follows traveled to Israel. Their Israeli headquarters is called Dimona. The African Hebrew Israelite Community Dimona experienced great suffering in their struggle to establish a viable community. The determination of the Dimona sustained them in their efforts to become a part of the Israeli nation.

Today the Dimona are recognized in the country of their adoption. They number about 2,000 in Israel. Several thousand more are in the United States of America, where their administrative headquarters is in Washington, D.C. The movement has attracted great attention throughout the world. In 1980 an official committee of the Israeli Knesset recommended that the Hebrew Israelites be granted permanent residence and land on which to settle and practice collective farming.

Holy days and the Sabbath are strictly observed in accordance with the Old Testament. Dimona prefer a vegetarian diet. Residing in Israel for more than 25 years uniquely qualifies them to conduct tours for African-Americans with a focus on the African presence in the Holy Land: "A community of 15 scholars and historians from within the ranks of the Hebrew Israelites performed the research, wrote the initial text, and coordinated the photography for the landmark African Heritage Study Bible. This included providing documentation on more than 1,000 footnotes and other references."[24]

The African Hebrew Community carries out a strong publishing endeavor. Numerous tracts and books set forth their position as Hebrew Africans. Ben Ammi writes in one of his numerous books:

> "God gave us the true rest day, the seventh day (Saturday), designed to keep us continually in the knowledge and true worship of the one God. It was also set aside as a memorial to God's Creation. However, the Europeans have pushed upon the deluded world the observance of a day on which the pagans worship the sun. The first day of the pagan week, called Sunday, is the day on which the pagans worship the all-conquering sun. It is not the Lord's day, and has absolutely nothing to do with the resurrection of Jesus, to which its existence is attributed.
>
> "Sunday was designated as the first day of the week, according to pagan tradition, because of the adversary's refusal to accept the way of life set forth by God. . . . The day used today as the Sabbath was originally called Sun day of worship. But to deceive the whole world, they made it one word Sunday—and said it was the day of the Lord. But we can plainly see when we simply separate and give its original form, the sun-day is still the day of the pagan sun worship. No people have changed their god or manner of worship except the Children of Israel, the sons of God."[25]

Ben Ammi also says: "Contemporary apostate Christianity has a new Sabbath (Sunday, or the first day, rather than Saturday, the seventh day), cycles of time, holidays, contempt for the Law, prophecies that are no more, and no worship of the holy one of Israel none of which were ever consecrated by Yeshua. Consequently, we may absolutely conclude none of the latter believers are/were followers of Yeshua the Hebrew Messiah."[26]

It should be of interest to Africans in diaspora that most of the Hebrew Christian movements seize upon the Sabbath as a mark of identity and also of protest against the European Latin Church. Ben Ammi speaks for a much larger constituency than the Dimona.

End Notes

[1]Daneel, p. 35.

[2]"The Abayudaya Jews of Uganda," Web page.

[3]Mbiti, p. 249.

[4]*Ibid.*, p. 251.

[5]Karst, letter.

[6]*Ibid.*

[7]Isichei, p. 65.

[8]*Ibid.*, p. 202.

[9]McKey.

[10]Lemon Report.

[11]*SDA Statistical Report for 1996.*

[12]McKey.

[13]*Ibid.*, p. 29.

[14]Nortey.

[15]*Ibid.*

[16]*Ibid.*, p. 36.

[17]*Ibid.*

[18]*Ibid.*

[19]Deanne Shapiro, "Factors in the Development of Black Judaism," in C. Eric Lincoln, *The Black Experience in Religion* (Garden City, N.Y.: Doubleday, 1974), pp. 258.

[20]*Ibid.*, p. 259.

[21]*Ibid.*

[22]*Ibid.*, p. 263.

[23]*Ibid.*, p. 269.

[24]*Howard University Directory.*

[25]Ben Ami-Ben Israel, *God, the Black Man, and Truth* (Washington, D.C.: Communicators Press, 1982), p. 194.

[26]———, *Yeshua the Hebrew Messiah or Jesus the Christian Christ* (Washington, D.C.: Communicators Press, 1996), p. 31.

CHAPTER ELEVEN
TOMORROW

"This is the purpose that is purposed upon the whole earth: and this is the hand that is stretched out upon all the nations. For the LORD of hosts hath purposed, and who shall disannul it? and his hand is stretched out, and who shall turn it back?" (Isa. 14:26, 27).

"Every matter that has a beginning must also have an end" (African proverb).

Parable for Today

The young African lad's story that we referred to in an earlier chapter is a parable for today. It strikes all the right themes. There is a twofold emphasis: the ancient biblical Sabbath and the second coming of Messiah Jesus. This is a parable for our times because the little fellow's story reflects trends and directions in African theology today. The story anticipates an end, closure: "The King is coming back!"

While the theologies of the West are de-emphasizing Scripture, African theology moves in the other direction toward a more serious biblical orientation. The African resonance to end-time/last-day issues is reflected in the declaration of Nigerian evangelicals: "In the light of the imminent return of our Lord Jesus Christ, who says, 'Surely I am coming soon'(Rev. 22:20), we see evangelism as an urgent task for the church."[1]

Mark R. Shaw, one of the younger missionary theologians, asks the question, "What does such a futuristic and Christ-centered eschatology offer to Africa?" In answer, he quotes a thoughtful comment about Western Christianity by David Bosch:

> "We [Evangelical Christianity] too easily identify God's will and power with ours. . . . It belongs to the essence of Christian teleology [movement toward God's ideal future] that it doubts that the eschatological vision can be fully realized in history. . . . The ultimate triumph remains uniquely God's gift . . . if we turn off the lighthouse of eschatology we can only grope in darkness and despair."[2]

The lad's parable covers a period of time salvation history from the Ascension to the Second Coming. The true focus is the great king who had 10 sons. "Then one day the king decided to go on a journey." In His parousia (Second Coming) parables, Messiah Jesus hints that there will be an apparent delay between His ascension and His second coming:

"For the kingdom of heaven is as a man traveling into a far country, who called his own servants, and delivered unto them his goods" (Matt. 25:14). "For the Son of man is as a man taking a far journey, who left his house, and gave authority to his servants, and to every man his work, and commanded the porter to watch" (Mark 13:34). "And he called his ten servants, and delivered them ten pounds, and said unto them, Occupy till I come" (Luke 19:13).

Sabbath holds the narrative together. During the interval between Jesus' ascension and return, the prime minister was charged with the responsibility of caring for His sons (the Ten Commandments): "While I am away, take care of my sons." In the story, it was the prime minister's attempt to remove the fourth son the fourth being the fourth commandment, the Sabbath commandment that provoked the king's wrath. The prime minister's substitution of his son in place of the king's son is unconscionable.

The punch line to the story, of course, is that "the King is coming back!"

Those African Christians who have suffered so intensely understand the nature of the conflict. It is Messiah Jesus against the Caesars of this world. In New Testament times, Christians were familiar with these realities. They had to face them every day. It was indeed Christ or Caesar. And they developed a language, encoded in symbols and imagery, to deal with the situation, which theologians call apocalyptic. This is why the book of Revelation appeals so powerfully to African Christians and African Christians in diaspora.

Today, as never before, demonic powers are at work. Another dimension must be addressed, a special kind of discourse is needed, a new vocabulary. As Messiah Jesus said, the situation calls for "new bottles," a new orientation.

The African prophets looked for a city. Their land had been confiscated. The graves of their ancestors had been defiled. Sundkler is convinced that "the book of Revelation has kindled in the heart of the Zionist prophet a longing to enter the heavenly Jerusalem."[3]

African Christians charged the missionary churches with evading their questions about the prophetic passages of the Bible, especially Daniel and the Revelation. A Zambian Anglican who later became a Seventh-day Adventist said of his first church:

> "When I asked them about the Bible they would not give me true answers. I was very much puzzled about Daniel and Revelation. But they said, 'these are only dreams. You need not read those books. They are very hard and nobody can understand those books. It is

better to read the Gospels.' But there was a great demand in my mind to understand these."[4]

Early African-American preachers were also much into the powerful symbolism of the so-called apocalyptic Scriptures—the books of Revelation, Daniel, and Ezekiel—and the apocalyptic sayings of Jesus (Matthew 24; Mark 13; Luke 21) and Paul (2 Thessalonians 2:1-10).

Why does the book of Revelation especially appeal to African people on the continent and in diaspora? In some measure, it is because in this literature (apocalyptic), God is in control, in spite of the way things may seem to be. Passages such as Revelation 11:12 and 21:5, 18 picture a God who is omnipotent. In the book of Revelation we find the end of the story, and God is still in command. African-American Christians are fond of saying, "Everything is going to be all right. God is on His throne; all is right with the world." This word speaks of things that have not taken place as if they have already come to pass. The apocalyptic vision helps Christians to live in God's future while still in the present.

The great African prophets saw themselves as God's advance agents. They were convicted that Yahweh was bringing about a new age for His people. One of the characteristic features of the prophetic message is its expectation of things to come, things which must "shortly come to pass" (Rev. 1:1). There is a future orientation in their teaching. The African prophets were anxious that the people personally feel God's call to prepare themselves for a coming act of God and to seek their salvation.

They made strong demands on the religious faith of their followers. They went right to the root of the problem of morality, showing that all morality involves the heart and is something internal. There was urgency in their message. Turn to God now; destroy the fetishes now; break off from sin now; stop, cease, desist, be baptized now! They were convinced that justice and morality will ultimately triumph in this world because this is God's plan, and He has the power to make it succeed.

The Bantu prophets placed a great deal of emphasis on the New Jerusalem and its gates (Rev. 21:2, 12). The sermons of the African-American preaching fathers and the African-American spirituals also use the New Jerusalem symbolism and its gates very effectively. The lyrics of the spiritual declare that there are "twelve gates to the city, hallelu!" The church and its spiritual leaders were "the holders of the keys."

In the setting of the Nazarite Church, "the Sabbath is the key, so that the gates may be opened"[5] (these are the words of Nazarite hymn No. 212). The followers of William Saunders Crowdy thanked God for the prophet who "brought us the keys." A common theme in Sabbatarian Israelite dreams is approaching the gates of the city and being told they need to have the key—the Sabbath.

Shembe's Prophecy: How the Sabbath Was Restored to His Followers

> "Surely the Lord GOD will do nothing, but he revealeth his secret unto his servants the prophets" (Amos 3:7).
>
> "And they that shall be of thee shall build the old waste places: thou shalt raise up the foundations of many generations; and thou shalt be called, The repairer of the breach, The restorer of paths to dwell in" (Isa. 58:12).

Isaiah Shembe and William Saunders Crowdy saw themselves as restorers of the Eden Sabbath, not simply for Africans and the descendants of Africans, but for all people. Becken, Hexam, and Oosthuizen have done extensive oral history study among Shembe's followers. They report the following eyewitness account, as told them by Aaron Grumede and Petros M Dhlomo:

> "When we were on the mountain Nhlangakazi in January 1922, Shembe said: 'Our Father and I have concealed something here on the mountain, when the great ancient kingdoms abolished the day of the Lord. When God had created heaven and earth and all things, He rested on the Sabbath day and said: "You people, let us rest on this day." Because of its restrictions, the ancient kingdoms tried to push it aside and chose the day, which they liked, the Sunday, and they said, that they praised the resurrection of the Lord on that day. But the Sabbath was a great blessing to those who observed it, and when somebody asked God for something, God gave it to him in those ancient days because of this Sabbath day.'
>
> "The Congregation asked the Beginner of the Way, that God may restore this day to them, if we would agree to it, because they liked it. The lord said: 'No, my children, I am afraid to bring this your petition to Jehova; because when something has been lost from home, it does not come back. For when this day will become too difficult to keep for you, what will you do? For it has been abolished, and it will not come back. It may destroy all of you together with your coming generations. Therefore, I am afraid to ask this for you from Jehova.' The congregation was weeping, because they wished, that the Sabbath should be restored. When they had heard its rules and its blessings, they promised to try hard to keep its rules and regulations.
>
> "After a few days following this petition of the congregation there on the mountain Nhlangakazi, the lord rose and said: 'My children, I inform you, that Jehova has accepted your request and agreed to give you the Sabbath day. But I don't know how this will be. For with this announcement of today, the old Sunday, on which

> you used to worship, is no longer among you. Today, we return to the day of God, on which He rested after creating heaven and earth, and told us, that He also should rest on this day. Today, I place this yoke on your shoulders, together with your children and your coming generations.' The congregation accepted all these words. In this way, the Sabbath day was restored."[6]

Here is an actual occurrence that has found its way into oral history, an overview of the Sabbath as divine institution, the saga of the perennial controversy, man's refusal to yield supreme authority to His Creator. The responsibility is placed squarely on "the great ancient kingdoms" that abolished the day of the Lord. Shembe always refers to Sabbath as the day of the Lord Yahweh's day. In Shembe's theology, the Sabbath is rooted in Creation.

Yahweh's explicit command to the people was, "You people, rest on this day." Shembe sees the covenant aspect of Sabbath. We rest, and in doing so, we join Jehovah in His rest: "For he that is entered into his rest, he also hath ceased from his own works, as God did from his" (Heb. 4:10).

We have already seen that in many African societies there is a work/rest rhythm that is firmly imbedded in the culture. Yahweh invites humankind to enter His rest, His "cathedral of time." In the African view, this is not something completely metaphysical, intangible, "spiritual." Sabbath is something concrete and substantial, comprehensible to every human being, the ultimate sign of Yahweh's territorial authority: "Worship him that made heaven, and earth, and the sea, and the fountains of waters" (Rev. 14:7).

The cosmos is His domain. "Do not trespass here!" There are physical boundaries, a day consisting of seconds, minutes, hours "evening and morning" with a definite beginning and a definite end.

Pardon Mwansa, a Zambian scholar, informs me that in the Bemba language Sabbath means "to stop." Actually, it does not just refer to stopping in general, but to knock off, to stop working.[7] Again, the African idea of Sabbath is bound up with rest, and that rest is tied to a specific day. Yahweh deals in specificities; He sets boundaries.

Shembe points out the natural antipathy on the part of the ancient kingdoms toward the Sabbath. The Sabbath has its restrictions; it is a binding covenant that the King enjoins upon His subjects. It is to be expected that earthly rulers should resist the rule of Yahweh. They view it as a threat to and a dilution of their authority, and would rather have the people say, "We have no king but Caesar."

The tendency of all human rulers is toward absolute power and authority, which is Yahweh's prerogative. They find the covenant aspect of Sabbath too restrictive, too binding. Furthermore, it interferes with commerce as well as with carnal pleasure (see Isa. 58).

"Because of its restrictions," Shembe says, "the ancient kingdoms tried to push it aside and chose the day which they liked, the Sunday, and they said that they praised the resurrection of the Lord on that day."

Shembe recognizes that Africa has no Sunday tradition. Sunday is always an import to Africa, brought to its shores by Europeans. In this he is identifying those "great ancient kingdoms" that "abolished the day of the Lord." Clearly, these powers are the imperial church and her successors, who imposed the imposter day upon their subjects. The institution of Sunday was a deliberate choice. Sabbath was made a day of mourning and fasting; Sunday was made a day of feasting and happiness.

When Shembe says, "Because of its restrictions, the ancient kingdoms tried to push it aside," does he have in mind the centuries-long Ethiopian struggle to maintain the integrity of the ancient biblical Sabbath? He is certainly indicating that the change was not only inappropriate, but that it could not really alter God's basic contract with humanity: "My covenant will I not break, nor alter the thing that is gone out of my lips" (Ps. 89:34).

Nor could any human substitution override the preordination of Yahweh or replace His special seal. The change of Sabbath could never obtain the approval of God. It was not His choice. Human beings have had the audacity to prefer their own choice over Yahweh's, but in so doing, they have disdained their Creator's gift.

The resurrection of Jesus is given as the reason for their choice, but Shembe refuses this line of reasoning and insists that the Sabbath has always been a great blessing to those who have observed it. The Old Testament idea of covenant is not a contract or agreement between equals. It is not something hammered out at the bargaining table. It is something imposed on subjects and vassals by a superior personage. It is always unilateral: "For who hath known the mind of the Lord? or who hath been his counsellor" (Rom. 11:34).

"But the Sabbath was a great blessing to those who observed it, and when somebody asked God for something, God gave it to him in those ancient days because of this Sabbath day." This is in the spirit of Isaiah 56 and 58, where great blessings accrue to those who turn aside from their ways to follow Yahweh.

Shembe sees the Sabbath issue as bringing conflict: "I'm afraid to bring this your petition to Jehova; because when something has been lost from home, it does not come back. For when this day will become too difficult to keep for you, what will you do? . . . It may destroy all of you together with your coming generations. Therefore, I am afraid to ask this for you from Jehova." This is an amazing statement and corresponds with the predictions of Daniel and Paul, who pointed out that a power would come to world prominence that would attempt to "change God's times and laws" (Dan. 7:25).

Paul speaks about a man of sin: "Let no man deceive you by any means: for that day shall not come, except there come a falling away first, and that man of sin be revealed, the son of perdition; who opposeth and exalteth himself above all that is called God, or that is worshipped; so that he as God sitteth in the temple of God, showing himself that he is God" (2 Thess. 2:3, 4). And John the revelator has his number (Rev. 13:18).

Shembe was right when he predicted the day will come when it will be too difficult for them to keep "this day": "And that no man might buy or sell, save he that had the mark, or the name of the beast, or the number of his name. Here is wisdom. Let him that hath understanding count the number of the beast: for it is the number of a man; and his number is six hundred threescore and six" (Rev. 13:17, 18).

Shembe is forthright with the people. He said there would be difficulty associated with this day, hardship, persecution. If I understand the testimony of the biblical witnesses correctly, controversy over this day has much to do with the final showdown between those cosmic forces to whom the people of earth give their supreme allegiance, Messiah Jesus or the enemy of all righteousness.

"These shall make war with the Lamb, and the Lamb shall overcome them: for he is Lord of lords, and King of kings: and they that are with him are called, and chosen, and faithful" (Rev. 17:14).

But the people agreed to all that Shembe said and made covenant with God: "Gather my saints together unto me; those that have made a covenant with me by sacrifice" (Ps. 50:5).

The Sabbath is not to be taken lightly, because it involves the sovereignty of God, His right to govern His creation, to establish His universal reign. African Christians, and indeed, all Christians everywhere who embrace Yahweh's day of rest, see the Sabbath in this wider setting.

End Notes

[1]Mark R. Shaw, *The Kingdom of God in Africa: A Short History of African Christianity* (Grand Rapids, Mich.: Baker Books, 1996), p. 281.

[2]*Ibid.*, p. 282.

[3]Sundkler, p. 293.

[4]Isichei, p. 5.

[5]Sundkler, p. 290.

[6]Irving Hexham and Gerhardus C. Oosthuizen, eds., *The Story of Isaiah Shembe*, Hans-Jurgin Becken, trans.(Queenstown, Ontario: Mellon, 1997), pp. 94, 95.

[7]Pardon Mwansa, research paper.

CHAPTER TWELVE

THE LARGER VISION

"Open ye the gates, that the righteous nation which keepeth the truth [the commandments of God] may enter in" (Isa. 26:2).

There is a big picture, a larger canvas, a cosmic television screen, on which the great drama is playing itself out from the African perspective, in an African key. African and Old Testament concepts exhibit a startling similarity. African stories about creation and the origin of human beings, the fall of humankind and their rebellion against God, recall the Old Testament Scriptures.

In one African creation story, the Sky God is angry with his children because they fight each other. However inadequate this description may be, it is not antithetical to the depiction of the Hebrew prophets. In the Apocalypse of John, the imagery and symbolism are straight out of the Old Testament. The law court is the organizing principle.

In Old Testament times, especially the times of the judges, the decisions were made at the gates. The elders gathered here and heard the cases, and at the gates the antagonists and protagonists presented their cases with vigor. The judges listened attentively. Friends and witnesses were allowed to speak. The drama was played out to conclusion. When the decision was given, all the people agreed. Often they burst out in praise of the wisdom of the judge.

In Daniel's court, the followers of Yahweh were pronounced in the right. In the book of James, it is the poor of this world, the heirs of the kingdom, who are justified by verdict. The book of Revelation takes all of these strands and weaves a tapestry of cosmic judgment and justice. In the book of Revelation, John has the officers of the court presenting to the saints affidavits of victory, testaments of their loyalty to Yahweh. "Blessed are they that do his commandments, that they may have the tree of life, and may enter in through the gates into the city (Rev. 22:14)." They have "a right to the tree of life and may enter into the Gates of the city."

In fact, to carry the law court scene further, the great accuser, Satan, is drummed out of court, disbarred! Paul's words again are to the point: "Let God be true and every man a liar!" In biblical terms, those whom the verdict favors are, indeed, the elect. They go through the gates.

Justice and Equity

The Sabbath speaks of justice and equity. Africans, who have suffered much at the hands of cruel rulers, domestic and foreign, resonate to the idea of justice. In a famous speech to the Maryknoll Sisters, Julius Nyerere said: "Kindness is not enough; charity is not enough. . . . The church must work with the people in positive tasks of building a future of social justice."[1]

Lawrence A. Jones, speaking of the African-American slave, says: "On the one hand, their primary faith was anchored in the convictions concerning sovereignty, righteousness, justice, and [the] mercy of God. They looked forward to the New Jerusalem the city of God."[2] Messiah Jesus is concerned about justice.

In Isaiah 56 we find a time frame. Yahweh's judgments are imminent; His "righteousness is to be revealed." There is a latter-day setting. Yahweh calls for a revival in covenant faithfulness among His people, those who profess to serve Him. The Sabbath covenant is enjoined upon every member of the community, ordinary people, "strangers who have joined themselves to the Lord," eunuchs, outcasts. Yahweh promises to bring them all to His holy mountain, His house of prayer.

The playing field is enlarged to include the entire human family: "Everyone that keepeth the Sabbath from polluting it, and taketh hold of my covenant" (Isa. 56:6). In the Hebrew prophet's view, "taking hold of," or observing, the Sabbath is a kind of pledge or loyalty oath to Yahweh. There is definitely a covenant aspect here (see verses 4 and 6). Yahweh universalizes the covenant when He says: "Yet will I gather others to him, beside those that are gathered unto him" (verse 8). He offers this covenant to "all people."

Evangelical Christians proclaim often and with great fervor that Jesus is Lord. But at the same time, they fail to recognize that Messiah Jesus declared with great authority that "the Son of man is Lord even of the sabbath day" (Matt. 12:8). "Therefore the Son of man is Lord also of the sabbath" (Mark 2:28).

Sabbath to Jesus meant liberation, freedom, human dignity, and self-worth. This is the true meaning of the proclamation "Jesus is Lord." Sabbath, therefore, stands for the Lordship of Jesus Christ. Africans on the continent and in the diaspora must bring this critical matter of the day of worship to the biblical test, and under the Lordship of Christ, as many of their fellow Christians have done. They must follow the testimony of Scripture, even if it means rejecting the traditions of the ancestors.

The biblical significance of the Sabbath of the Lord, as we have shown, is rooted in Creation. Many theologians deny that the Sabbath is a Creation ordinance. They insist that the Sabbath was made by Moses for the nation of Israel only (see Ex. 16; Deut. 5:12-15). The deep issue at stake in this theological debate is the credibility of the Creation record in Genesis 1, 2, and its reflection in the fourth commandment in Exodus 20.

One American theologian gave this assessment of the origin of the Sabbath:

> "According to the canon of Scripture, the 'creation interpretation' of the Sabbath is affirmed to be theologically prior to the 'redemption interpretation.' This means, therefore, that the Sabbath is always binding upon all men whether they obey it or not! In the redemption of Israel from Egypt, the Sabbath is not established for the first time, but is reestablished; the moral law is not first published at Sinai, but is re-published there.
>
> "Hence, because the law of the Sabbath is grounded in the order of creation itself and pertains to all creatures, the traditional Christian interpretation of the Sabbath as a ceremony now abolished by Jesus Christ is incorrect".[3]

Hans K. LaRondelle, Adventist theologian, states: "The basic motive of the threefold message of Revelation 14 is that of restoration! It serves the same purpose as Isaiah's call to a backsliding Israel [in] Isaiah 58:1."[4]

I refer again to Shembe's warning: "For when this day will become too difficult to keep for you, what will you do? . . . It may destroy all of you together with your coming generations." Shembe's prediction is not at variance with the biblical testimony. The cosmic endgame will involve a showdown over the issue of worship. And Sabbath is at the heart of worship.

It is the Lordship of Christ, obedience to Yahweh's commandments, that brings us to the showdown: "Here is a call for the endurance of the saints, those who keep the commandments of God and hold fast to the faith of Jesus" (Rev. 14:12, NRSV). "Then the dragon was angry with the woman, and went off to make war on the rest of her children, those who keep the commandments of God and hold the testimony of Jesus (Rev. 12:17, NRSV).

> "In particular, he [Shembe] emphasized that only through observation of the Sabbath could the Zulu nation be fully restored to its independence and former glory.
>
> . . . We can safely say that the mission of Isaiah Shembe was to restore the dignity of the Zulu person and the independence of the Zulu nation, who suffered greatly when they resisted the invasions of their country first by the Boers and later the British.
>
> "The aim of Isaiah Shembe was to restore his people to the previous glory, and this, he believed, could be done on the basis of God's presence among the Zulu people in the same way as God had revealed His presence to ancient Israel. In 1913, two years after he founded the Church of the amaNazaretha, he had a vision which led

> him to declare that the church accepted the Sabbath as God's holy day instead of the Christian Sunday. As a result of this vision, he considered the Sabbath to be the key to Zulu fortunes because it was the test of true obedience to God."[5]

Shembe in Africa and William Saunders Crowdy in America both recognized the importance of the ancient Creation Sabbath to the welfare of Africans and people of African descent. The Sabbath is the key, because it brings with it awareness of our common ancestry, our relationship to Yahweh, the Father, the great Nana. It also makes us keenly aware of our responsibility before Yahweh. Obedience in all things is required of the sons and daughters of the Most High God.

Shembe and Crowdy chose the Creation Sabbath, which was and still is a radical option. The aim of Crowdy's movement was to "perpetuate a union among the saints of Christ and maintain a correspondence with all other churches of God throughout the U.S. and the whole world. We therefore purpose to maintain and keep the commandments of God and the sayings of Jesus according to the Bible."[6] Compare this text from the book of Revelation: "Here is the patience of the saints: here are they that keep the commandments of God, and the faith of Jesus" (Rev. 14:12).

Crowdy believed that the Sabbath was the appropriate day of worship because it had African roots.

Tale of Two Cities

> "The Old Testament prophet, in fact, may be regarded as a privileged press-reporter admitted to sessions of the heavenly Privy Council, in order that he may subsequently publish to Israel what is God's secret policy, and what part Israel is to play in implementing it. By the same token, John, believing that the church faces an immediate life-and-death battle, which is not theirs alone but God's, is summoned to the control room at Supreme Headquarters."[7]

I have referred to the powerful appeal of the New Jerusalem to the African prophets. They "looked for a city." However, this is to be expected because of their emphasis on eschatology the last days and the end-time. The biblical description of the ultimate habitat appeals to landless people wherever they happen to live. The motif appeals also to Christians in all lands, of all races, in the developed world and in the so-called developing countries. Every committed follower of Messiah Jesus is, to some extent, an exile, a permanent minority, a part of a counterculture community.

There are two symbolic cities that dominate the landscape of salvation history. These two cities, Babylon and the New Jerusalem, spoken of by the Hebrew prophets, loom large, especially in the book of Revelation, the most thoroughly Old Testament book of the New Testament.

John the revelator skillfully uses the Old Testament to craft a brilliant description of a dazzling city of imposing power and fabulous wealth that rewards those who imbibe its idolatrous philosophy and self-indulgent lifestyle. The prophet exclaims:

> "'O Babylon, city of power! In one day your doom has come!' . . . No one buys [your] . . . cargoes of gold, silver, precious stones and pearls; fine linen, purple, silk and scarlet cloth; every sort of citron wood, and articles of every kind made of ivory, costly wood, bronze, iron and marble; . . . of cinnamon and spice, of incense, myrrh and frankincense, of wine and olive oil, of fine flour and wheat; cattle and sheep; horses and carriages; and bodies and souls of men. . . . 'Woe! Woe, O great city, dressed in fine linen, purple and scarlet, and glittering with gold, precious stones and pearls!'" (Rev. 18:10-16, NIV).

Extremely self-confident, "in her heart she boasts, 'I sit as queen; I am not a widow, and I will never mourn'" (verse 7, NIV).

However, it is all an illusion smoke and mirrors. Babylon is really a city of slavery and death whose power is sustained by sorcery: "By your magic spell all the nations were led astray" (verse 23, NIV). Its doom is already pronounced: "Woe! Woe, O great city, O Babylon, city of power! In one hour your doom has come!" (verse 10, NIV). "Babylon will be thrown down, never to be found again" (verse 21, NIV).

In contrast to Babylon is "Jerusalem that is above [which] is free, and she is our mother" (Gal. 4:26, NIV). Clearly, the New Jerusalem is a city of freedom and truth, a city of life and light: "But you have come to Mount Zion, to the heavenly Jerusalem, the city of the living God. You have come to thousands upon thousands of angels in joyful assembly" (Heb. 12:22, NIV).

Babylon, Major Paradigm

Christians of the African diaspora have placed a great deal of emphasis on the Exodus motif. It has served well. But if one follows the path or sweep of the prophets, the movement of their prophecies toward time's end, the Babylon motif becomes more pertinent and relevant. African-American theologians are suggesting a new paradigm based on a recapitulation of the Babylonian captivity and the Jewish diaspora: "In contemporary Black culture the configurations of captivity and diaspora appear most compelling."[8]

Babylon is the major prophetic paradigm of our times, the master symbol that speaks to the present realities. The Babylon metaphor is the final depiction of ultimate reality, stark and shocking. Only in the apocalyptic portions of Scripture, especially Daniel and Revelation, is evil really shown up for what it is. We must keep in mind that apocalyptic is a different world of discourse, with a vocabulary and word pictures all its own.

What, then, is Babylon? A city in opposition to God. Its citizens "will make war on the Lamb, and the Lamb will conquer them, for he is Lord of lords and King of kings, and those with him are called and chosen and faithful" (Rev. 17:14, NRSV). Babylon is the city of the counterfeit, the great illusion, the last and final representation or manifestation of accumulated evil in totality.

If Egypt is a place of physical bondage, of forced labor, of the taskmaster's lash, then Babylon is a place where there is the attempt to make slavery pleasant. The ultimate captivity is not physical, but spiritual, psychic, mental. Babylon is the epitome of deceit. In the first literal Babylonian captivity, the people were given garden plots. Captive youth were given scholarships to the university; they were integrated into the larger society.

Babylon swallowed up people, suffused and absorbed them. Many of the captives became wealthy and succumbed to the "good life." Most refused to leave this good life to face the arduous, even dangerous, task of rebuilding Jerusalem and the temple. It was difficult to hear the prophet's message in the midst of a city of such sophistication and pleasure. Babylon's culture is a culture of the senses. Babylon is built on a mirage, an illusion. Babylon's inhabitants are intoxicated, deluded.

There is the attempt on the part of Babylon to make slavery seem as freedom. Babylon's slaves are drunk with the "wine of her fornication." They like it. Babylon gives the appearance of being progressive, liberal, permissive. Our Black foreparents would have used the word conjure: "Satan is a liar and a conjurer too. If you don't watch out, he'll conjure you!"

The Babylon motif becomes more dominant in history's twilight era. The Babylon motif obtains in a time and place of prosperity good economy, an advanced civilization, swollen with hubris and pride of accomplishment. Babylon's citizens commend themselves, toast themselves, drink to themselves. They suffer the ultimate delusion. All are slaves, even the elite, the ruling class. Everyone in Babylon is a victim of some sort. The underclass is deceived to the extent that they envy and imitate the "beautiful crowd," who are as much in slavery as they, held captive without physical walls.

The Sabbath as token of remembrance and identity becomes increasingly important to the followers of Messiah Jesus, who must live in a culture that aggressively seeks to destroy the power of these tokens of remembrance:

"Moreover also I gave them my sabbaths, to be a sign between me and them, that they might know that I am the LORD that sanctify them. And hallow my sabbaths; and they shall be a sign between me and you, that ye may know that I am the LORD your God" (Eze. 20:12, 20). The exiles must keep the memory alive of who they are and where they have come from, their roots.

Sabbath, that ancient institution from Eden, reminds us that we are stewards and not proprietors. Sabbath saves us from giving ultimacy to any institution or organization other than the kingdom of God. Sabbath calls for the worship of Yahweh: "Fear God, and give glory to him; for the hour of his judgment is come: and worship him that made heaven, and earth, and the sea, and the fountains of waters" (Rev. 14:7, 8).

Sabbath means that we believe in God as a perfect Creator. George Elliott says: "It [Sabbath] is set as the perpetual guardian of man against that spiritual infirmity which has everywhere led him to a denial of the God who made him, or to the degradation of that God into a creature made with his own hands."[9]

We must not buy into the corrupt system that the biblical writers call Babylon. (The Israelite African churches used Jesus' and John's term "the world" in ways that suggest the meaning of Babylon; see John 17:14, 25; 1 John 2:15-17.) This would be to exchange physical bondage for the greater spiritual bondage. African-Americans must take care that, while demanding their piece of the pie, they do not fall victim to the seductive dream. Christians, followers of Yahweh, must resist giving in to the corrupt system of this world.

Sabbath focuses on the Creator God as the one who invests His creation with meaning and value, and it points to Yahweh as owner-operator. Sabbath is a covenant, a golden clasp, that binds God to His children. His children find their identity in Sabbath. This sign of purity and ownership (2 Tim. 2:19) also serves as seal and imprimatur, Yahweh's instrument of liberation and His super affirmation of the value of the man whom He has created.

Yahweh's Lawsuit

> "Hear the word of the LORD, ye children of Israel: for the LORD hath a controversy with the inhabitants of the land, because there is no truth, nor mercy, nor knowledge of God in the land. By swearing, and lying, and killing, and stealing, and committing adultery, they break out, and blood toucheth blood. Therefore shall the land mourn, and every one that dwelleth therein shall languish, with the beasts of the field, and with the fowls of heaven; yea, the fishes of the sea also shall be taken away" (Hosea 4:1-3).

"God forbid: yea, let God be true, but every man a liar; as it is written, That thou mightest be justified in thy sayings, and mightest overcome when thou art judged" (Rom. 3:4).

One of the Akan appellations for the High God is the great Nana. This is the name that is used to describe Yahweh as the universal Father. It corresponds somewhat to the Christian concept of the fatherhood of God. Danquah states it quite eloquently when he says:

"The Great Ancestor (the Nana) is the great Father, and all men of the blood of that ancestor are of him, and are of one blood with all other men created of his blood and breath. Life, human life, is one continuous blood, from the originating blood of the great source of that blood. The continuance of that blood in the continuance of the community is the greatest single factor of existence . . . anything short of that ideal makes life a degradation, a contradiction of what men of the ancestral blood, one in the Great Ancestor, should be inspired by."[10]

The great Nana is displeased by man's inhumanity to man. He is displeased whenever the social contract is broken: "The discipline of the universal Nana would demand that if there is even one person, one race, one nation, which puts others in a bad light, does damage to them, then the universal community is bad."[11] An elderly Nyasaland man put it this way:

"A good town is where the head man and the older people are respected by all, and where they, in their turn, give thought to all, even the children. It is only a good town where the young have respect for their fathers and mothers and all their relations, and where no person makes an attempt to do damage to another. If there is even one person who puts others in a bad light, or does damage to them, then the town is bad."[12]

In the African view, as well as in the vision of the Hebrew prophets, it is people's inhumanity to their fellows that pollutes the earth and brings its inhabitants under the judgment of God. Therefore, the great Nana institutes a lawsuit against the nations. He intends to bring closure to man's rebellious activity. Rebellion must have an end!

Danquah insists that man must discover the Nana of ultimate being, who is, in fact, the father of us all. The great Nana brings lawsuit because people have forgotten Him or do not understand or acknowledge Him as universal father: "Until man at last discovers the Nana of ultimate being, and not merely a small family or race or tribe or ethnic group, or larger unit of humanity such as Western or Asiatic, he stands under the judgment of God."[13]

This Akan understanding of the judgment and justice of God corresponds to Paul's great statement of belief: "Because he hath appointed a day, in the which he will judge the world in righteousness" (Acts 17:31).

Yahweh sees this failure to recognize Him as the supreme Nana as an attempt to place Him in a box, to manipulate Him, to use Him, to reduce Him to the status of tribal god, and to deny Him His position as Father of all human beings in African terms, to conjure Him.

There is a social contract that Yahweh imposed upon the human family at Creation (see 2 John 5). The Sabbath is a sign of the relationship existing between God and His people, a sign that they are His obedient subjects, that they keep holy His law. The observance of the Sabbath is the means ordained by God of preserving a knowledge of Himself and of distinguishing between His loyal subjects and the transgressors of His law.

The Akan would say that the great Nana is aggrieved when this contract is broken, even in the slightest degree. The Hebrew prophets would say Yahweh is wounded. He remonstrates with the people. His anger is aroused. This is the basis of the Hebrew prophets' message about judgment and justice. Justice is more important than benevolence. In the Akan concept of Nana and the biblical concept of the Fatherhood of God, Yahweh links man and his Maker "in relationship that is communal from its first beginnings."[14]

The entire old Testament is about this lawsuit. This is how the Hebrew prophets thought of it. And on behalf of Yahweh, they present a bill of particulars. They explain what it is that constitutes breach of contract. The suit is initiated because of the sins of the people the breaking of the social contract.

Bill of Particulars

Isaiah Shembe took the "ancient kingdoms" to task for violating this contract. "Because of its restrictions, the ancient kingdoms tried to push it [Sabbath] aside and chose the day, which they liked, the Sunday." When the "ancient nations" (the European ecclesiastical establishment) deliberately changed the day of worship from Saturday to Sunday, Yahweh was aggrieved because human beings had acted unilaterally and presumptuously. A dissonant note was brought in that fractured the harmony and peace that Yahweh wished for His children to enjoy.

The prophet Daniel makes the specific charge in the seventh chapter of his book: "And he shall speak great words against the most High, and shall wear out the saints of the most High, and think to change times and laws: and they shall be given into his hand until a time and times and the dividing of time" (Dan. 7:25). Here is reference to those ancient kingdoms the Latin Church that assumed the prerogatives of the Most High God, and, in fact, did attempt to change Yahweh's royal law.

John the revelator develops the bill of particulars in greater detail:

> "For all nations have drunk of the wine of the wrath of her fornication, and the kings of the earth have committed fornication with her, and the merchants of the earth are waxed rich through the abundance of her delicacies. . . . For her sins have reached unto heaven, and God hath remembered her iniquities. . . . How much she hath glorified herself, and lived deliciously, so much torment and sorrow give her: for she saith in her heart, I sit a queen, and am no widow, and shall see no sorrow.
> . . . And the merchants of the earth shall weep and mourn over her; for no man buyeth their merchandise any more: the merchandise of gold, and silver, and precious stones, and of pearls, and fine linen, and purple, and silk, and scarlet, and all thyine wood, and all manner vessels of ivory, and all manner vessels of most precious wood, and of brass, and iron, and marble, and cinnamon, and odours, and ointments, and frankincense, and wine, and oil, and fine flour, and wheat, and beasts, and sheep, and horses, and chariots, and slaves, and souls of men" (Rev. 18:3-13).

Man, in his exuberance, drunken with the maddening wine of Babylon, is guilty of the worst kinds of abuse of power. The merchants and the rulers of earth conspired to rob and enslave all people that dwell on earth. "The great men, the captains, and the mighty men" (Rev. 6:15) is the way the revelator describes it.

In tampering with the contract the law of Sinai, and especially the fourth commandment of that law the Latin Church has defied Yahweh. They have removed that commandment from the law the fourth which makes all men equal.

The Court Sits in Judgment

It is good that the great Nana rises up in judgment: "At the set time that I appoint I will judge with equity" (Ps. 75:2, NRSV). In order to maintain his moral authority in the universe, Yahweh must act at a point in time! We could say, in His own time, at a time of His choosing. "Rise up, O LORD, in your anger; lift yourself up against the fury of my enemies; awake, O my God; you have appointed a judgment" (Ps. 7:6, NRSV)." "Let the assembly of the peoples be gathered around you, and over it take your seat on high" (verse 8)."

"The LORD judges the peoples; judge me, O LORD, according to my righteousness and according to the integrity that is in me" (verse 7).

His Fatherhood, His Nanahood, has been challenged: "Arise, O God, plead thine own cause: remember how the foolish man reproacheth thee daily" (Ps. 74:22). "Arise, O God, judge the earth: for thou shalt inherit all nations" (Ps. 82:8). "Lift up thyself, thou judge of the earth: render a reward to the proud" (Ps. 94:2). "Yea, let God be true, but every man a liar; as it is written, That thou mightest be justified in thy sayings, and mightest overcome when thou art judged" (Rom. 3:4).

The judge is the most awesome figure in the Old Testament. He combines in his person the executive, judicial, and legislative functions. In the Old Testament there is also the ideal king, who is the real moral force in the nation the righteous defender and champion of the poor and the powerless. Psalm 72 is written for the ruler of God's people as one who is directly accountable to Yahweh. In the African setting, this would be the Nana or the chief; he rules under God.

> "Give the king your justice, O God, and your righteousness to a king's son. May he judge your people with righteousness, and your poor with justice. May the mountains yield prosperity for the people, and the hills, in righteousness. May he defend the cause of the poor of the people, give deliverance to the needy, and crush the oppressor" (Ps. 72:1-4, NRSV).

In the African culture, the chief was required to reflect the virtues of the great Nana. He was expected to embody all the characteristics of nobility and justice that are seen in the great Nana.

The chief must maintain the peace and harmony of the community. He must not allow any of his subjects to mar the good name or reputation of the kingdom. It is his duty to cleanse the camp of evil. The people expect no less. The Hebrew prophets call on Yahweh to rise up and execute judgment.

In the book of Revelation, the prophet John sees Yahweh fulfilling this role. He judges the universal community of nations and removes evil from their midst. His rising up results in a good community in which justice and equity prevail. The great Nana cannot leave the cosmos in disorder. He must restore shalom, that is, right relations and just conditions.

Daniel sees a court preparing for judgment:

> "I beheld till the thrones were cast down, and the Ancient of days did sit, whose garment was white as snow, and the hair of his head like the pure wool: his throne was like the fiery flame, and his wheels as burning fire. A fiery stream issued and came forth from before him: thousand thousands ministered unto him, and ten

> thousand times ten thousand stood before him: the judgment was set, and the books were opened" (Dan. 7:9).

Final Outcome

The Old Testament prophets envisioned the establishment of Yahweh's righteous rule in the creation. It will take strength and determination to accomplish this, but the prophets assure us that this will become a reality on "earth, as it is in heaven."

> "This is the purpose that is purposed upon the whole earth: and this is the hand that is stretched out upon all the nations. For the LORD of hosts hath purposed, and who shall disannul it? and his hand is stretched out, and who shall turn it back?" (Isa. 14:26, 27).

In order to accomplish His ultimate purpose for this planet, Yahweh will effect a greater deliverance than He did in Egypt. This time the whole world and all of its peoples are involved:

> "On that day the Lord will extend his hand yet a second time to recover the remnant that is left of his people, from Assyria, from Egypt, from Pathros, from Ethiopia, from Elam, from Shinar, from Hamath, and from the coastlands of the sea. He will raise a signal for the nations, and will assemble the outcasts of Israel, and gather the dispersed of Judah from the four corners of the earth" (Isa. 11:11, 12, NRSV).

This grand theme comes through in the preaching and writing of the great African prophets. As the people of Africa who belong to Messiah Jesus look toward the New Jerusalem, city of their longing, one of the Nazaretha hymns seems appropriate:

> "O Mountain Eagle
> lift thy mighty wing
> we need thy shelter,
> Thou rock of our fathers.
>
> We have no fortress
> other than thee
> In which to find shelter,
> We thy wayward creatures.
>
> We stand before thee
> O beautiful hen,

Thou dost not love
Jerusalem alone.

O love us and hatch us
Wondrous Hen!
We dwell in thy kingdom,
Our Hen of Heaven.

O Lord, bring it forth,
this Ekuphakameni,
Just as a hen
loveth her chickens.

O Jerusalem, Jerusalem!
How great was my longing
to gather thy children
under my wing, But they would not.
Thus thou art left desolate" (Hymn No. 101).

Sundkler, who reprints the hymn, adds this fitting comment:

"In that light the Zulu prophet sees his heaven and his church. To him, these two focusing points in life are the refuge from a bitter and cold world; mighty and warming wings; 'shelter in the time of storm.'"[15]

Yahweh Reverses the Stream

The same river that streamed out of Eden streams into the New Jerusalem, having run its course. John the revelator paints a verbal fresco of the ideal city. It is actually the depository of all that is good, all that has outlasted the ravages of time, all that which has survived, possessions and people; Yahweh has saved the best. This is meaning of the term *remnant.*

"And in the spirit he carried me away to a great, high mountain and showed me the holy city Jerusalem coming down out of heaven from God. It has the glory of God and a radiance like a very rare jewel, like jasper, clear as crystal. It has a great, high wall with twelve gates, and at the gates twelve angels, and on the gates are inscribed the names of the twelve tribes of the Israelites; on the east three gates, on the north three gates, on the south three gates, and on the west three gates. And the wall of the city has twelve foundations, and on them are the twelve names of the twelve apostles of the Lamb. The angel who talked to me had a measuring rod of gold to measure the city and its gates and walls. The city lies foursquare, its length the same as its width; and he measured the city with his rod, fifteen hundred miles; its length and width and height are equal. He also measured its wall, one hundred forty-four cubits by human measurement, which the angel was using. The wall is built of jasper, while the city is pure gold, clear as glass. The foundations of the wall of the city are adorned with every jewel; the first was jasper, the second sapphire, the third agate, the fourth emerald, the fifth onyx, the sixth carnelian, the seventh chrysolite, the eighth beryl, the ninth topaz, the tenth chrysoprase, the eleventh jacinth, the twelfth amethyst. And the twelve gates are twelve pearls, each of the gates is a single pearl, and the street of the city is pure gold, transparent as glass. I saw no temple in the city, for its temple is the Lord God the Almighty and the Lamb. And the city has no need of sun or moon to shine on it, for the glory of God is its light, and its lamp is the Lamb. The nations will walk by its light, and the kings of the earth will bring their glory into it. Its gates will never be shut by day and there will be no night there. People will bring into it the glory and the honor of the nations. But nothing unclean will enter it, nor anyone who practices abomination or falsehood, but only those who are written in the Lamb's book of life" (Rev. 21:10-27).

"Then the angel showed me the river of the water of life, bright as crystal, flowing from the throne of God and of the Lamb through the middle of the street of the city. On either side of the river is the tree of life with its twelve kinds of fruit, producing its fruit each month; and the leaves of the tree are for the healing of the nations. Nothing accursed will be found there any more. But the throne of God and of the Lamb will be in it, and his servants will worship him; they will see his face, and his name will be on their foreheads. And there will be no more night; they need no light of lamp or sun, for the Lord God will be their light, and they will reign forever and ever" (Rev. 22:1-5).

The climax of the struggle is described in word pictures that speak across all of the divides that separate the family of man: racial, social, ethnic, gender etc. John's prose can only be called sublime:

"After this I beheld, and, lo, a great multitude, which no man could number, of all nations, and kindreds, and people, and tongues, stood before the throne, and before the Lamb, clothed with white robes, and palms in their hands" (Rev. 7:9).

"And the nations of them which are saved shall walk in the light of it: and the kings of the earth do bring their glory and honour into it. And the gates of it shall not be shut at all by day: for there shall be no night there. And they shall bring the glory and honour of the nations into it. And there shall in no wise enter into it any thing that defileth, neither whatsoever worketh abomination, or maketh a lie: but they which are written in the Lamb's book of life" (Rev. 21:24-27).

This is the destiny of the human family. God will not abandon it:

"For as the new heavens and the new earth, which I will make, shall remain before me, saith the LORD, so shall your seed and your name remain. And it shall come to pass, that from one new moon to another, and from one sabbath to another, shall all flesh come to worship before me, saith the LORD" (Isa. 66:22, 23).

One of the African proverbs says: "Hope is the pillar of the world." According to the Hebrew prophets, that hope is grounded in Yahweh's future: "Surely there is a future, and your hope will not be cut off" (Prov. 23:18, NRSV).

"For I know the plans I have for you, says the LORD, plans for welfare and not for evil, to give you a future and a hope" (Jer. 29:11, RSV).

"There is hope for your future, says the LORD" (Jer. 31:17, RSV).

End Notes

[1]Isichei, p. 326.

[2]Lawrence A. Jones, "They Sought a City," in C. Eric Lincoln, ed., *The Black Experience in Religion* (Garden City, N.Y.: Doubleday Anchor, 1974), p. 7.

[3]Herbert W. Richardson, quoted in Hans K. LaRondelle, *How to Understand the End-time Prophecies of the Bible* (Sarasota, Fla.: First Impressions, 1997), p. 358.

[4]LaRondelle, p. 358.

[5]Hexham, *Scriptures*, pp. Xxvi, xxviii.

[6]Wynia, p. 53.

[7]G. B. Caird, *The Revelation of St. John* (New York: Harper and Row, 1966), p. 60.

[8]Theophilus H. Smith, "The Spirituality of African-American Traditions," in Louis Dupre and Don E. Sailers, eds., *Christian Spirituality* (New York: Crossroads, 1989), p. 409.

[9]George Elliot, quoted in Bacchiocchi, p. 73.

[10]Danquah, p. 28.

[11]*Ibid.*, p. 127.

[12]*Ibid.*, pp. 126, 127.

[13]*Ibid.*, p. 139.

[14]*Ibid.*, p. 25.

[15]Sundkler, p. 294.

WORKS CITED AND RECOMMENDED

Achtemeier, Elizabeth. *The Old Testament and the Proclamation of the Gospel. Philadelphia,* Westminster, 1980.

African Heritage Study Bible. Edited by James Peebles, 1994.

African Traditional Religion in South Africa: An Annotated Bibliography. Edited by David Chichester et al. Westport, Conn.: Greenwood, 1997.

Alvarez, Francisco C. *Narrative of the Portuguese Embassy to Ethiopia.* Reprint, London: Hakluyt Society, 1996.

Alves, Rubem A. *Tomorrow's Child: Imagination, Creativity, and the Rebirth of Culture.* New York: Harper, 1972.

Anderson, Marian. *My Lord What a Morning.* Reprint: Madison: University of Wisconsin Press, 1992.

Anderson, Vernon A. "Witchcraft in Africa A Missionary Problem." Ph.D.diss., Southern Baptist Theological Seminary, 1942.

Andrews, John Nevins. *History of the Sabbath and First Day of the Week.* 2d edition, enl. Battle Creek: Adventist Pub., 1873.

Awoniwi, Joel. *Sabbath in Yoruba Land Before Christianity.* 2nd edition. Ile Ife, Nigeria, n.d.

Azevedo, Mario J., ed. *Africana Studies: A Survey of Africa and the African Diaspora.* Durham, N.C.: Carolina Academic Press, 1993.

Bacchiocchi, Samuele. *Divine Rest for Human Restlessness.* Berrien Springs: Bacchiocchi, 1980.

______. *From Sabbath to Sunday: A Historical Investigation of the Rise of Sunday Observance in Early Christianity.* Rome: Pontifical Gregorian University, 1977.

Barrett, David B. and Todd M. Johnson. *International Bulletin of Statistical Research.* January, 1998.

Barth, Markus. *Justification.* Grand Rapids: Eerdmans, 1971.

Baumann, H. *Schopfung und Urzeit des Menschen im Mythus der Afrikanischen Volker*. Berlin: 1936. Second edition, 1964.

Beckett, W. Timothy II. "Remnant Children of Israel." Paper, Dallas, 1993.

Ben Ammi-Ben Israel. *God The Black Man And Truth*. Washington: Communicators Press, 1982.

Ben Ami-Ben Israel. *Yeshua the Hebrew Messiah or Jesus the Christian Christ*. Washington: Communicators Press, 1996.

Bernal, Martin. Black Athena, Vol. I. *The Afroasiatic Roots of Classical Civilization: The Fabrication of Ancient Greece, 1785-1985*. New Brunswick: N.J.:Rutgers, 1987. Vol. II. *The Archeological and Documentary Evidence*. Rutgers, 1991.

Bettenson, Henry, ed. *Documents of the Christian Church*, 2nd edition. London: Oxford, 1963.

Birch, Bruce C. *Let Justice Roll Down: The Old Testament, Justice, and Christian Life*. Louisville: Westminster John Knox, 1991.

Blyden, Edward W. *Christianity, Islam, and the Negro Race*. Edinburgh: 1969; Reprint, Chesapeake, Va.: ECA Assoc., 1993.

Bonwick, James. *Egyptian Belief and Modern Thought*. Reprint, London: African Publication Society, 1983.

Branson, Roy. "The Sabbath in Modern Jewish Theology." In *The Sabbath in Scripture and History*. Edited by Kenneth A. Strand. Washington: Review and Herald, 1982, 266-77.

Brueggemann, Walter, *Genesis. Vol. I of Interpretation: A Bible Commentary for Teaching and Preaching*. Louisville: Westminster John Knox, 1991.

Burton, Keith A. "Western European Imperialism and the Literary Suppression of the African Fidelity to the Biblical Sabbath." Paper presented to Sabbath in Africa Project, 1993.

Caird, G. B. *The Revelation of St. John*. New York: Harper and Row, 1966.

Calloway, Henry. "A Xhosa Reproves a Missionary." In *The Treasury of African Folklore*. Edited by Edward Courlander. New York: Marlowe, 1956, 440-41.

Chatelain, Heli. "The A-M Bundu of Angola." In *The Treasury of African Folklore*. Edited by Harold Courlander. New York: Marlowe, 1956, 286-92.

Clapp, Rodney. *A Peculiar People: The Church as Culture in a Post-Christian Society*. Downer's Grove, Ill: InterVarsity Press, 1997.

Copher, Charles B. *In Stony the Road We Trod: African American Biblical Interpretation*. Edited by Cain Hope Felder. Minneapolis: Fortress Press, 1991.

Courlander, Harold. *The Treasury of African Folklore*. New York: Marlowe, 1996.

Daneel, M. L. Quest for Belonging, Vol. I. *Old and New in Southern Shona: Independent Churches*. Hawthorne, N.Y.: Mouton, 1971.

Danquah, Joseph B. *The Akan Doctrine of God*. London: Lutterworth, 1944.

Diop, Cheikh Anta. *The Cultural Unity of Black Africa*, 2nd edition. Chicago: Third World Press, 1989.

DuBois, W. E. B. *Souls of Black Folk*. New York: Fawcett, 1961.

Eliade, Mircea, editor-in-chief. *Encyclopedia of Religion*. New York: Macmillan, 1986.

______. *Patterns in Comparative Religion*. Translated by Rosemary Sheed. New York: Sheed and Ward, 1958.

Epstein, Isadore, ed. *The Babylonian Talmud: Hebrew-English Edition*. Revised edition. Trans. Jacob Schacter and H. Freedman. London: Soncino Press, 1969.

Felder, Cain Hope. *Troubling Biblical Waters*. Bishop Henry McNeal Turner Studies in North American Black Religion; Vol. 3. Maryknoll, N.Y.: Orbis, 1989.

Gates, Henry Louis. *The Signifying Monkey*. New York: Oxford University Press, 1988.

Getui, Mary. "Possible Sabbath-keeping Traditions Among Abagusii of Western Kenya." A Report for the Sabbath in Africa Project. Kenyatta University, Sept., 1995.

Gibbon, Edward. *The Decline and Fall of the Roman Empire*. Reprint, 6 Vols. London: Dent Everyman, 1910.

Gowan, Donald E. *From Eden to Babel: A Commentary on the Book of Genesis 1 - 11*. Grand Rapids: Eerdmans, 1985.

Hall, Douglas J. *The Stewardship of Life in the Kingdom of Death*. Grand Rapids: Eerdmans, 1992.

Hamilton, Jeffries M. "The Rest Is Commentary: A Reading of the Ten Commandments." *Quarterly Review*, 13 (Fall 1993): 25-37.

Hansberry, William Leo. *Pillars in Ethiopian History: The William Leo Hansberry African History Notebook*, Vol. I. Edited by Joseph E. Harris. Washington: Howard University Press, 1974.

Hastings, Adrian. *The Church in Africa: 1450-1950. Oxford History of the Christian Church*. New York: Oxford University, 1994.

Henry, Carl F. "Where is Modern Theology Going?" *Christianity Today*. 12 (1 March 1968): 3-7.

Heschel, Abraham. *The Earth is the Lord's and The Sabbath*. Reprint. New York: Harper and Row, 1966.

Hexham, Irving, ed. *The Scriptures of amaNazaretha of EkuphaKameni*. Queenstown, Ont.: Mellon, 1993.

Hexham, Irving and Gerhardus C. Oosthuizen, eds. *The Story of Isaiah Shembe*. Translated by Hans-Jurgin Becken. Queenstown, Ont.: Mellon, 1997.

Heye, Bekele. "The Sabbath in Ethiopia." Master's thesis. Andrews University, 1968.

Isichei, Elizabeth A. *A History of Christianity in Africa*. Grand Rapids: Eerdmans, 1995.

Johnson, James Weldon. *God's Trombones*. New York: Penguin Books, 1927.

Jones, Lawrence A. "They Sought a City." *In The Black Experience in Religion*. Edited by C. Eric Lincoln. Garden City, N.Y.: Doubleday Anchor, 1974, 6-22.

Jones, Reginald L., ed. *Black Psychology*. 3d rev. ed. Berkeley: Cobb and Henry, 1991.

Karst, Gary. "Sabbath Keepers in the Sudan." Letter. General Conference of Seventh-day Adventists, Dec. 6, 1995.

Keidel, Levi O. *Black Samson: An African's Astounding Pilgrimage to Personhood*. Carol Stream, Ill.: Creation House, 1975.

Lampe, G. W. H., ed. *Cambridge History of the Bible, Vol. II*. Cambridge: Cambridge University Press, 1969.

LaRondelle, Hans K. *How to Understand the End-time Prophecies of the Bible*. Sarasota, Fl.: First Impressions, 1997.

Lemon, Philip F. "*The Kasai Story.*" Written for Duane McKey by the retired president of the Quebec Conference of Seventh-day Adventists, 1986.

Maxwell, C. Mervyn. *The Message of Daniel.* God Cares, Vol. I. Boise: Pacific Press, 1981.

Malisha, Lukas. *Christianity in Africa.* London: Mission Book Service, 1987.

Mbiti, John. *African Religions and Philosophy.* London: Heineman, 1989.

_____. "The Encounter of Christian Faith and African Tradition." *In Theologians in Transition.* Edited by James M. Wall. New York: Crossroads, 1981.

McKey, F. Duane. "History and Analysis of the Relationship Between the Seventh-day Adventist Church and Several Independent Churches in the Kasai Province of Zaire, 1972-1985." Dissertation, Andrews University, 1989.

Mekouria, Tekele Tsadek. *In General History of Africa, Vol. II.* Ancient Africa. Edited by G. Moktar.UNESCO, Berkeley: University of Calif., 1980.

Ngetich, Sammy. "Possible Sabbath Traditions in Africa: The Case of the Kalenjin People." Paper presented to the Sabbath in Africa Project. Barston: University of East Africa, Jan. 1995.

Niebuhr, H. Richard. *The Kingdom of God in America.* Hanover, N.H.: University Press of New England, 1988.

Noble, Frederic Perry. *The Redemption of Africa: A Story of Civilization.* Chicago: Revell, 1899.

Nortey, Jacob J. "Independent African Churches—Are They Genuinely Christian?" *Spectrum,* 20 (Dec. 1989): 29-37.

Odom, R. L. "The Sabbath in the Great Schism of A.D. 1054."*Andrews University Seminary Studies,* 1 (1963), 74-80.

Okinda, Josiah. "Possible Sabbath-Keeping Traditions in Pre-colonialist Africa: A Study of the Luo People in Kenya." Paper presented to the Sabbath in Africa Project. Barston: University of East Africa, Jan. 1995.

Owusu-Mensa, Kofi. "Onyamee Kwamee (The Akan Saturday God of Saturday)." Paper, n.d.

Pakenham, Thomas. *The Scramble for Africa: The White Man's Conquest of the Dark Continent from 1876 to 1912.* New York: Avon Books, 1992.

Parfitt, Tudor. *The Thirteenth Gate: Travels Among the Lost Tribes of Israel*. Bethesda, Md.: Adler and Adler, 1987.

Parrinder, E. G. *African Traditional Religion*. London: 1962.

Pauw, B. A. *Christianity and the Xhosa Tradition*. Oxford: Clarendon, 1958.

Payne, A. Wardel, ed. *Howard University Directory of African-American Religious Bodies*. Washington: Howard University Press, 1995.

p'Bitek, Okot. *African Religions in European Scholarship*. Kampala: East African Lit. Bureau, 1970. Reprint. African Heritage Classical Research Studies. Chesapeake, VA: ECA Assoc. 1997.

Peterson, Frank L. *The Hope of the Race*. Nashville: Southern Publishing, 1934.

Raboteau, Albert J. *A Fire in the Bones: Reflections on African-American Religious History*. Boston: Beacon Press, 1995.

______. *Slave Religion: The Invisible Institution in the Antebellum South*. New York: Oxford University Press, 1978.

Rattray, R. S. *The Ashanti*. London: Oxford University Press, 1923.

Rice, Gene. "The Curse that Never Was." *Journal of Religious Thought*, 29 (1972): 13.

Sanneh, Lamin. *West African Christianity: The Religious Impact*. Maryknoll, NY: Orbis, 1983.

Sednak, Kojo-Duffu. "The Knowledge of the Creator Embedded in African Culture." Paper. May 6, 1990.

Shank, David A. *Prophet Harris: The "Black Elijah" of West Africa*. Edited by Jocelyn Murray. Boston: Brill Acad., 1994.

Shapiro, Deanne. "Factors in the Development of Black Judaism." *In The Black Experience in Religion*. Edited by C. Eric Lincoln. Garden City, NY: Doubleday, 1974, 254-272.

Shaw, Mark R. *The Kingdom of God in Africa: A Short History of African Christianity*. Grand Rapids: Baker Books, 1996.

Smith, Theophilus H. "The Spirituality of Africa-American Traditions." *In Christian Spirituality*. Vol. 3, Post Reformation and Modern. Edited by Louis Dupre and Don E. Saliers. New York; Crossroads, 1989, 372-414.

Speiser, Edward A., ed. *Genesis*. Anchor Bible Series, Vol. 1. New York: Anchor Doubleday, 1964.

Strand, Kenneth A. "The Sabbath and Sunday from the Second through Fifth Centuries." In *The Sabbath in Scripure and History*. Edited by Kenneth A. Strand. Washington: Review and Herald, 1982, 323-332.

Sundkler, Bengt G. *Bantu Prophets in South Africa*. New York: Oxford University Press, 1961.

Tinney, James S. "Black Jews: A House Divided." *Christianity Today*, 15 (7 Dec. 1973): 52-53.

Ullendorff, Edward. *The Ethiopians: An Introduction to the Country and People*. London: Oxford University Press, 1960.

Van Sertima, Ivan, and Larry Williams, eds. *Great African Thinkers. Vol. I. Cheikh Anta Diop*. New Brunswick, NJ: Transaction, 1986.

Vansina, Jan. *Oral Tradition as History*. Madison: University of Wisconsin Press, 1983.

Vyhmeister, Werner. "The Sabbath in Asia" and "The Sabbath in Egypt and Ethiopia." In *The Sabbath in Scripture and History*. Edited by Kenneth A. Strand. Washington: Review and Herald, 1982, 151-189.

Wainwright, Geoffrey. *A Doxology: The Praise of God in Worship, Doctrine and Life*. New York: Oxford University Press, 1980.

West, Cornel. *Prophetic Fragments*. Grand Rapids: William B. Eerdmans, 1988.

Westermann, Claus. *Creation*. Translated by John J. Scullion. Philadelphia: Fortress, 1974.

______. *Genesis 1-11*. Minneapolis: Augsburg, 1984.

White, Ellen G. "The Bible to Be Understood by All." *The Signs of the Times*, 20 (20 August 1894): 643-44.

______. *Christ's Object Lessons*. Nampa, Idaho: Pacific Press, 1990.

______. *The Desire of Ages*. Nampa, Idaho: Pacific Press, 1940.

______. *Early Writings*. Hagerstown, Maryland: Review and Herald, 1945.

______. *Education*. Nampa, Idaho: Pacific Press, 1903.

______. *The Faith I Live By*. Hagerstown, Maryland: Review and Herald, 1958.

______. *The Great Controversy*. Nampa, Idaho: Pacific Press, 1911.

______. *Patriarchs and Prophets*. Nampa, Idaho: Pacific Press, 1913.

______. *Prophets and Kings*. Nampa, Idaho: Pacific Press, 1943.

______. *The Southern Work: Reprinted from Articles and Letters of 1891-1899*. Hagerstown, Maryland: Review and Herald, 1966.

______. *Sons and Daughters of God*. Hagerstown, Maryland: Review and Herald, 1955.

______. *That I May Know Him*. Hagerstown, Maryland: Review and Herald, 1964.

______. *This Day with God*. Hagerstown, Maryland: Review and Herald, 1979.

______. *Thoughts from the Mount of Blessing*. Nampa, Idaho: Pacific Press, 1929.

______. "*Ye Did It to Me*." The Signs of the Times, 19 (7 August 1893): 614.

Whitehouse, Jerald W. Global Center for Adventist-Muslim Relations. Personal Interview.

Williams, Joseph. *Hebrewisms of West Africa: From Nile to Niger with the Jews*. Toronto: Longmans Green, 1930. Reprint, Baltimore: BCP Books, 1998.

Wright, Christopher J. H. "Editorial: Deuteronomic Depression." *Themelios 19* (Jan. 1994): 3-4.

Wynia, Elly M. *The Church of God and Saints of Christ: The Rise of Black Jews*. New York: Garland Publishing, 1990.

Yangson, Samuel. Unpublished paper. 1980.

909 917-5836